The Private Practice of Behavior Therapy

A Guide for
Behavioral Practitioners

APPLIED CLINICAL PSYCHOLOGY

Series Editors:
Alan S. Bellack, *Medical College of Pennsylvania at EPPI, Philadelphia, Pennsylvania,* and Michel Hersen, *University of Pittsburgh, Pittsburgh, Pennsylvania*

Recent Volumes in this Series

BEHAVIORAL ASSESSMENT AND REHABILITATION OF THE TRAUMATICALLY BRAIN DAMAGED
Edited by Barry A. Edelstein and Eugene T. Couture

COGNITIVE BEHAVIOR THERAPY WITH CHILDREN
Edited by Andrew W. Meyers and W. Edward Craighead

HANDBOOK OF BEHAVIORAL GROUP THERAPY
Edited by Dennis Upper and Steven M. Ross

ISSUES IN PSYCHOTHERAPY RESEARCH
Edited by Michel Hersen, Larry Michelson, and Alan S. Bellack

A PRIMER OF HUMAN BEHAVIORAL PHARMACOLOGY
Alan Poling

THE PRIVATE PRACTICE OF BEHAVIOR THERAPY
Sheldon J. Kaplan

RESEARCH METHODS IN APPLIED BEHAVIOR ANALYSIS
Issues and Advances
Edited by Alan Poling and R. Wayne Fuqua

SEVERE BEHAVIOR DISORDERS IN THE MENTALLY RETARDED
Nondrug Approaches to Treatment
Edited by Rowland P. Barrett

SUBSTANCE ABUSE AND PSYCHOPATHOLOGY
Edited by Arthur I. Alterman

TREATING ADDICTIVE BEHAVIORS
Processes of Change
Edited by William R. Miller and Nick H. Heather

The Private Practice of Behavior Therapy

A Guide for Behavioral Practitioners

Sheldon J. Kaplan

Private Practice
Jacksonville, Florida

Plenum Press • New York and London

Library of Congress Cataloging in Publication Data

Main entry under title:

Kaplan, Sheldon J.
    The private practice of behavior therapy.

    (Applied clinical psychology)
    Bibliography: p.
    Includes index.
    1. Behavior therapy—Practice. 2. Behavior therapy. I. Title. II. Series. [DNLM: 1.
Behavior Therapy. 2. Private Practice—organization & administration. WM 425 K178p]
    RC489.B4K34   1986   616.89′142′068   86-12197
    ISBN 0-306-42193-3

© 1986 Plenum Press, New York
A Division of Plenum Publishing Corporation
233 Spring Street, New York, N.Y. 10013

Printed in the United States of America

To my wife, Harriett, and sons, Lee and Kevin,
for their patience, love, and loyalty to me
not only during the preparation of this text, but always.

Preface

Entering a full-time private practice and forsaking the comforts of a regular paycheck was a difficult decision for me. Fortunately, I was able to begin my practice on a part-time basis in space rented from two physician friends. By using my behavior skills for self-management and organization, I was then able to help my practice grow so that, with some trepidation, I moved into a full-time practice. I have continued to maintain my practice according to the same ethical, professional, and business assumptions discussed in this book.

One of the reasons for my writing this book is that, at the time I was beginning my practice, there was no one text that helped me begin or to explain what "nuts and bolts" issues I needed to consider. As my practice has grown, I continued to see a need for a resource text to help the beginning therapist get started. I decided to describe the assumptions, methods, and issues that I have used so as to present a discussion of timely issues relevant to the practice of behavior therapy.

This book is the result of an idea that arose out of a chapter I wrote for Volume 17 of *Progress in Behavior Modification*, edited by Michel Hersen, Richard M. Eisler, and Peter M. Miller. Within this text, I have tried to pull together not only all the pertinent behavioral literature I could find but also traditional clinical psychology and business literature as well. In this manner, the clinician can have a broad-spectrum look at establishing and maintaining a behavior therapy private practice.

Chapter 1 presents a comparison of behavior therapy with clinical psychology as well as the advantages and disadvantages of a behavioral practice. Chapters 2 and 3 describe the methods for getting started and conducting the practice. Getting and "nurturing" referrals as well as the methods for intake, assessment, treatment, and follow-up of a client are some issues in these chapters.

Chapter 4 outlines and briefly discusses the various procedures from all areas of behavior therapy used in clinical practice, whereas Chapter 5 provides the therapist with the ethical standards and guidelines for professional services. Chapters 6 and 7 detail various "tools of the trade" such as recording and treatment forms, equipment, texts, computers, and continuing education.

In Chapter 8, I discuss various issues relating to being a behavioral consultant to agencies, schools, retardation centers, and businesses. The growing influence of employment assistance programs, health maintenance organizations, and preferred providers organizations provides a new market for short-term, effective treatment such as is available through behavior therapy.

In Chapter 9, the "nuts and bolts" business issues of practice are discussed. Financially, "getting started" and "keeping going" one's practice is a never-ending challenge of monitoring expenses and minimizing overhead. On the other hand, developing quality services and earning a good reputation for such services will greatly offset overhead expenses to ensure that the practitioner "survives" as well as is financially comfortable in the public marketplace.

Chapter 10 presents some case histories from my practice that exemplify the variety of clinical populations and problems served. In Chapter 11, I have provided the clinician with a discussion of several issues relating to the new directions in the field. Certification and licensure, peer review, considerations of treatment regarding "setting events," and the influence of behavior therapy in the formulation of social policy are some examples.

The intent of this text is to provide the beginning and practicing clinician with the basics of establishing and maintaining a behavior therapy private practice. Though a variety of issues are discussed and highlighted in this book, the clinician must continue to rely on expertise, experience, and innovation, clinically and from a business standpoint. It is hoped that this guide will assist the clinician in this endeavor.

Acknowledgments

I would first like to thank Michel Hersen for suggesting the idea of a behavior therapy private practice text. I also express my thanks to Eliot Werner for giving me the opportunity to publish this volume with Plenum Press.

There are many people who have contributed professionally to the work on which this book is based. I wish to thank my associate and friend, Stephanie D. Kuhling, for providing me with professional support and time in the exchange of ideas that have led to a successful and effective practice of behavior therapy. I wish to acknowledge also the support of the rest of my staff: Michael Sisbarro, Jennifer Glock, and Robert Woods.

It is often said that without a highly competent office secretary and office manager, a business can not function. This is true in my office. With the calm persistence of my office manager, Denise Griggs, my office does run efficiently, smoothly, and in a very professional manner. My thanks to her as well.

Finally, I wish to acknowledge the time, effort, and patience of my wife who read, proofed, and otherwise helped in the preparation of the manuscript, and to Lori Sistrunk and Lisa Hatcher for typing the manuscript.

Contents

Behavior Therapy
Foundations for Clinical Practice

The science of psychology is a multifaceted discipline that examines all aspects of human behavior. From research, psychologists have been able to describe and explain the hows and whys of behavior based on the tenets of experimental, social, personality, physiological, and behavioral psychology. Applied psychology has sought to integrate this scientifically obtained information, formulate hypotheses, and develop methods of treating a variety of clinically significant problems in settings such as public service agencies, hospitals, schools, clinics, and private practice. Behavior therapy has, in its brief history, evolved as one of the most viable forms of applied psychology used in these settings.

1.1. DEFINITION OF BEHAVIOR THERAPY

Despite the fact that behavior therapy has established itself as a viable therapeutic approach, there is no single definition generally agreed to represent the field by those calling themselves behavior therapists. Brown, Wienckowski, and Stolz (1975) define behavior therapy as the application of principles of experimental psychology to socially significant problems for the purpose of alleviating human suffering and to enhance human functioning. Included in this definition is the requirement that the behavior therapist systematically monitors and evaluates the effects of the treatment procedures applied. The goal of behavior therapy is, of course, to improve the self-control of the client by expanding his or her behavioral repertoire of skills and abilities. Behavior therapy attempts to do this by manipulating the consequences of the individual's behavior from the immediate environment. Wilson and O'Leary (1980) view behavior therapy as simply a collection of principles and techniques involving changing behavior; Kazdin and Wilson (1978) view behavior therapy as an empirically based technology of behavior change, whereas Krasner (1982) views behavior therapy techniques entirely as methods of self-control. Wolpe (1973), on the other hand, views behavior therapy in a more elaborate fashion. That is, Wolpe sees this approach as a discipline in which the therapist, though attentive to the emotional needs of the client, conceptualizes the presenting problems according to principles of learning and neurophysiology. Treatment involves the manipulation of the complex interaction of the client's behavioral repertoire with his or her physiology whether the stimulus is external or internal, simple or complex, and whether the response is motoric, autonomic, or imaginal.

1.2. COMPARISON OF BEHAVIOR THERAPY WITH TRADITIONAL CLINICAL PRACTICE

Behavior therapy and clinical psychology can be compared and contrasted on several dimensions (Woolfolk & Richardson, 1984). First, clinical psychology arose from the work of Freud, the humanists, and the neo-Freudians. Inherent in each of these psychodynamic approaches is a "value" system that specifies some optimum level of human functioning (often varying from discipline to discipline regarding what is optimum human functioning). Behavior therapy, on the other hand, is based on a rather long history of experimental psychology in which empirically tested clinical procedures have been developed from this research. Behavior therapy assumes no such value system or perceived functioning level, but rather targets goals mutually agreed upon by therapist and client relating to the presenting problem only, and not on more global life issues, as does clinical psychology. Behavior therapy separates itself from value and attempts to relate predominately more to fact.

Second, the thrust of behavior therapy is based on its strong opposition to the role of the medical or disease model in the explanation of behavior. Traditional clinical psychology adheres to this medical model. By doing so, it frequently attaches generalized labels to "kinds" of people, whereas behavior therapy focuses more on what specific behaviors are dysfunctional (deficits, excesses, and lacking stimulus control) that need to be changed.

Third, contemporary behavior therapy has emphasized rationality and logic in the treatment of clients since its precognitive days. With the assimilation of the cognitive approaches (Beck, Ellis, Meichenbaum, and others) into the realm of behavior therapy, the focus of treatment is on logical thinking, rational behavior, and effective problem solving. Clinical psychology, on the contrary, is more concerned with exploring and developing one's feelings rather than with the more cognitive activity of present-day behavior therapy.

Finally, because objectivity and fact are basic tenets of behavior therapy, all monitoring, implementation of treatment procedures, and goals in a behavior therapeutic approach are firmly grounded in the data and in the objective development of a level of appropriate behavior determined jointly by the therapist and client. Goals in traditional clinical psychology are based on theories of personality not usually amenable to empirical test, are more normative, and are frought with subjectivity.

1.3. THE GROWING INFLUENCE OF BEHAVIOR THERAPY

O'Leary (1983) in his presidential address to the Association for the Advancement of Behavior Therapy (AABT) referred to the success of behavior therapy in a variety of settings and its growing influence on the helping professions. He emphasized the increased prevalence and professional recognition of behavior therapists as evidenced by the amount of published articles in behavioral and nonbehavioral journals, the proportionally large amount of research grants obtained by behavioral researchers, and by public and professional acknowledgment of the effectiveness of behavioral treatment methods for clinically and socially significant problems.

O'Leary cites a variety of statistics relating to the prevalence of those who call themselves, and practice as, behavior therapists. First, the two major orientations of treatment for child clinical psychologists are psychodynamic and behavioral. In a survey of pediatric psychologists, 59% of them indicated that they were behaviorally oriented, whereas only 39% said that they preferred the psychodynamic approach. For psychologists working with adults, they, too, indicated a greater preference for the behavioral orientation than for the psychodynamic approaches. Finally, a sample of the professional graduate schools of psychology and practitioners from the National Register indicated that the behavioral approach was among the top three orientations preferred for therapy.

Professional publications have also seen a rise in the number of behavioral research and application articles. O'Leary indicates that there has been a tremendous influence by behavior therapy in these journals. A large majority of articles on psychological treatment involve some aspect of behavior therapy. Further, the number of research grants from the Psychosocial Treatments Research Branch of the National Institute of Mental Health (NIMH) have been largely in favor of behavior therapy treatment-outcome studies. Of those grants awarded in 1982, 74% of them were given to behavioral researchers. In addition, this fact is so impressive to the NIMH that this government facility is considering asking behavioral researchers to study nonbehavioral methodologies because of their excellent track record in behavioral outcome studies.

To determine the public's image of behavior therapy, O'Leary reviewed and rated newspaper articles for the *New York Times* from 1965 to 1983. Of course, in the days of misuses and abuses of behavior therapy and behavior modification, the field received a great deal of bad press and was viewed as using psychosurgery, or techniques similar to those used in Stanley Kubrick's film *A Clockwork Orange,* and brainwashing. From 1968 to 1978, behavior therapy was, therefore, viewed as predominately negative. However, from 1979 to 1983, newspaper articles describing behavior therapy techniques and the field's general approaches have been generally positive and quite favorable.

Finally, in a review of various areas of clinical behavioral intervention, O'Leary also found favorable indications of the strong and growing influence of behavior therapy. Azrin and his associates' successful work in the field of retardation, marital therapy, job finding, and alcoholism, Lovaas's longitudinal research in the field of autism, Patterson's studies with aggressive boys, O'Leary's work with hyperactivity, Rachman's treatment of agoraphobia, Jacobson's research with marital discord, and Beck and his associates' work with depression all have resulted in techniques that the practitioner can apply with at least moderate effectiveness and that are empirically demonstrated to relieve human suffering.

In summary, there is an obvious growing influence of behavior therapy on the fields of psychology, psychiatry, and mental health in general. Behavior therapy has such promise that researchers are looking toward ways of influencing social policy and mental health standards in both the public and private sectors of our society.

1.4. THE ADVANTAGES AND DISADVANTAGES OF A PRIVATE PRACTICE IN BEHAVIOR THERAPY

Browning (1982) has discussed many advantages and disadvantages of private practice, regardless of treatment orientation. Private practice affords an individual freedom to direct what work is done, when to work, how much is earned, and allows for immediate feedback of one's successes. However, the practitioner also becomes an administrator who can get bogged down in red tape. The practitioner is personally responsible for success or failure in the practice, and self-management contingencies are necessary to get through what Browning terms the "roller coaster effect" of referrals and services in private practice.

Behavior therapy has, in the past, been maligned as a viable means of treating behavioral and emotional problems. Early claims of the approach being nothing more than bribery, being too "controlling," "manipulative," "mechanical," and too "simplistic" still linger in the public and private sectors. Abuses of this approach in the 1970s resulted in litigation that altered how practitioners of behavior therapy applied their knowledge. Out of this litigation came such policies as fully informed consent, a statement of rights for the retarded, those with psychopathology, and those in prison, the requirement of peer review committees to ensure that the rights of the client are protected, and the consideration of the least restrictive alternatives for treatment of client problems. With such controversy, there are many professional risks and some benefits one must consider, over and above those typically associated with a traditional private practice, before beginning a behavior therapy practice (Drash & Bostow, 1981).

The first obvious advantage is that the field of behavior therapy is presently enjoying more credibility and wider use by psychologists and other counseling professionals (Smith, 1982). Progress has been made in the field, and there is greater diversity of available techniques for treating different clinical problems.

Smith (1982), in an article discussing current trends and therapists' preferences for different types of therapies, found that behavioral and cognitive/behavioral psychology represented one of the strongest trends in counseling and clinical psychology today. In a questionnaire sent to clinical and counseling psychologists, approximately 58% of the respondents indicated that the most influential psychotherapists in the field of psychology today were from the behavioral and cognitive orientations (e.g., Bandura, Beck, Ellis, Lazarus, Meichenbaum, and Wolpe). Approximately 45 to 50% of those polled indicated that books and authors currently most representative of the counseling and psychotherapy field were written by these behavioral and cognitive/behavioral psychologists. According to Smith, therefore, current directions in therapy emphasize an integration of the behavioral, social, cognitive, and physiological techniques frequently associated with behavior therapy.

Second, the therapist can provide to the client a practical approach to resolving the presenting problems better than in more traditional forms of psychotherapy (Stolz, Wienckowski, & Brown, 1975; Wolpe,

1973). Specifically, in behavior therapy, presenting problems are viewed as learned behavior and emotion, which are maintained by the current environment, both inside and outside of the body. Operational definitions of such events, combined with a functional analysis of how the client's problems developed and have been maintained, allow for the use of scientific procedures that have been shown to be of a least moderate effectiveness. The therapist and client set clearly defined therapeutic goals. The client can then logically see when these goals are achieved, whereas the therapist can then modify treatment as the data reflect such a need to do so.

Third, as pointed out by Eysenck (1960, 1964) and Wolpe (1973), behavior therapy is more efficient and, therefore, more cost-effective for the client. Success rates are reported at 70%, 80%, and 90% (Kaplan, 1982; Swan & MacDonald, 1978; Wolpe, 1973) using behavior therapy, whereas rates of 40 to 50% are typical in traditional forms of therapy. The number of sessions typical for behavior therapy averages approximately 30, as compared to greater than 100 sessions for traditional psychotherapy and psychoanalysis. If psychotherapy averages $50 to $75 per hour (Drash & Bostow, 1981; Kaplan, 1983; *Psychotherapy Finances*, 1984; Whalen, 1978), the client realizes substantial savings. In a questionnaire submitted to the private clients of this author, a similar success rate of 80% was obtained. Furthermore, long-term follow-up data of 1 to 2 years reflected a 70 to 75% maintenance of the effects of treatment.

Fourth, behavior therapy can address populations of clinical problems not usually amenable to traditional forms of psychotherapy. Retardation, autism, social skills deficits, sexual dysfunction, phobic reactions in children and adults, and learning disabilities are some examples. Hence, behavior therapy can provide a greater referral base because of its diversity of techniques.

Finally, there is much emphasis in behavior therapy toward training the client to serve as his or her own therapist while the referred problems are being resolved. Because the behavioral model is one that emphasizes a reeducation of how behavior and emotions develop (Ellis, 1975; Wolpe, 1973), the client is then in a better position to avoid future problems due to this reeducation process. This model is more efficient than traditional approaches, which can continually reinforce a dependent client–therapist relationship.

The disadvantages of a private practice in behavior therapy cannot be ignored, however. In its youth, behavior modification and therapy was often viewed, simplistically, as the "M & M" science. Second, independent behavioral practitioners may still suffer from the stigma and bad press due to misinterpretations and misrepresentation by the media.

Turkat (1979) and Turkat and Feuerstein (1978) gave much evidence for the negative image of behavior therapy, and the role that the media has played in stigmatizing behavior therapy. Wicker (1974) and Nordheimer (1974) have written articles that have done much to misrepresent behavior therapy as "Chinese torture," "brainwashing," and "sensory deprivation." Although behaviorists have attempted to correct this negative viewpoint by emphasizing fully informed consent, client rights, peer review, and least restrictive alternatives in the use of behavioral techniques, the negative image, unfortunately, still lingers.

Third, professionals who practice traditional clinical psychology and psychiatry are prone to view the behavior therapist with much skepticism and, possibly, ridicule. There is still some hesitance by traditionalists toward viewing this pragmatic approach to therapy as a powerful means of helping clients. Rather, this approach may be viewed more as being narrowly limited in the scope of problems that it addresses. Referrals may be made to the behavior therapist for treating a child's bedwetting or thumbsucking or an adult's phobias, but treating depression, sexual problems, family difficulties, and other "deeper" psychological difficulties is left to the traditional psychotherapist and psychiatrist. Fortunately, this problem is lessening in its influence, as has been implied by Smith (1982).

Fourth, the public has, for so long, been exposed to the medical model for dealing with problems. Those of the lay public who believe that psychological difficulties are manifestations of some inner illness are less likely to enter therapy based on a learning theory approach to resolving clinically significant problems. Clients may not want to be presented with an explanation as to how various antecendents and consequences have contributed to the development of the frequency, duration, and topography of their behavior problems. Clients may not want to correct their problems through behavioral tasks but may "believe," instead, that change in their suffering is solely the responsibility of the therapist. The expectations of the client may be for a more psychodynamic explanation and problem resolution where the therapist is the authoritarian and omnipotent resolver of conflict.

Last, there are economic disadvantages for the private practitioner in behavior therapy. The length of therapy time is shorter and requires a wider referral base than more traditional psychotherapy, which emphasizes long-term therapy. The shorter the time of treatment, the more clients are needed to maintain one's practice. Also, there is less "front-end loading" (Drash & Bostow, 1981) in that traditional psychotherapy often requires comprehensive and costly psychological testing before therapy, which can generate sizable incomes for these services alone.

By contrast, the behavior therapist is more concerned about direct—rather than indirect—measures, so that income to maintain a private practice may have to be generated in other ways. Furthermore, insurance companies still vary as to whether they will accept for reimbursement the services of the behavior therapist. "Freedom of choice" legislation and a greater recognition of the effectiveness of behavior therapy (Birk *et al.*, 1973) have, to some extent, lessened the economic dangers of a behavioral practice.

2

Getting Started in a Behavior Therapy Private Practice

The methods and mechanics for setting up and nurturing a behavior therapy private practice cannot be found in the research literature. As Goldfried (1983), Lubetkin (1983), and Wachtel (1977) suggest, clinical observations and a clinician's experiences are important, even though unsystematic, criteria for the successful practice of behavior therapy. The beginning therapist should have guiding principles on which to base his or her practice, a plan for getting referrals, and some ideas as to what services will be provided as the early stages of planning a practice begin.

There are a variety of texts on the subject of private practice (Browning, 1982; Keller & Ritt, 1983; Pressman, 1979). The assumptions for the establishment of a private practice discussed in these texts involve a number of issues. First, the beginning clinician must determine whether he or she has the professional competence and the skills to provide the broad-based mental health services that are usually provided in private practices. With sufficient consideration given this issue, the clinician must then determine what problems and populations will not be served and those that will. Second, there is an increased need for the clinician to have excellent organizational skills. By organizing the operation of a clinical practice from a business as well as from a professional standpoint, the clinician is better able to provide quality services, track the client's progress and problems, monitor the myriad business responsibilities and problems that can arise, and have the time to continually upgrade the overall delivery system of services of the practice. Third, the therapist must have sufficient self-management skills to keep the practice operating, to adhere to the regimen of case review and management, to self-reinforce appropriate clinical behaviors, and to provide self-corrective feedback when errors of judgment or procedure occur. Finally, the beginning practitioner must be prepared for the heavier demands on his or her family, due to increased time and responsibilities devoted to the practice. The therapist may sometimes get behind schedule and then work late the remainder of the day into the evening hours. Workshops are often given after clinical hours in the evening. Professional meetings are also convened in the evening hours. Emergencies such as potentially suicidal clients, child abuse evaluations, and court testimony may further disrupt the schedule.

For the behavior therapist, there are additional assumptions that are very important to an independent practice. The behavior therapist beginning in private practice assumes the following:

1. *The behavior therapist can survive in the public marketplace.* As Smith (1982) states, there is a decline in the use of more psychodynamic approaches in favor of behavior and cognitive/behavioral therapeutic techniques. Therefore, an individual practitioner using these methods will be more successful with his or her clients and, therefore, build and maintain a large referral base.

Drash and Bostow (1981) discussed the benefits of a practice of behavior therapy in terms of getting referrals. Behavior therapy can give greater assurances of rapid progress and results, is very pragmatic in its treatment approaches, reduces the length of time needed for treatment, is more suitable to prepaid therapy plans due to its focus on short-term but effective treatment, and is more broad-based in that it can address a wider range of clinical problems than can traditional psychotherapy.

2. *A "general practitioner" behavioral approach facilitates referrals and a broad base of services.* The applied behavioral research community has addressed a diversity of problems and populations, including parent training, child behavior disorders, child abuse, depression, learning difficulties, retardation, family conflict, autism, marital discord, job-finding skills, aloholism and other substance abuse, sexual dysfunction, community energy consumption, fears and nervous habits, and stress-related disorders. Taking a "general practitioner" behavioral approach means being able to treat behaviorally an assortment of these and other clinical problems. The behavior therapist must assume the general practitioner's role for two reasons. First, it provides the therapist with continually different cases to treat and, thus, requires close contact with the professional literature in many different areas. Such variability in referred problems helps avoid "burnout" and facilitates professional development. Second, diversity in the problems treated in a behavior therapy

private practice allows for more referrals from different sources. This diversity then forms a wide referral base on which to run a private practice. The behavior therapist can serve as a behavioral consultant writing treatment programs for schools, retardation facilities, clinics, business and industry, (conducting workshops on stress management, assertiveness training, and behavior modification), develop a job-seekers club, weight control and smoking cessation groups, conduct parent training groups, and conduct therapy with children, adolescents, and adults individually and in groups. Such diversity facilitates a regular flow of client referrals.

Within the context of a broad-based referral system, one can define some limits of specialization. Fishman and Lubetkin (1983) indicate that a "lion's share of referrals" may occur in the specialty area that the clinician may select (e.g., phobias, sexual disorders, social skills deficits, or tics). However, it is recommended that the clinician first get established in the community as a behavior therapist, and then gradually begin to limit the practice or some portion of the practice to some specialty area. This approach thus avoids too much specialization and a narrowing of the flow of referrals to the practice.

3. *The behavior therapist is often the "stepchild" in the community.* As stated previously, an independent practitioner of behavioral psychology is likely to be looked upon by fellow colleagues and other helping professionals as having a practice that is limited in scope. Referrals, therefore, may be for discrete problems, such as tantrums, bedwetting, and phobias, whereas the "deeper rooted" problems are believed to be best dealt with in long-term traditional psychotherapy.

4. *It is lonely for the behavior therapist in the private practice community.* Even one's fellow psychologists may look upon the behavior therapist as one who takes a narrow view of psychotherapy. One may, therefore, be isolated professionally from other practitioners in the community. Professional development must rest, then, on attendance at periodic behavioral seminars in cities near and far, the annual conventions of the Association for the Advancement of Behavior Therapy (AABT) or the Association of Behavior Analysts (ABA), or reading cover to cover one's journals and books. In the United States, there are, of course, geographic areas where there is a larger distribution of behavior therapists in practice. These individuals can meet to discuss particularly perplexing client problems, professional and business experiences in practice, and the recent innovations in the field of behavior therapy.

5. *Reeducation of the professional community and lay public is a necessary part of private practice.* Despite the fact that behavior therapy has enjoyed greater exposure, the professional community and lay public still may view its tenets and techniques with outdated claims of bribery, use of

M & M's, or the "carrot-and-stick" approach. It is vital that the behavior therapist be invited to speakers' bureaus, and talk at medical and dental society meetings, PTA meetings, or on radio and television about the field of behavior therapy, its advantages, its criticisms, and its contributions. These attempts to correct public and professional misconceptions as described by Turkat (1979) can facilitate referrals, greater recognition, and credibility of the behavior therapist in the community.

6. *Reeducation of the client toward a behavioral analysis approach should accompany behavioral assessment and intervention of the referred problems.* In therapy with clients, a behavioral approach is a rather novel and scientific way to analyze the client's difficulties. The client may have misconceptions about his or her difficulties (Wolpe, 1973), and these misconceptions can inhibit progress by the client. Briefly educating the client as to how his or her maladaptive behavior was generated and how modification of the contingencies in the environment in conjunction with other behavioral and cognitive/behavioral procedures can influence more adaptive behavior, can facilitate treatment, and teach the client to be his or her own therapist.

7. *Objective assessment and evaluation measures are a vital part of behavior therapy private practice.* In order to define the extent of the effectiveness of the behavioral procedures being used, it is vital for the therapist to require the client to collect data on the frequency, rate, latency, and/or duration of the targeted problem. Data sheets and graphs should be an integral part of the client's file. This objective data collection and presentation allows the therapist to troubleshoot the prescribed procedures, as well as to give feedback of progress to the client.

8. *Behavior intervention methods should, in most all cases, be based upon researched and published procedures showing at least moderate success.* This is an obvious assumption for the behavior therapist. In planning treatment, the therapist should refer to the literature on the presenting problem. This literature review forces the professional to stay current with the basic and applied research literature and provide support for the proposed methods of treatment. This assumption also suggests the need for taking continuing education courses for upgrading one's skills.

9. *A broad-spectrum behavioral approach encompassing the five roots of behavior therapy—behavior modification, classical conditioning, social learning and self-control, cognitive psychology, and psychophysiology—is very effective for treating the diversity of problems referred.* One can expand the scope of services that are offered by practicing broad-spectrum or multiform behavior therapy. The availability and variety of the procedures developed in behavior therapy provide the therapist with a greater selection of procedures effective for a diversity of problems and client populations.

10. *Working long hours beyond client or agency contact hours is necessary for a successful private practice.* Like any other psychology practice, time beyond contact hours is necessary for report writing, treatment planning, case management, administrative duties, practice promotion, and correspondence. In a behavior therapy practice, writing behavior programs during hours after the scheduled session time is additionally necessary for keeping up with client progress, needs, problems, and goals for treatment. This program planning, coupled with the other general practice responsibilities, can make for long working hours.

11. *Developing a business perspective as well as clinical perspective will maintain one's practice and enable it to prosper financially and grow professionally.* The clinician must continually be aware of, and implement, sound business practices that involve collections, accounts receivable, accounts payable, taxes, insurance reimbursements, employee and business insurances, investments, IRAs, Keogh and profit-sharing plans, and legal and professional liability and expenses. In doing so, cash flow is maximized to offset overhead, there is a reasonable profit margin, and the business is well organized. The clinician must continually be aware that his or her practice is also a business, so that decisions can be based on not only what is good for the practice professionally but also from a business standpoint.

2.1. GETTING REFERRALS

Getting referrals has often been referred to as "beating the bushes." This phrase, at least, implies that the practitioner seeks every avenue for building up his or her referral sources. As Fishman and Lubetkin (1983) point out, there is no substitute for a good reputation for getting referrals. There are, however, indirect as well as direct methods for developing a flow of referrals to the office. As one's practice begins, effectiveness and an overall good reputation must follow to maintain these sources of referrals.

2.1.1. Indirect Methods

Some methods of presenting oneself to the public usually do not result in a large number of direct referrals and are more indirect in their value as referral sources. Being on radio or television talk shows, writing an article for local, state, or national lay magazines or newspapers, or being quoted as an expert in newswriter's articles on pertinent issues are usually, by experience, trickling sources of referrals. However, as Lubetkin (1983) points out, exposure on *local* talk shows and being quoted as an expert in specialized science sections of the *local* newspaper are more productive indirect methods of getting referrals. These practices do serve overall to educate the public about behavior therapy so that when the need arises, the public and various professionals will understand more what behavior therapy is and is not, and who is identified as a behavior therapist. Once educated, the public and professional realms will then refer more clients to the behavior therapist. As reported in a recent issue of *Behavior Therapist* (Keane, 1983), AABT has created a media committee to facilitate greater favorable media coverage of events and conventions in major cities across the country. Such coverage may demystify and "rehumanize" the process of behavior therapy.

Browning (1982), in his book on private practice issues, refers to the "seed principle" for getting referrals and expanding one's practice. Basically, this author suggests that by providing gratis services in the beginning of one's practice for such situations as hardship cases and workshop hours, these early seeding efforts will return many referrals to increase the client load. The author presents no data in support of this principle, but research can be found in the behavioral literature to lend credence to such an approach. In studies of social comparison processes (Hake & Vukelich, 1973; Hake, Vukelich, & Kaplan, 1973), results suggest that persons tend to establish a reciprocal and cooperative relationship in which reinforcers can be mutually earned and provided. Azrin, Naster, and Jones (1973) applied this principle to the analysis and treatment of marital discord. For the clients treated, reciprocity counseling helped establish an environment in the home in which spouses could once again serve as reinforcers for each other. Similarly, when workshops are provided or therapy services are rendered gratis, the principle of reciprocity, providing reinforcers to the one who reinforces, may operate. Hence, Browning's seed principle may have some validity for the development of referrals.

2.1.2. Direct Methods

The direct methods of getting referrals involve both the lay public and professional sectors in the community. Professionally, it is advisable for the independent practitioner who is beginning in practice to:

1. Establish a listing in the telephone directory as a behavior therapist (the telephone directory may be a poor source of referrals, depending upon the different regions of the country). Checking with the local

professional psychological association regarding how to advertise taste-
fully in the newspaper, on the television and radio, or in the telephone
book is suggested (Fishman & Lubetkin, 1984). The yellow pages ads
can even be in boldface type for emphasis to potential clients. If a larger
block or display ad is chosen, this can be expensive and may not return
the necessary amount of new referrals to justify the expense. However,
if desired, the advertising division of the phone company will help
design an ad at no extra charge that conforms to the ethics of the profession. Also, when placing the ad strategically in the yellow pages listing,
Fishman and Lubetkin suggest the "Clinic" heading, as their clients
report referring to this heading first in the search for a therapist.

2. Give pertinent and timely talks to such professional groups as
dental and medical societies and the local bar association.

3. Visit family practitioners, internists, and pediatricians to discuss
services because these physicians see a variety of family difficulties.

4. Present programs to the grand rounds of physicians at various
hospitals on subjects of interest.

5. Talk with judges, individually and as a group.

6. Obtain privileges at the local psychiatric hospitals.

7. Do in-service training for teachers and principals.

8. Get appointed to the variety of professional boards such as the
Mental Health Association, Association for Retarded Citizens, and child
guidance clinics.

9. Obtain contracts for services through the Department of Health
and Rehabilitative Services, the Veterans Administration, Division of
Vocational Rehabilitation, Foster Care, and other public and private
agencies.

10. Introduce oneself to the professionals in the vicinity of the
office.

11. Consider offering lower fees than your colleagues as one begins
practice.

12. Teach courses at a local university because an excellent referral
source comes from faculty and former students at a university.

In the lay community, similar steps must be taken to insure referrals
will continue to the practice. Such methods include getting appointed
to lay boards, such as a private school board of directors. Also, placing
one's name on all speakers' bureaus of groups in the community, such
as Kiwanis, Rotary, the Masons, Pilot Club, Junior League, Parents without Partners, National Council of Jewish Women, Knights of Columbus,
and others will, by speaking about issues in behavior therapy, help
identify one with behavioral psychology. Giving free workshops to
churches, private schools, or other community groups on a periodic

basis, advertising these workshops in the local newspaper, and conducting them on site in churches, schools, or hospitals is an excellent method of exposure and source of referrals.

One of the most important direct methods of gaining referrals is through attaining the goals set in therapy with a client and in successfully completing treatment. The client will tell his or her friends, who will then refer themselves, also. Such word-of-mouth referral proceeds geometrically, not arithmetically. The best referral is by a satisfied client. That client will also relate improvement to the family physicians, who may then refer their other clients. Of course, client satisfaction is not necessarily related to successfully mastering goals established in treatment. Even if the client does not attain the treatment goals, the fact that the professional practitioner has maintained a personal relationship with this client and has provided quality services is also extremely important.

2.2. "NURTURING" REFERRALS: KEEPING A STEADY FLOW

There are many methods for getting referrals, but there is only one method of keeping them. That is, as Lubetkin (1983) and Fishman and Lubetkin (1983) point out, successfully maintaining a private practice in behavior therapy requires the independent practitioner to establish and "nurture" a personal relationship with other professionals, the lay public, and, of course, the client. Although not necessarily behavioral terminology, nurturing can be operationally defined to include but not be limited to such behavior as the following:

1. Socializing with referring professionals at parties, sports, or other social/professional functions.

2. Sending "thank you" notes or letters to referring professionals stating appreciation for their referral and confidence in the services provided.

3. Calling the referring professional to discuss his or her appraisal of the client's difficulties and concerns *before* treatment.

4. With the permission of the client, calling the professional who referred him or her to provide an update of the client's progress *during* treatment, where appropriate. This is an especially important response to a physician's referral. Oftentimes, a physician will refer a client and never hear about the client's progress. Setting up a regular schedule of calling the referring physician to update the client's progress is important to the physician and increases the likelihood of further referrals.

5. Sending a copy of the behavioral/psychological evaluation to the referring professional (physician, psychiatrist), during and after treatment, for his or her records and review. Such reporting allows for that

referring professional to continue with the treatment of the client's problems pertinent to his or her specialty.

6. Occasionally taking extra time with a client beyond the scheduled 50-minute hour (if such extra time does not interfere significantly with the next hour's client) to more thoroughly complete the therapy session. Such extra time spent puts emphasis quite properly on the *personal* relationship rather than purely on the business relationship. Clients are more apt to refer other clients who are looking for a competent, professional, *and* personable therapist more interested in providing professional services, rather than operating strictly as a business.

7. Using *rapport building* and relationship enhancement (Ford & Kendall, 1979; Goldstein, 1980; Swan & MacDonald, 1978) techniques before the therapy session gets underway and throughout the session. Such variables as therapist "credibility," "empathy," "warmth," and "self-disclosure" are, according to Goldstein, important to the progress of the client in therapy. These terms do need to be operationalized to be useful in practice. Questioning and discussing nontherapy matters with the clients, such as outside interests they have, an ill child, their car repairs, or recent vacations allow for an easy transition to discussing more critical issues. This personal, rather than mechanical, approach to each therapy hour is highly beneficial to word-of-mouth referrals. Such referrals are a major source of the client load.

8. Giving talks on subjects that appeal to a respective group of people. Topics for such groups should be tailored to the requests from the group (e.g., stress management techniques for the high-level executive). The titles of such talks need to be timely and "catchy" (Lubetkin, 1983). Using humor and engaging in relaxed mannerisms (smiling, joke telling, using compliments and friendly quips to the audience) during the talk are also part of this nurturing of referral sources (i.e., good public relations).

9. Spending extra time answering questions after a talk or workshop as well as snacking afterward with the audience over coffee and donuts is an excellent method of establishing the personal relationship with these referral sources.

2.3. PROFESSIONAL SERVICES OFFERED BY THE BEHAVIOR THERAPIST

There are a variety of services that the behavior therapist can provide through the private practice. The following is a list and description of these different services.

2.3.1. Individual Therapy

Individual therapy service constitutes the backbone of the clinical end of the practice. In individual therapy, the variety of clinical problems referred are subject to therapeutic intervention. Such individual therapy may involve adjunctive sessions with parents, spouses, teachers, or other significant others in the client's environments.

2.3.2 Behavior Group Therapy

Group therapy based on the Lieberman (1980) and Rose (1977) models of behavior group therapy is an excellent addition to the practice. Such a group can serve as a resource for the client in individual therapy, for the client who experiences difficulty in social situations, and for the client who cannot afford individual therapy but whose problems can be legitimately dealt with in a group setting after some initial individual sessions have been conducted to determine such a need. Fees for this service are usually much lower than for individual therapy. Assertive training, social skills training, and other closed-ended issues can be dealt with in groups.

In group therapy, groups are usually somewhat homogeneous. Clients are taught to define their problematic behavior and cognitions, count target behaviors to change, and roleplay and implement treatment procedures with the group members and therapist, similar to individual therapy. Role playing, support, reinforcement, and generalization are obvious benefits of group therapy to the individual client.

2.3.3. Behavioral Evaluations

Many facilities seek out the services of qualified behavior therapists to assist them in a variety of ways. The entire facility may be in need of an evaluation of its overall service delivery program with regard to its behavioral services to its clients. Such treatment facilities as retardation centers, state hospitals, schools, and mental health and child guidance clinics secure the services of the behavioral consultant to evaluate the strengths, weaknesses, and deficits of the facility for its eventual improvement. Second, the facility may be in need of specialized evaluation services for the purpose of providing assistance with dangerous or difficult clients when previous behavior procedures have met with little success. The behavioral consultant can observe the client, talk to his or her trainers, and develop a treatment plan appropriate to the problems presented.

2.3.4. Parent Training

Parent training is an important area of child treatment, whether used as adjunct to individual child therapy or exclusively as the primary method of treatment. A structured approach to teaching parents effective methods for child rearing and in dealing with specific clinical problems of children is an important service that the behavior therapist can provide through the private practice.

2.3.5. Marital Therapy

The field of marital therapy has seen rapid development of procedures helpful in relieving the problems of marital discord. The behavioral clinician who chooses to provide marital therapy services either as a specialty or as a regular service of the practice needs to ensure that he or she is well read on the recent literature and expert in the innovative procedures currently in that literature.

2.3.6. Sex Therapy

The procedures of sex therapy developed by such therapists as Masters and Johnson, LoPiccolo, and Lobitz are highly effective for such clinical problems as premature ejaculation, frigidity, impotence, and vaginismus. This is a specialized area, and certification as well as continuing education may be needed to provide these services.

2.3.7. Job-Finding Training

The procedures developed by Azrin, Flores, and Kaplan (1975) have served as the framework for job-finding clubs around the United States. These procedures are highly applicable to programs through the Department of Vocational Rehabilitation and university career counseling centers.

2.3.8. Agency and Hospital Consultation

The behavior therapist/consultant can secure agency contracts to provide behavioral services for in-service training, the structuring of entire behavioral programs, or behavioral evaluations as described previously. Also, the behavior therapist can obtain hospital privileges to assist the medical professional on such issues as medication compliance, pain management, and other such behavioral and somatic issues.

2.3.9. Business Consultations

With the recent advent of health maintenance organizations (HMOs), preferred provider organizations (PPOs), and employee assistance programs (EAPs), the behavior therapist is in the unique position of providing short-term evaluations and treatment as well as being able to conduct training seminars on such business-related issues as stress management, assertiveness training, time management, and parenting for the career employee.

2.3.10. Biofeedback Therapy

Biofeedback is used by therapists as an adjunct to psychotherapy (e.g., electrodermal responses in desensitization, EMG training for relaxation training exercises). Biofeedback is also used to deal directly with psychosomatic stress-related disorders such as migraine headaches, insomnia, tension headaches, Raynaud's disease, and spasmodic torticollis.

3

Conducting a Private Practice in Behavior Therapy

3.1. GENERAL COMMENTS

As indicated in Chapter 2, the mechanics for setting up and maintaining a behavior therapy private practice are not found in the research literature. Goldfried (1983) points out that the behavioral clinician's work is not a science or an art but a craft. That is, there is a plethora of research articles validating clinical behavior therapy procedures. However, their application to the problems of individual clients is under less controlled conditions than in the research settings and is, certainly, less systematic at times (Swan & MacDonald, 1978). Although there is a technology of therapeutic change, the application of behavior techniques in private practice is best done by the professionally sensitive and experientially trained behavior therapist, that is, the skilled behavioral craftsman. Successful behavior therapy is, thus, largely the result of a clinician's experience (Lubetkin, 1983; Wachtel, 1977) rather than the mere result of knowledge of the straightforward application of treatments of choice for specific problems. Beck, Rush, Shaw, and Emery (1979) caution the therapist in viewing behavior therapy as "gimmick oriented."

Behaviorists are not very comfortable with subjective terminology and nondefinable phenomena such as therapist "sensitivity," which is part of "craftsmanship." However, this term can be defined operationally. "Sensitivity" may then include the skills a therapist demonstrates in identifying all antecedent and consequent events, describing the behavior topographically, gathering data on the client's behaviors, and determining which antecedents and consequences are currently maintaining the client's difficulties. "Sensitivity" must also include social reinforcement and relationship enhancement techniques in order to maintain social control over the client's behavior (i.e., rapport).

3.2. PROCEDURAL CONCERNS FOR THE PROVISION OF BEHAVIOR THERAPY SERVICES

The therapist beginning to organize a private practice is often concerned about how a practice is best structured. Issues relating to intake, assessment, treatment, and evaluation of the client's presenting problems must be addressed, and procedures must be specified to conduct an effective and successful practice of behavior therapy.

The discussion that follows is a description of the approach taken by me in each of these procedural issues. Certainly, this description is not the *only* approach but serves merely to provide a structural outline for novice and experienced therapists to follow in their practices of behavior therapy. The intake process simply involves the client's or client's guardian filling out the appropriate intake questionnaire(s) prior to seeing the therapist. The structure of this questionnaire is important in that, in addition to the basic personal data requested (age, sex, school, parents, siblings), questions regarding the individual's presenting problems (frequency, duration, antecedents and consequences) are also asked. For the child or adolescent, a family and developmental medical history may be completed by the parents in addition to a statement of problems and desired goals in treatment. For the adult, the latter two forms (statement of problems and desired goals) are also requested. Such a comprehensive intake is highly informative and quickly places the therapist in the midst of analyzing the client's problems almost before seeing the client. The more quickly therapy can be started and completed, the more cost-effective it is for the client. Of course, it is naive to think that the therapist can solve the client's problems before thoroughly questioning the client. Rather, the intake helps shorten the process considerably with respect to time, money, and suffering by the client. As part of the intake process, a therapy treatment agreement is presented to the client for his or her signature (S. Berkowitz, personal communication, November, 1983).

The Appendix to this chapter is an example of the client–therapist treatment used by the author. This therapeutic agreement specifies the therapist's qualifications, where these qualifications are listed, what behaviors are expected of the client (or client's guardian), and those to be expected of the therapist. Issues relating to treatment fees, confidentiality, insurance, and appointment cancellations are also written in the treatment agreement. This agreement is then discussed in detail with the client during the first session so that any misconceptions about therapy can be cleared up and any questions the client has may be answered. Of course, the analysis of the client's problems may come several sessions after the initial session at which time an evaluation will be done with the client or client's guardian.

3.3. RELATIONSHIP ENHANCEMENT AND RAPPORT BUILDING

It is a rather straightforward task for academicians to plan curricula that teach the behavioral steps needed to functionally analyze a client's difficulties. It is, however, much more difficult to teach "rapport building" and relationship enhancement techniques to therapists. Nonetheless, these skills are vital to the therapeutic process and to treatment outcomes. Ford (1978) has documented the importance of a client–therapist relationship that facilitates behavior change. It seems clear that some nonspecific factors of this relationship have to operate in order for behavior change to occur. Relationship enhancement methods serve to increase the reinforcement value of the therapist. Goldstein (1980) suggests that structuring the session in such a way as to inform the client of the therapy process and of its desired outcomes facilitates a greater therapist-to-client working relationship. Therapist characteristics, as described by Goldstein, should involve "expertness, credibility, and empathy." Beck et al. (1979) suggest that an effective therapist demonstrate warmth, accurate empathy, and genuineness. Although these terms are quite subjective "under-the-skin" phenomena, it is very important for the therapist to be able to:

1. explain clearly and concisely the analysis of the client's problems and how they will be treated;
2. compliment the client for appropriate behavior while using direct but tactfully stated critical statements to reduce client inappropriate behavior;
3. smile and use humor with the client where appropriate;
4. make caring statements about the client and client's family, as long as such statements do not strengthen inappropriate behavior in the session;

5. use for oneself the skills that the therapist is teaching as a model for the client; and
6. use self-disclosure statements when necessary for greater rapport building and relationship enhancement.

In addition to these behaviors, Beck *et al.* suggest that the optimal relationship between client and therapist involves a therapist who can accurately empathize with the client's feelings and attitudes and who expresses empathetic, sympathetic, and understanding statements regarding the client's problems. Other characteristics are that the therapist make no value judgments critical of the client's difficulties and behave in such a way that the client can readily discuss his or her problems assured of therapist "sensitivity" and professional intuitiveness.

Turkat and Brantley (1981) suggest, however, that the vague therapist characteristics suggested by Goldstein (1980) and Beck *et al.* (1979) have to be operationalized and research done on each dimension before inclusion of these nonspecific factors into counseling. However, the fact that 58% of respondents in a survey of behavior therapists (Swan & MacDonald, 1978) are already using these techniques suggests that these methods, in whatever form, are already part of successful behavior therapy. Further research on these issues would, of course, improve treatment outcomes.

3.4. INITIAL SESSION

In the treatment of children, usually the initial session is with the parents of the child. Phillips and Mordock (1970) and Holland (1970) outline procedures for conducting behavior therapy with children. The parents are made an integral part of therapy so as to effect change in their behavior that, in turn, will modify the child's behavior by altering the child's environment. Some questions directed toward the parents during the initial session are:

1. What are all the problems?
2. What is their frequency, duration, latency, and rate?
3. What has been tried thus far?
4. What are the reinforcers and punishers in the child's environment?
5. Has the child seen a therapist previously?
6. What are the developmental factors that have brought the child to this point?

7. What are positive behaviors the child demonstrates (i.e., behavioral assets)?
8. Describe the sibling and peer relationships.
9. Does the child demonstrate additional problems, such as fears, phobias, nervous habits, nervous tics, bedwetting, or nightmares?
10. Describe the child's behavior and achievement in school.
11. How often does the parent verbally and physically praise the child versus how often do the parents verbally reprimand and impose punishment of the child?

The therapist then attempts to translate these vague and general descriptions of the child's problems into objective statements and goals.

After the parents are thoroughly questioned, they are given a quiz developed by O'Dell, Tarler-Benlolo, and Flynn (1979) that tests their knowledge of parenting skills and behavior modification. The results of this test are then compared with the results of the same test given after the parents have read *Parents Are Teachers* (Becker, 1971) and *Families* (Patterson, 1971), on which this test is based. As the parents begin reading these texts, they usually begin modifying the home environment to reflect a more positive approach to parenting. Parents are also asked to increase the frequency of praise to their child from the point of the initial interview onward as a first means of modifying their child's behavior.

In the initial session with an adult, much time is spent discussing the nature of the adult client's difficulties. The antecedents and consequences for each problematic behavior, the topography, frequency, duration, latency, rate of the behavior, and the possible historical contributions to the development of the referred problems are all discussed. The initial interview is based on questions similar to those suggested by Wolpe (1973).

Once the (child or adult) client's problem has been explored thoroughly, it is necessary, as Wolpe (1973) points out, to educate the client to understand behavior therapy and to clear up misconceptions about his or her problems. The client can be educated by a number of different methods, such as (a) use of a didactic presentation by the therapist on behavior modification and therapy; (b) an assignment to read books such as *I Can If I Want To* (Lazarus & Fay, 1975) or *A New Guide to Rational Living* (Ellis, 1975); (c) a demonstration of a completed behavior program with graphs, data collection sheets, and procedural descriptions; or (d) a series of videotapes or films available through various publishers or through a nearby university library system on such topics as reinforcement theory, cognitive therapy, social learning through imitation and modeling, and biofeedback and self-control. Clearing up a client's anxiety based on misconceptions about the nature and severity of his or her difficulties is often an important first step in treating the client's problems.

3.5. ASSESSMENT, FORMS, AND PROCEDURES

In addition to this intake information, initial interview, and reeducation phase, it is also advised that a series of paper/pencil questionnaires be given to the client to complete after the first session. Parents are given a statement of goals and observations of their child's behavior, a frequency chart to keep track of the problem behaviors, a reinforcement survey for their child to complete, and the assignment to record the number of praise statements and criticism statements they make in the week before the next scheduled visit with the child. Adults may be asked to self-monitor the target behaviors and complete several questionnaires. A life history questionnaire (Cautela, 1977; Lazarus, 1971; Wolpe, 1973), the Self-Rating Behavior Scale (Cautela, 1977), the Revised Willoughby Questionnaire for Self-Administration, the Bernreuter S-S Scale (Wolpe, 1973), a fear survey (Wolpe & Lang, 1969), an assertive inventory (Gambrill & Richey, 1975; Rathus, 1973) and the Beck Depression Inventory (Beck, 1978b; Beck, Ward, Mendelson, Mock, & Erbaugh, 1961) are suggested forms. It is also advised that a locus-of-control questionnaire be administered to determine the client's typical methods of solving his or her problems. Some behavioral clinicians may wish to use standard psychometric testing as well as the MMPI as adjunctive data.

In addition to this standard general assessment package, the clinician may want to explore, in detail, the various aspects of the client's presenting problems. Thus, a specialized assessment may need to be done. The following is a list of some of these paper/pencil questionnaires used for the assessment of specialized problems.

Behavior Modification
1. Frequency of praise and criticism statements by parents and teachers
2. Parent Record Sheet (Forehand & McMahon, 1981)
3. Frequency chart for counting maladaptive behaviors
4. Marlatt's (1976) Drinking Profile
5. Marital Pre-Counseling Inventory (Stuart & Stuart, 1973)
6. Child Behavior Checklist (Achenbach & Edelbrock, 1979)

7. Parent Attitude Test (Cower, Husk, Beach, & Rappoport, 1970)
8. Walker Problem Behavior Identification Checklist (Walker, 1976)

Pavlovian/Classical Conditioning
1. Cues for Tension and Anxiety Scale (Cautela, 1977)
2. Daily Monitoring Forms for Relaxation Exercises (Cautela, 1977)
3. State-Trait Anxiety Inventory for Adults and Children (Spielberger, 1973)
4. Covert Conditioning Survey Schedule (Cautela, 1977)
5. Aversive Scene Survey Schedule (Cautela, 1977)
6. Imagery Survey Schedule (Cautela, 1977)

Bandura/Social Learning
1. Social Anxiety and Social Performance Survey schedules (Cautela, 1977)
2. Vignettes of social situations for simulation and role playing for children and adults (Edelson & Rose, 1978)

Cognitive Restructuring
1. Rational Self-Help Form (Ellis, 1976)
2. Daily Log of Dysfunctional Thoughts (Beck, 1978a)
3. Daily Mood Rating Form and Self-Monitoring Log (Clarkin & Glaser, 1981)

Biofeedback and Physiological Reconditioning
1. Tension and Migraine charts (Stroebel & Sandweiss, 1979)
2. Pain Rating Scale (Williamson, Labbé, & Granberry, 1983)
3. A life stressors profile

Clients are typically quite cooperative in completing the many questionnaires they have been given. It is helpful to explain to the client that information on these forms will help to assess the major facets of the client's functioning and dysfunctioning. Recommending to the client to break up the time filling out these forms is advised.

Swan and MacDonald's (1978) national survey of behavior therapists indicated that adequate assessment of the client's presenting problems was one of the most important responsibilities of the therapist. Much has been written on the subject of assessment and how best to do adequate assessment of a client's difficulties (Barlow, 1981; Heinrich, 1978; Kanfer & Saslow, 1969; Kazdin, 1984; Lazarus, 1976; Nelson & Barlow, 1981; Nelson & Hartmann, 1981).

Kazdin (1984) discusses different approaches to the assessment and diagnosis of childhood disorders. However, these approaches are equally applicable to the assessment and diagnosis of the problems presented by adults. The three types of assessment and diagnosis are the methods detailed in the third edition of the *Diagnostic and Statistical Manual of Mental Disorders* or DSM-III (American Psychiatric Association, 1980), multivariate assessment, and, of course, behavioral assessment. The DSM-III is a general description of a client's problems based on a theoretical framework and on various descriptive and statistical characteristics. Concepts used to describe client problems in the DSM-III vary in their description of the problems' severity.

The therapist first considers a client's *symptoms*. From this group of symptoms, the therapist may indicate that the client has a *syndrome*, or group of behaviors, affects, and cognitions that covary in some way. A *disorder* is more complex than a syndrome in that more can be said about a disorder. There may be some biological correlates, a natural course of the disorder that is somewhat predictable and not attributable to any other disorder. The most severe classification is that of *disease*. Within this classification, the pathology of the difficulties are known, as is the etiology and path of the psychopathological process, according to Kazdin. Additional dimensions of this multilevel approach to assessment and diagnosis include the therapist's considering the breadth, chronicity, onset, and various contextually related factors to the clinical problem.

The second of Kazdin's review of assessment procedures is the multivariate analysis. In this approach, factor analysis is used to develop a constellation of symptoms along some arbitrarily labeled dimension. There are, in fact, various rating scales based on this multivariate approach. The Behavior Problem Checklist by Peterson (1961) and the Child Behavior Checklist by Achenback and Edelbrock (1979) describe such dimensions as shyness, depression, and social withdrawal as typical classes of symptoms grouped in this factor analysis approach. Like the DSM-III approach, the multivariate approach has many procedural and conceptual problems that make it less than maximally acceptable in the analysis of clinical problems.

The third approach is the behavioral diagnostic and assessment approach. This method focuses on how to treat a client's problems rather than on some taxonomic system. Within this system, the therapist moves away from being concerned about categorizing problems to more diverse descriptions that lead to treatment of the problems. This behavior-analytic approach does have procedural problems if viewed strictly from a pro-diagnostic view because most behavior analysts avoid psychiatric diagnoses and labels.

Nelson and Hartmann (1981) as well as Heinrich (1978) define *behavioral assessment* as the identification of responses and their controlling variables that include both environmental and organismic variables so as to alter behavior. These authors conceptualize behavioral assessment as a funnel-like approach in which, initially, a broad-based analysis is followed by a more restricted analysis once the targeted behaviors have been identified. This approach is similar to the differentiation between macroanalysis and microanalysis in which all the presenting problems are identified, after which the microanalysis explores each specific problem. Nelson and Hartmann also suggest that during the initial assessment sessions, verbal content information, such as the wide variety of life areas affected by the client's problems, and the nonverbal content not directly related to the problems, such as general appearance and behavior, characteristics of speech, thought content, mood or affect, sensorium functions, intelligence, insight and judgment, be explored. These authors also agree that, along with this interview format, broad-based questionnaires should be completed by the client. Thus, the nature of these authors' assessment involves, as suggested here, an initial interview, a stimulus-organismic-response-consequence (SORC) analysis, nonverbal or verbal content not related to the referred problem, questionnaires, self-monitoring, stimulation and role playing (Flowers & Booream, 1980), physiological measures, IQ or academic tests, and naturalistic observations.

Kanfer and Saslow (1969) have developed an elaborate but quite time-consuming format for the assessment of a client's problems. Here the therapist classifies behavior according to behavioral excesses, deficits, and assets and issues of self-control with an analysis of the maintaining consequences of each. The authors also incorporate a developmental and sociological/cultural analysis of the individual's behavior and environment akin to the organismic variables analyzed by Nelson and Hartmann (1981) and Heinrich (1978). Unfortunately, this assessment procedure is a very lengthly one and can be very unwieldy. A therapist with a 30- to 40-hour per week caseload might find it difficult to use this valuable assessment tool. Nonetheless, it does offer the therapist a thorough format of behavioral assessment.

Lazarus's (1976) multimodal analysis of behavior is a very useful and efficient way of assessing a client's difficulties. The BASIC ID, representing (B) behavior, (A) affect, (S) sensory, (I) imagery, (C) cognitions, (I) interpersonal, and (D) drugs, for adults, or for children—school issues—allows the therapist to differentiate the vague complaints of the client into distinct categories for intervention. It is also possible that the SORC analysis can be superimposed on the multimodal approach for each area in which problems are identified.

Nelson and Hartmann (1981) indicate that assessment does not only occur in the initial portions of therapy but also throughout the treatment process. Repeating the dependent measures periodically throughout treatment to include questions, direct observations, self-monitoring data, and physiological measures is a way of continually monitoring the effectiveness of treatment.

3.6. EVALUATION

From all of the information supplied—the intake and question-naires, notes from the one-to-two interviews, and results of the paper/pencil tasks—an evaluation of the problems presented for treatment can then be written. In accord with the AABT Guidelines for Human Services, it is recommended that a written evaluation be provided to the client (or the client's guardian). This written evaluation coincides with the commitment made in the general treatment agreement, which states that the therapist agrees to "describe in detail, and give . . . the rationale for the intervention techniques" needed to assist the client in meeting the mutually agreed upon objectives in therapy.

The format for this written evaluation is as follows:

1. Personal Data
   a. Client Name
   b. Address
   c. Age
   d. School or occupation
2. Statement of the problem with operational definitions
3. Functional analysis of the presenting problem(s)
   a. Antecendents, consequences and reference to behavioral topography
4. Long-term goals in therapy
5. Short-term goals in therapy
6. Methods of measuring the targeted behaviors
7. Proposed methods of treating the targeted behaviors
8. Literature references that support the use of these procedures
9. Risks and benefits of treatment for each behavior
10. Projected length of treatment

After the written evaluation has been read by the client and discussed with the therapist, and questions are answered to clarify terminology and procedures, fully informed consent can then be assumed. However, getting the client's signature to acknowledge fully informed consent may be advised. The next step is to begin the treatment of the targeted behaviors, cognitions, anxieties, and fears. Behavioral contracting for specific week-to-week goals is a frequent treatment approach to develop client compliance (Goldiamond, 1975a; Homme, Csayni, Gonzales, & Rechs, 1970). In this specific contract, the therapist and client agree to accomplish certain goals by the next session or by several sessions as enroute objectives to the longer term therapeutic objective. Contracts are then revised or rewritten as the short-term goals are achieved as specified in the evaluation.

A great deal of organization is needed in the conduct of the behavior therapy private practice. It is vitally important that the therapist keep track of the overall treatment plan, what procedures are to be used in which sessions, progress or problems and specific treatment, termination, and follow-up. Fortunately, behaviorists thrive on reducing a technical skill to a clerical task for simplicity, and they have developed a number of forms that allow the therapist to follow the client from intake, assessment, treatment, evaluation, and termination (maintenance and generalization) to follow-up.

3.7. COMPOSITION OF THE THERAPY HOUR

In a past survey of members of the private practice special interest group of the Association for the Advancement of Behavior Therapy (Kaplan, 1983) and other sources (Browning, 1982; Survey of Psychological Services, 1979), information regarding therapy by psychologists has been gathered. For example, the length of the therapy hour is usually 50 minutes with a 10-minute break for making notes in that client's record, to make phone calls to clients and other therapists, and to prepare for the next hour's client. Some therapists have shortened the therapy hour to 45 minutes to allow for these duties. Therapists typically see their clients weekly and sometimes twice per week.

During the therapy hour, a variety of activities are planned. The therapist first reviews the client's homework assignments, graphs the data collected by the client, and discusses the progress and problems related to the completion of these tasks. The "troubleshooting" done by the therapist may involve correcting problems of client noncompliance and attendance, difficulties in data collection, improper application of the treatment procedures, and the ineffectiveness of these procedures. Upgrading short-term goals toward the long-term goals stated in the written treatment evaluation is discussed (Goldiamond, 1975a). Next, the therapy techniques planned for that session (e.g., assertiveness training, contracting, systematic desensitization) are implemented. Finally, the therapist recommends and discusses with the client certain home-work assignments pertinent to the current point of therapy and overall treatment plan for the next week. A behavioral contract may be written for the completion of these assignments from week to week.

The therapist may want to provide the client with a folder in which a copy of the treatment agreement, the written evaluation, data collection forms, homework assignments, and specific treatment recommenda-tions are kept. Much care should be practiced in this optional procedure with regard to ensuring the confidentiality of the client if such a folder is lost, misplaced, or in legal cases, ends up as evidence in court.

Although this systematic approach to therapy seems straightfor-ward and somewhat simplistic, it certainly is not. Rather, the complexity of client problems precludes an inexperienced and mechanical applica-tion of the treatment regimen but demands much skill, experience, and "intuition" on the part of the therapist when problems arise in therapy. The treatment procedures are easily administered; however, the idio-syncrasies or organismic variables (Heinrich, 1978; Kanfer & Saslow, 1969) of the client combined with the referred problem require the finesse and expertise obtained by clinical training and experience. Goldfried (1983) states that there are few rules for the selection of appropriate techniques and that the behavioral literature does not portray adequately what occurs in clinical behavior practice. Goldfried suggests that the experience and "wisdom" of the behavior practitioner is an essential ingredient to the successful formulation of effective methods in clinical behavior therapy.

3.8. HOMEWORK ASSIGNMENTS, CLIENT COMPLIANCE AND NONCOMPLIANCE, AND TROUBLESHOOTING PROBLEMS IN THERAPY

What the client does between sessions is very crucial to the outcome of therapy. Though what is done during the therapy hour is critical to the client's relief from suffering, there is greater assurance for this out-come if the therapist assigns tasks to the client to complete between sessions and the client complies with these assignments.

Shelton and Levy (1981a) surveyed the use of homework assign-ments in the contemporary behavior therapy literature. Their findings indicate that homework assignments are frequently reported in this lit-erature, which suggests a heavy use of such assignments. What is not known is what are the specific components of homework assignments that influence client compliance and how best to make such assignments.

As a part of their research, Shelton and Levy (1981b) have written a text on homework assignments and compliance. These authors cite three reasons clients do not comply with assigned tasks: (a) the client does not have the necessary skills to complete the tasks; (b) the client holds certain cognitive assumptions that interfere with the completion of the assignment; and/or (c) the client's environment supports and provides conditions for noncompliance.

In order to prevent noncompliance, these authors posit 11 propositions that attempt to correct those conditions that might set the opportunity for noncompliance, and instead, increase the likelihood of compliance. These 11 propositions of compliance enhancement are as follows:

1. The therapist must ensure that the assignment is so detailed as to include all the response and stimulus elements necessary to increase the desired behavior.

2. The therapist should not assume that the client possesses the skills necessary to complete the assignment but instead should give direct training of these skills utilizing instructions, coaching, modeling, imitation, reinforcement, and feedback as is needed.

3. All compliance should be reinforced via therapist praise, phone calls by the client to the therapist when a task is completed, through behavioral contracts, and by contacts with significant others in the client's environment.

4. The therapist's use of graded task assignments, starting with very simple tasks and then gradually increasing the complexity and time involved in completing the task, helps to increase client compliance with statements of commitment to change.

5. The therapist should take every opportunity to cue the client to complete the assigned tasks through the use of written assignments on no-carbon-required (NCR) paper, having the client make signs or provide other visible reminders in his or her natural environment, the therapist's making phone calls to the client, the use of timing devices (wristwatches, alarm clocks, a phone ringing), and the reminder by significant others enlisted to aid the client in the completion of homework.

6. The client should make a public commitment to comply to the assigned tasks.

7. The client is to be encouraged to make a private commitment to him- or herself to comply as a means of reinforcing the belief system necessary to follow through with the completion of tasks.

8. The client is to be required to use cognitive rehearsal as a strategy toward successfully completing assignments.

9. The therapist should attempt to anticipate those variables that increase the likelihood of noncompliance and develop strategies for reducing the negative effects of these influences.

10. The therapist should closely monitor the client's completion of the assigned tasks through such means as self-monitoring and monitoring by significant others in the client's environment.

11. In cases of significant noncompliance, the therapist may wish to consider the use of paradoxical intention and other such strategies.

Propositions 9 through 11 address the issues of countertherapeutic beliefs and behavior by the client that affect the completion of the assigned tasks. Beck *et al.* (1979) also discuss the methods and problems associated with homework assignments. Beck *et al.* suggest that each homework assignment be clear and specific, that it be made appropriate to each point of therapy, and that the conditions necessary to do the homework be clearly outlined for the client. Further, these authors indicate several countertherapeutic beliefs that interfere with homework assignments such as the client's viewing the assignments as nothing more than common sense, viewing him- or herself as unchangeable, understanding the conceptual basis for the therapist's giving the assignment but indicating an inability in making the behavior part of his or her repertoire, wanting guarantees of cures for his or her faulty beliefs and behaviors, viewing the assignments as only dealing superficially with the client's problem, predetermining that the approach taken in therapy is not helping, and reporting feeling too overwhelmed at the crucial time to engage in the assigned alternative and appropriate behaviors. Behaviors in therapy that are counterproductive involve the client's refusal to talk, the client's continually coming late and/or missing appointments, the client's indicating that he or she is too busy to complete the assignments, and the client's talking too much or tangentially rather than speaking to the issue of his or her difficulties. Other problems include the lack of parent consistency or compliance in following the recommendations of the therapist for child management, excessive emotional responses demonstrated by the parent that serve to undermine the behavioral procedures prescribed, and the client's refusal to accept the principles of learning as an explanation of how behavior develops and how behavior can be influenced.

Troubleshooting, thus, involves correcting problems of client noncompliance and attendance, difficulties in data collection, improper application of the treatment procedures, and the ineffectiveness of these treatment procedures. Problems of client noncompliance may be handled by the therapist more clearly specifying the homework assignments or by tactfully but directly questioning the clients about those beliefs and behaviors and their underlying assumptions that currently interfere with their homework and therapy. Difficulties in data collection may be due to the therapist's overconcern about the complexity of data needed from the client or may be due to the client's view that data collection is too much work, should not be the responsibility of the client, and is not pertinent to his or her "real" problems.

Improper application of the treatment procedures may be due to the therapist's not practicing the appropriate procedures for the referred problems in simulation or in role-playing tasks, or not observing the use of the procedures in the naturalistic settings. If the treatment procedures are proven ineffective for the referred problem, it is the therapist's responsibility either to modify the existing procedures based on other existing research literature or to choose alternative, more restrictive procedures for the amelioration of the client's difficulties.

3.9. TERMINATION AND FOLLOW-UP

Once the treatment goals have been achieved, termination is to be discussed and planned with the client. Termination is usually accomplished by gradually increasing the amount of time between visits toward the projected length of treatment until there is joint agreement by both the client and the therapist for complete cessation of therapy sessions. A reasonable schedule for termination involves scheduling the client every other week at first, then every third week, then once per month for a period of 2 to 3 months before sessions are no longer scheduled. In this manner, relapse is of lower probability due to the ongoing but gradually diminishing contact with the therapist.

Maintaining contact with the client after therapy has been successfully completed is important. Such follow-up can be done by merely calling the client on the phone to inquire generally about the client's adjustment and progress relative to the referred presenting problems or by developing a standardized questionnaire that surveys the client's progress along various dimensions. Lazarus (1971) has developed a questionnaire that the client completes for the purpose of evaluating the therapy services, the success of treatment, and therapist effectiveness. The questionnaire can also be completed in a telephone contact, but the therapist must avoid biasing the client toward giving positive answers due merely to some halo effect of the therapist's contact. Lazarus attempts to avoid such bias by putting a disclaimer in the body of the questionnaire that urges the client to appraise accurately the success of treatment and the current degree of severity of the previously referred problems. It is recommended that follow-up be conducted at 3 months, 6 months, 12 months, 18 months, and 24 months after therapy has been successfully terminated. These intervals approximate research follow-up procedures and attempt to measure the degree of durability and generalization of the treatment procedures over time as well as the degree to which the client has learned to be his or her own therapist.

Follow-up after the client has terminated therapy is important for several reasons. First, it gives the therapist information about the treatment effectiveness as well as feedback about his or her performance as a therapist for that client. Second, such follow-up presents to the former client the view that the therapist has concern about the client even after therapy has been discontinued. Last, because of this expressed concern, that client is likely to recommend that therapist by word of mouth to others who may be in need of assistance. A satisfied client is, of course, the best form of advertising one's professional expertise and care for clients.

APPENDIX

CLIENT–THERAPIST TREATMENT AGREEMENT

I am a psychologist licensed in the state of _____. I received my Ph.D. from _____ University in _____and have been working with children, adolescents, and adults, individually and in groups since receiving my doctorate. My education, background, and experience are listed in the American Psychological Association's Biographical Directory.

In my work, I have found that it is best to specify clearly the form and content of the relationship that you and I are about to enter into by drawing up a list of clearly defined treatment agreements. By spelling out the service that I have to offer, you as the (patient, patient's representative) consumer can best judge whether this is the service that you are seeking. You are also in a better position to evaluate whether you are satisfied with the services. I am completely committed, both professionally and personally, to providing you with the highest quality service.

This contract, or list of treatment agreements, is an aid to help you receive the service that you desire. It is also your assurance that I am well aware and respectful of your basic rights to know the exact nature of the treatment relationship that we have entered into, as well as knowing the treatment objectives and techniques to be developed and implemented.

Please carefully consider the terms of this contract and feel free to discuss any of the agreements with me. By signing the contract, you and I will have agreed to participate fully in the services described unless we mutually agree to revise, or add to, any of the provisions, or until you choose to terminate the service.

Please retain a copy of these agreements and do not hesitate to ask questions or make suggestions and comments at any time.

THERAPIST

1. I will discuss with you and/or your child and help assess objectives and identify goals to be achieved during the treatment.

2. I will discuss with you and/or your child, describe in detail and give you the rationale for the intervention technique(s) that I feel will assist you in meeting your objectives.

3. I will discuss with you the anticipated benefits as well as the possible undesirable effects, if any, associated with these procedures.

4. I will ask you and/or your child to do "homework" and to bring the homework with you to our next session. This will be discussed in detail during each session. The homework will consist generally of two elements:

    A. implementing the technique(s) that we discuss and agree upon, and

    B. making written recordings (i.e., counting, tallying) of events taking place at home.

5. I will monitor our progress each week, discuss and make revisions in the intervention techniques when needed and periodically summarize enroute progress in order to continue towards the specified goals.

Other Agreements

1. _____
2. _____
3. _____

PATIENT

Treatment Procedures

1. After discussing the objectives and the treatment procedures, I freely agree to implement the procedures and work toward the achievement of the objectives, knowing full well the possible desirable and undesirable effects.

2. I agree to complete accurately my weekly "homework" assignment(s) and to bring it with me to the next session, so that the effectiveness of the intervention procedures can be evaluated.

Confidentiality and Termination

1. I specify that the use of any information regarding my identity, stemming from my sessions with you, will remain strictly and absolutely confidential, unless I give written permission to the contrary.

2. I have been assured of my right to terminate participating in the treatment program at any time, for any reason, without needing to explain and without any penalty.

Fees and Appointments

1. I agree to provide you with the following compensation for each 50-minute hour weekly session: $_____.

2. I understand that it is preferred that payment for services be made on a session-by-session basis.

3. I further agree that I shall keep all scheduled appointments, unless a personal emergency occurs, and shall give at least 24 hours notice of my intention to cancel any appointment.

4. I understand that to cancel an appointment, I must either speak to you directly, or leave a specific message regarding cancellation at your office phone number (___) _____.

5. If I do not cancel my appointment at least 24 hours in advance, I understand that I will be charged one-half the amount for that session whether I am in attendance or not.

6. I further understand that I am totally responsible for all payments. It

is I who am being billed for services that I receive and not my insurance company, should I have such insurance covering the service. All arrangements and commitments for insurance are between myself and the insurance company only, and not between the therapist and the insurance company. I understand that the therapist and his secretary will, however, assist me in filling out any insurance forms I have to reimburse me for the services provided.

Date:_____

Patient or Patient's Representatives:

Signature: _____

Signature: _____

Therapist:

Signature: _____

This Client–Therapist Treatment Agreement specifies the responsibilities of the therapist and client as well as other information pertinent to beginning therapy. Reprinted by permission of S. Berkowitz (personal communication, November, 1983).

4

A Review of Common Treatment Procedures in Behavior Therapy

Behavior therapy has had a short history but a long past. This diverse field has developed as a result of the contribution of the early logical positivists in philosophy, the early learning theorists, the social learning and cognitive theorists, and the physiologists as well. In fact, the roots of behavior therapy have evolved from five separate directions in psychology.

The early learning theorists (Hull, 1943; Skinner, 1938; Thorndike, 1933; Watson & Rayner, 1920) contributed enormously to the development of sound principles of learning and behavior. Skinner's book *The Behavior of Organisms* and other such works (Ferster & Skinner, 1957; Skinner, 1953) were major contributions that provided various principles and techniques of operant conditioning to the field of psychology. Principles such as reinforcement, punishment, schedules of reinforcement, and extinction are the basic foundations of operant conditioning. Skinner's followers applied these principles based on research of animal behavior to the study of human behavior. For example, Azrin and his colleagues have applied these principles to the development of techniques for problems of psychotic, retarded, and normal children and adults (Ayollon & Azrin, 1968; Azrin & Foxx, 1971, 1974; Azrin & Lindsley, 1956; Azrin & Nunn, 1973; Azrin & Powers, 1975; Azrin & Wesolowski, 1974; Azrin, Kaplan, & Foxx, 1973; Azrin, Naster, & Jones, 1973; Azrin, Sneed, & Foxx, 1974). From such application of these operant procedures by these and many other applied researchers, the field of behavior modification has evolved.

Classical conditioning is the second "arm" of this multifaceted field of behavior therapy. Pavlov (1927), Anrep (1920), and Sherrington (1906) contributed to the field through their early studies of reflexive behavior, whereas later behavioral researchers studied the emotional concomitants of aversive conditions in animals (Azrin & Holz, 1966; Azrin, Hutchinson, & Hake, 1966; Brady & Hunt, 1955; Brady, Porter, Conrad, & Mason, 1958; Estes & Skinner, 1941; Masserman, 1943; Sidman, 1960). Joseph Wolpe (1958) extended these findings to the analysis of human emotional behavior. His studies of fears and phobias led to the development of various classical conditioning techniques to reduce the debilitating emotional reactions of fear, anger, and anxiety and their accompanying behavior problems, such as smoking, overeating, sexual deviance, and phobic reactions to a variety of environmental conditions.

Albert Bandura's (1962) work on vicarious learning through modeling and imitation, "self-efficacy," and self-control added a third pillar to the foundations of behavior modification and therapy. His studies and those of his colleagues on imitation, vicarious processes, and identification (Bandura, 1965, 1968; Bandura & Hustan, 1961; Bandura, Ross, & Ross, 1963) to induce behavioral, affective, and attitudinal changes (Bandura, Blanchard, & Ritter, 1969) on self-monitoring and self-reinforcement systems (Bandura & Kupers, 1964; Bandura & Whalen, 1966; Bandura, Grusec, & Menlove, 1967), and on aggression (Bandura & Walters, 1959; Bandura, Ross, & Ross, 1963) contributed greatly to the analysis of "internal" and "external" behavioral/emotional events that occur as a result of social learning conditions.

The cognitive psychologists—Beck, Ellis, Lazarus, Kazdin, Kendall, Mahoney, Goldfried, and Meichenbaum—have been the leaders of the most recent and rapidly developing root of this field. Their studies of cognitive events and the creation of a cognitive/behavioral approach to modifying internal thoughts provides an added dimension to the analysis and modification of covert and overt behaviors. Ellis (1962) developed a theory that faulty and irrational styles of thinking are the cause of most psychological disorders. His view, that by challenging thoughts that are irrationally based, both one's feelings (emotions) and behaviors can be altered, has received increased attention by therapists (Rimm & Masters, 1974).

Aaron Beck has also contributed to the field of cognitive theory and practice through such works as *Cognitive Therapy and the Emotional Disorders* (1976) and *Cognitive Therapy of Depression* (1979). Beck views his treatment approach as an "active, directive, time-limited, structured approach" whose underlying assumption is that an individual's affect and behavior are determined by the manner in which the world is cognitively structured by the individual. These cognitions are based on schemata, the client's attitudes and assumptions, which have developed from past experiences. Lazarus (1976) developed multimodal behavior therapy, which is an integration of cognitive, physiological, and behavioral variables. These elements are used to determine the antecedent and organismic conditions of the individual's psychological difficulties to be dealt with in therapy. Mahoney (1974), Goldfried and Merbaum (1973), Kazdin (1978), and Kendall and Hollon (1979) all have attempted to bring the two positions—cognitive theory and behavioral technology—together for the purpose of producing therapeutic change in the client.

Biofeedback and its related methods (autogenic training, somatic and positive imagery) represent the fifth arm of behavior therapy. In 1963, Neal Miller attempted to disprove the hypothesis of Gregory Kimble that the autonomic nervous system was not amenable to voluntary control. During the 1960s and early 1970s, Miller and his associates (DiCara & Miller, 1968; Miller, 1969; Miller & Banuazizi, 1968; Miller & Carmona, 1967; Miller & DiCara, 1968) conducted animal research that ultimately demonstrated that the autonomic nervous system was subject to such voluntary control. From this research, clinicians and researchers such as Basmajian (1974), Brown (1974), Benson (1975), Schwartz (1972), and others (see Yates, 1980) were able to extend these findings to human behavior and to demonstrate control of such autonomic functions as heart rate, blood pressure, muscle tension, skin temperature, skin conductance, respiration, and gastrointestinal activity.

During the development of the field of biofeedback, Hans Selye (1974) described the adaptation syndrome through which the body copes with stress. Stress, according to Selye, is a function of autonomic, genetic, and environmental variables. The adaptation syndrome begins with the *alarm* stage in which the body gears up to prepare for and cope with a sudden stressor. The second stage is called the *resistance* stage. It is here that the body tries to cope for some prolonged time, making autonomic adjustments in the body to sustain it through the perceived stressor. Finally, the *exhaustion* stage is the point at which the body begins "break down" in the area in which it is genetically programmed to be the weakest (i.e., heart failure, strokes, migraine headaches, ulcers, dermatitis, cancer, etc.). With the advent of biofeedback and its related methods, these procedures provide the mechanism to prevent the destructive progression through these stages of stress to distress.

Out of each of these fields of behavior therapy have come many methods of treatment. Use of the clinical techniques described from only one of the five areas may be termed "narrow-band behavior therapy," whereas a more integrative approach utilizing all of these areas may be termed "broad-spectrum behavior therapy" (Lazarus, 1967, 1971). In recent years, there has been an increasing emphasis on utilizing a broad-spectrum behavior therapy approach in clinical practice (Beck, 1976; Ellis, 1974; Humphreys & Beiman, 1975; Lazarus, 1976; MacDonald, 1975; Meichenbaum, 1977; Smith, 1982). It is evident that broad-spectrum behavior therapy has become a more widely practiced mode of treatment.

The purpose of this chapter is to review the many different methods of intervention that have been developed in each of these areas of behavior therapy. This review is not intended to provide the specific steps for implementing each procedure as it is assumed that the clinician entering private practice already has these skills in his or her repertoire. These procedures are deceptively simple, though the experienced and well-trained clinician will avoid the mechanical "quick fix" in favor of a more careful examination of the problems of the client before deciding on the treatment of choice. In addition, some of these procedures can be used individually, whereas others are used together in some combination (within or across the different areas of behavior therapy) deemed appropriate by the clinician and found to be effective in the research and clinical behavioral literature.

4.1. TREATMENT PROCEDURES

The following is a list of the various treatment procedures that have been developed in the different fields of behavior therapy. This list is not intended to be a comprehensive one but does outline the common methods of treating clinical problems in each area. Each procedure is defined, and some treatment considerations are given.

4.2. TRADITIONAL OPERANT CONDITIONING/BEHAVIOR MODIFICATION PROCEDURES

4.2.1. Positive and Negative Reinforcement and the Scheduling of Reinforcers

Definition. Any type of reinforcement involves increasing behavior from its baseline level. *Reinforcement* is defined as the process in which any stimulus that immediately follows a response—or in the case of negative reinforcement, the termination of an aversive stimulus following the response—increases the probability of that response's occurring again.

4.2.1.1. Continuous Reinforcement

Definition. Reinforcement is delivered following each instance of the response.

Treatment considerations. This procedure is only used in the early acquisition of the desired response and is terminated once the individual has learned the new behavior. Responses that are learned via this procedure are more subject to extinction than are other such schedules.

4.2.1.2. Intermittent Reinforcement

Definition. Schedules of reinforcement are predetermined based on the number of responses emitted, or on the amount of time that passes before the next response is reinforced. The most common schedules used in behavior modification programs are fixed ratio, fixed interval, variable ratio, and variable interval.

Treatment considerations. Each of these schedules of reinforcement generates different response patterns. The practitioner must decide which schedule is most appropriate based on the setting in which the response is desired. Also, the issue of maintenance and generalization must be considered because each schedule of intermittent reinforcement has a different topography under the conditions of extinction.

4.2.1.3. Differential Reinforcement of Other Behavior (DRO)

Definition. The delivery of reinforcement after a specified interval of time has elapsed during which some undesired behavior has *not* occurred defines the DRO procedure.

Treatment considerations. This procedure is typically used in tandem with other reinforcement and corrective procedures. Maximum length of the DRO interval should not exceed 30 minutes to 1 hour. However, the minimum length of the interval can vary, depending on the nature and extent of the problem behavior.

4.2.1.4. Differential Reinforcement of Incompatible Behavior (DRI)

Definition. The DRI procedure is one in which the reinforcer(s) that are maintaining some inappropriate behavior are removed while a more appropriate behavior incompatible with the maladaptive behavior is reinforced in its stead.

Treatment considerations. The practitioner must make sure that the alternative behavior is, in fact, incompatible, that extinction is carried out correctly, and that each instance of the more appropriate and incompatible behavior is reinforced to ensure the speedy acquisition of this alternative behavior.

4.2.1.5. *Differential Reinforcement of High (DRH) and Low (DRL) Rates of Behavior*

Definition. The DRL and DRH schedules are variations of differential reinforcement schedules. In both cases, a predetermined rate (low or high) is specified. If the individual responds in such a way that the desired rate is met in a defined interval of time, then reinforcement is delivered. If the desired rate is not met, then the interval recycles.

Treatment considerations. The DRL procedures have been used to reduce the rate of maladaptive behavior, primarily, whereas the DRH procedures have been used in work and other settings where work productivity and a high rate of behavior are the goal of treatment.

4.2.1.6. *"The Good Behavior Game"*

Definition. This is a procedure that combines a variable-interval schedule with a variety of reinforcement procedures and cuing methods. Specifically, individuals are reinforced according to a varied time basis. It is announced that when an audible bell rings and that when it is simultaneously observed that the individual is on task, then reinforcement will be forthcoming. The intervals planned for the audible bell are set by the trainer according to the predetermined periods of the selected variable-interval schedule. Reinforcement may be in the form of some primary reinforcer or by a point or token system.

Treatment considerations. The Good Behavior Game is typically used in groups such as in elementary school classes or in sheltered workshop settings where consistent on-task behavior is desired. The trainer must be aware of the potential of reinforcing off-task behavior by looking around the training area *after* the bell has gone off rather than immediately before or during the bell's tone.

4.2.2. Shaping

Definition. Shaping is commonly defined as the differential reinforcement of successive approximations to some complex terminal behavior.

Treatment considerations. Shaping is a very effective procedure; however, it is a very time-consuming one. The clinician must be careful not to remain at one of the steps in the list of successive approximations too long, to avoid sloppy use of the differential reinforcement procedure at each step, and to avoid making the distance between the successive approximations steps too large, which would otherwise cause a breakdown of the behavior.

4.2.3. Forward and Backward Chaining

Definition. Chaining involves the formation of a complex behavior by teaching each behavioral component of the chain separately and then putting them together in the form of some chained sequence of behavior. Backward chaining involves the development of the complex behavior by teaching the last component in the chain nearest to the primary reinforcers first and then working backward to the first component of the chain. Forward chaining starts with the first component of the chain and works toward the last component of the chain.

Treatment considerations. These procedures have been used with teaching the handicapped child and adult such life skills as toothbrushing, shoe tying, dressing, and walking. As with the shaping procedures, care must be taken by the practitioner to move from one step to another only if the individual has mastered the previous step and to insure that the reinforcers are being used properly.

4.2.4. Instructional Control

Definition. Instructional control involves giving the individual feedback about the correctness of his or her behavior via either physically guiding the client to the correct response, or by verbal feedback such as "yes" or "no," or using both.

Treatment considerations. Most individuals have response to instructional control in their repertoires, but for some children or handicapped children and adults this response has to be taught. Teaching an individual to comply with commands is an essential ingredient to the success of any behavior modification or behavior therapy treatment regimen.

4.2.5. Graduated Guidance

Definition. This procedure is one in which the therapist physically assists the client to perform some desired response. The therapist provides only enough manual guidance necessary for the client to perform the response. As the individual gradually makes the response on his or her own, the therapist can remove the guidance.

Treatment considerations. In the use of this procedure, the therapist should remain near the client to provide guidance to the extent that the client needs such assistance. Physical guidance may be withdrawn as the client makes the response unaided, but the therapist may need to "shadow" the client's hand so as to prevent any flow of movement other than toward the completion of the response. When such shadowing is no longer needed, the therapist may merely stand near the client to apprise the client of the therapist's presence. Graduated guidance is effective with clients who are deaf, blind, or without sufficient instructional control in their repertoires. This procedure should be used only if the client has failed to respond to verbal instructions or modeling by the therapist.

4.2.6. Prompting and Fading

Definition. These methods of instructional control gradually allow the client to make the desired response in a self-initiated manner. Prompting is a form of guidance that initially assumes that the client will not or does not have the skills to make the response in such a way that the trainer or therapist has to provide some degree of guidance. This guidance may be physical or verbal or may involve modeling by the trainer. Fading is defined as the gradual removal of these prompts once the response has been learned.

Treatment considerations. One of the most important considerations one must make in the use of these procedures is that it is very possible that the client may require the prompt in order to make the response and will not make this response when these prompts are faded. Thus, it is very important that the therapist provide only enough prompting to allow the client to make the response and to gradually require the client to make the response for the desired reinforcers as the frequency of the response increases. As the procedure of fading is used, the therapist has to be sensitive to the possibility of extinction of the response, which means thinning out the use of prompts assuming that they have some reinforcement value.

4.2.7. Reinforced Practice

Definition. This procedure is defined as one in which the client is given many opportunities to practice the desired response through the therapist's scheduling of such frequent opportunities. Each time the client practices the response correctly, reinforcement follows, thus ensuring the response will be retained in the repertoire.

Treatment considerations. In some situations when a client is learning a new response, there are not many opportunities for the response to be practiced in the natural environment. Therefore, the therapist may arrange situations in which the client can acquire and practice the response.

4.2.8. Extinction

Definition. Extinction is defined as the termination of the contingent relationship between some response and its maintaining consequences. Extinction results in a gradual decrease in the rate, force, duration, and topography of the response.

Treatment considerations. There are several very important considerations in the use of extinction. First, the reinforcers that normally maintain the response must be identified. Second, the contingent relationship between the response and the reinforcer must be able to be discontinued. Third, the therapist must ensure that the response undergoing extinction must not result in tissue damage to the client or to others, nor that there is a possibility of property destruction. Finally, the parents, staff, or other significant others in the client's environment must be aware that extinction initially results in an increase of the rate, force, duration, variability, or an increase in other inappropriate behavior as the response is undergoing extinction. In the use of extinction, the therapist must be aware of the possibility of increased aggressive behavior or other inappropriate behavior before deciding on the use of this procedure.

4.2.8.1. *Negative Practice*

Definition. This procedure is defined as one in which the client is required to engage repetitively and rapidly in some targeted problematic behavior each time he or she displays that inappropriate behavior. The client is prompted either by verbal statements or by graduated guidance by the therapist to make the response in this prescribed manner.

Treatment considerations. This procedure is usually used with small motor behaviors and should never be used with a targeted behavior that has some probability of resulting in tissue damage to anyone or that may result in the destruction of property. This procedure should also be used only in conjunction with a DRO or DRI procedure. Caution should be used with this procedure as the interval of time of massed practice has not been specified in the literature and has shown mixed results.

4.2.8.2 Stimulus Satiation

Definition. This procedure of response elimination involves the repeated presentation of the desired stimuli to the client for the purpose of reducing the attractiveness of, and influence by, that stimuli.

Treatment considerations. This procedure is confounded with negative practice and aversive control. Caution should be used with this procedure because there is a paucity of literature on its use and because this procedure may result in the exacerbation of the targeted maladaptive behavior.

4.2.8.3. Graduated Extinction or Habituation

Definition. This procedure is defined as the gradual reexposure of fear-evoking stimuli to a client to eliminate avoidance and other fearful behaviors. Exposure is done systematically and uses a hierarchy of fearful items presented on the dimension of least-to-most fearful situations of the phobic reaction.

Treatment considerations. The starting point of the hierarchy must be empirically established, and the items of the hierarchy must be selected and ordered carefully. The presentation of fear-evoking stimuli must be slow because it has been observed in the literature that there is a significant amount of anxiety produced with each presentation of a hierarchy item.

4.2.9. Punishment: Withdrawal of Positive Reinforcers

4.2.9.1. Exclusion Time-Out I

Definition. This procedure involves the immediate and temporary removal of a client from an activity contingent on the client's engaging in some targeted inappropriate behavior. The client is then required to sit in a chair, stand facing the wall, or is sent to his or her room for a period of time, usually 5 to 10 minutes.

4.2.9.2. Exclusion Time-Out II

Definition. In this time-out procedure, the client is removed from an activity for the same period of time and placed behind a screen or some other visual obstruction contingent on the client's exhibiting an instance of the targeted inappropriate behavior.

4.2.9.3. *Seclusion Time-Out*

Definition. Seclusion time-out refers to the procedure in which the client is confined to a room for the purpose of preventing the acquisition of or access to reinforcing stimuli contingent on the occurrence of some inappropriate behavior.

Treatment considerations. There are several important conditions that must be met in the use of time-out. First, any time time-out is used, the therapist must be aware that strong negative emotional behavior from the client will result. Consequently, the client must be observed unobtrusively and continuously so as to prevent the client from hurting him- or herself. Second, this procedure should not be used with clients who have epileptic seizures or self-injurious behavior. Third, all reinforcing stimuli must be identified and absolutely suspended from the client's access during time-out. Fourth, there must be a discrete signal that indicates the onset as well as the termination of the time-out period to be imposed. Fifth, the room in which the client is secluded is to be well-lighted, well-ventilated, and well-heated or -cooled. There should be no safety hazards, and normal standards of comfort must be observed. Sixth, the client should not be confined for more than 5 minutes beyond the point in which inappropriate behavior or other emotional behavior is being exhibited. Seventh, key locks should not be used on rooms in which the client is to be confined. Eighth, the client should be given some contractual agreement upon the end of the time-out period so that the client is apprised of the behaviors desired. Finally, as with all punishment procedures, time-out should only be used in conjunction with reinforcement procedures for highly desired and adaptive behaviors.

4.2.9.4. *Contingent Observation*

Definition. This procedure is a modified version of time-out except that the client is removed from the environment and required to observe another individual engaging in alternatively appropriate behavior incompatible with the behavior of the client that led to his or her removal. The client is then required to return to the group after a predetermined period of observation and engage in the behavior that the offending client observed was more appropriate. Once the client does model the appropriate behavior, the period of contingent observation is concluded, and reinforcement would then be delivered as the client returned to the group and began behaving appropriately as was observed.

Treatment considerations. Care must be taken not to provide reinforcement at the end of the period of contingent observation in such a way that disruptive behavior would be accidently reinforced. This procedure is often used in classrooms, day-care centers, residential facilities, and sheltered workshops. It can also be used with multisibling families.

4.2.9.5. Response Cost

Definition. Response cost is the removal of some positive reinforcer contingent on the occurrence of some targeted maladaptive behavior. Response cost may take the form of loss of privileges, possessions, or previously scheduled and highly desired activities.

Treatment considerations. This program should be used in conjunction with procedures for the reinforcement of appropriate and incompatible behaviors. Also, where appropriate, removal of the client's possessions should be subject to the approval of the client's parents or guardians. The use of some discrete signal should be used to indicate the onset of response cost. All previously determined reinforcers should be empirically demonstrated to be reinforcers and not be assumed as incentives. Finally, the reinforcer should, if at all possible, be logically related to the inappropriate response.

4.2.10. Punishment: Imposing Aversive Stimuli

4.2.10.1. Social Disapproval

Definition. This simple procedure is defined as the use of specific verbal statements and physical gestures as a consequence of a client's inappropriate behavior, which results in a decrease in such disruptive behavior.

Treatment consideration. The therapist must insure that such social disapproval be given in a somewhat elevated voice level, with a furrowed brow, with appropriate gestures, and with a statement of dissatisfaction given immediately upon the client's demonstration of the inappropriate behavior. Name-calling and other forms of verbally abusive language are prohibited.

4.2.10.2. Brief Physical Restraint

Definition. This procedure is defined as one in which the therapist physically restrains the client from engaging in some inappropriate behavior harmful to him- or herself or to others. Restraint is usually for a very brief period of time such as intervals of from 10 to 30 seconds.

Treatment considerations. The therapist must use this procedure in conjunction with DRO or DRI procedures. In addition, the therapist must consider the possibility that the client may become aggressive in response to such physical restraint, thereby exacerbating the original problem. Also, the therapist should avoid inadvertant reinforcement of the client's behavior during the period of physical restraint in such ways as through verbal statements, facial expressions, gestures, or visual contact.

4.2.10.3. Contingent Harmless Substances

Definition. This punishment procedure is defined as the delivery of such harmless substances as air flow, water mist, facial screening, or lemon juice contingent on the occurrence of the client's inappropriate behavior. It is used with behaviors that are typically dangerously aggressive or life threatening.

Treatment considerations. This procedure should be used in conjunction with DRO or DRI procedures. Also, these substances should be determined to be punishers prior to their usage. A physician should be consulted to ensure that these substances will not be harmful to the client.

4.2.11. Overcorrection

Definition. Overcorrection is defined as the set of procedures that require the client to correct a situation to a state better than when the client disrupted the environment with the occurrence of his or her inappropriate behavior. Each of the available overcorrection procedures is designed to be logically related to the disruptive behavior and is immediately made contingent on each of the disruptive behaviors. There are two major components that are common to each overcorrecton procedure. *Restitution* is based on the assumption that the client must correct the situation to a state better than before the disruptive behavior occurred, whereas *positive practice* requires that the client be given the opportunity to practice the appropriate behavior each time the inappropriate behavior occurs. There are several different types of overcorrection procedures. These procedures may be used in combination.

4.2.11.1. Household Orderliness Training

In this procedure, the client must not only correct the appearance of the environment he or she disrupted, but proper care of the environment must be learned by the client's engaging in such behaviors as dusting, moving furniture around, righting overturned chairs, vacuuming, mopping, and other such tasks practiced over a period of time of approximately 30 minutes.

4.2.11.2. *Social Reassurance (Apology) Training*

This procedure assumes that the client engaged in behavior that caused fear, worry, and concern among the others in the environment. To overcorrect this situation, the client is required to apologize by word, gesture, and expression to any client who was in the vicinity of the client's disruptive behavior. Suggested training is approximately 10 minutes.

4.2.11.3. *Oral Hygiene Training*

When the client comes into contact with harmful germs contracted by the client's biting others or mouthing contaminated objects or substances, he is required to brush his teeth and clean his mouth thoroughly by cleansing with toothpaste and by rinsing with oral antiseptic. Such cleansing prevents infection. Suggested training time is 15 to 30 minutes.

4.2.11.4. *Medical Assistance Training*

This procedure is used when a client has physically injured another individual. In the event that this has occurred, the client is required to comfort the other person as much as is possible, apply medicine and bandages to the person's injury, and fill out any medical forms necessary for the injured person. Suggested training time is not more than 30 minutes.

4.2.11.5. *Autism Reversal*

In cases in which the client exhibits autistic, self-stimulatory, and nonfunctional behaviors, autism reversal procedures are used to teach the client the appropriate use of the offending body part used in the self-stimulatory behavior.

4.2.11.6. *Habit Reversal*

For those who exhibit nervous habits, such as nail biting, thumb sucking, or tics, habit reversal procedures teach the client to use positive practice, competing response activities, relaxation procedures, and habit awareness exercises to eliminate the problematic behavior.

4.2.11.7. Theft Reversal

This overcorrection procedure is used for those individuals who steal the property of others. This procedure involves a return of the stolen property, the loss of the offending individual's own possession relative to the theft, social reassurance, and the client's being given the responsibility to protect the belongings of significant others in the environment for a predetermined period of time.

4.2.12. Minimeal Training

Definition. Clients who do not have the skills to feed themselves can be assisted in the acquisition of these skills by this procedure. Specifically, the client is taught correct usage of utensils, finger foods, a napkin, and other such skills through the use of frequent minimeal sessions in which graduated guidance, social reinforcement, and brief time-outs are used to help the client learn self-feeding.

Treatment considerations. Prior to the use of these procedures, the client must have a complete physical examination by a physician, regular monthly dietary and medical review, weight measures taken weekly, fluid intake measured daily, as well as frequency of urination and bowel movements being recorded and reported to the physician.

4.2.13. Token Economy

Definition. This is a highly complex procedure in which the client's behavior results in tokens being given contingent on specified appropriate behaviors. Tokens may be exchanged for a variety of reinforcers of a primary and secondary nature. A response-cost procedure is also part of this token economy system.

Treatment considerations. There are many factors to be considered in the use of the token economy system. First, someone trained in conducting such programs should be directing the program. Second, earning tokens should be based on the functioning level of the client. Third, maintenance and generalization must be planned so that when the client is no longer on the program, the natural consequences of the environment will ensure that the appropriate behaviors learned by the client will continue. Fourth, the behaviors that earn tokens must be precisely specified as well as those behaviors that lose tokens. Fifth, all items to be used as reinforcers must be specified. Sixth, tokens must be demonstrated as conditioned reinforcers and established as conditioned reinforcers prior to beginning the token economy. Seventh, clients must be required to spend their tokens. Eight, all token economies must be monitored and maintained by appropriate bookkeeping methods to ensure continuity of the program. Finally, every effort needs to be made to maintain a "balanced" economy so that such problems as inflation, hoarding, and satiation are avoided.

4.2.14. Behavioral Contracting

Definition. This procedure involves the written specification of the contingent relationship between the response required by the client and the reinforcer desired by the client. Contracting may be with the client, with the therapist, or with several significant others in the client's environment.

Treatment considerations. The writing of any behavior contract requires a clear, concise, and succinct definition of the desired response and the basis on which the reinforcers will be delivered. There must also be a provision for revising the agreement when either the agreement is met within the specified period of time or when the conditons have not been met and alternative contractual conditions need to be written. The time period for such contracts may be daily to weekly before revisions are made. Finally, all parties entering into the contract must do so without coercion or on the basis of inequality of conditions for the response requirement or the delivery of the reinforcement.

4.3. CLASSICAL CONDITIONING PROCEDURES

4.3.1. Progressive Deep Muscle Relaxation Training

Definition. This procedure was first developed in 1938 by Edmund Jacobsen as a means of relieving clients of stress and anxiety through a complex series of tensing and relaxing exercises of the major and minor muscle groups of the body. In the 1960s and 1970s, the procedure was modified from a 200-session format to a 2- to 3-session procedure. Specifically, the client tenses and relaxes major muscle groups such as the arms, legs, abdomen, neck and shoulders, face, and chest muscles in order to gradually learn the difference between tight muscles and very relaxed ones. By learning the "muscle sense" derived from this series of exercises, the client can begin to reduce the anxiety associated with the fearful stimuli in the client's environment.

Treatment considerations. Clients vary in their abilities to relax via these procedures. The literature indicates that some problems may arise in teaching relaxation exercises that may prevent the client from the acquisition of this skill. The client may have a fear of losing control, may suffer from self-consciousness, depression, physical pain, have difficulty keeping the eyes closed, have cognitive anxiety characterized by distracting and disturbing thoughts, experience fatigue or reduced mental alertness after such exercises, and show observable signs of muscular-skeletal tension though the client verbally reports no anxiety.

Other considerations involve the therapist's specifying the length of time the client tenses his or her muscles before counterposing "letting go" of the muscle tension. It is also important to make a tape of the relaxation training exercises actually done with the client. The client may take home this recording so that these exercises can be practiced in the same manner as specified in the training session. A personalized tape is often much more effective than a prerecorded tape by an unknown therapist. The therapist must ensure that the client does not depend on the tape to "make" him or her relax and should therefore plan to wean the client off of using the taped exercises from daily at first, to every other day, to every third day, to every fifth day, then to once per week as the relaxation response is acquired.

4.3.2. Systematic Desensitization

Definition. This procedure is defined as the pairing of muscle relaxation with scenes depicting situations that the client has reported has caused him or her a significant amount of anxiety. The assumption is that through this counterconditioning the client learns an alternative response to previously fearful stimuli, which ultimately results in the client's feeling more relaxed in these previously anxious situations. Several types of desensitization have been used with clients such as *imaginal,* the most common method that involves the client's imagining the fearful scene and then relaxing to it; *in vivo,* which involves the client's actually being in the natural setting of each scene described in the ascending hierarchy of anxiety; *group,* which is merely desensitization conducted with groups of people; and *automated,* which is the use of slide projectors and tape players to replace the therapist and to generate as similar a situation as *in vivo* as is possible.

Treatment considerations. The therapist must be concerned with the previously discussed potential problems of deep muscle relaxation, the determination of the fear theme presented by the client, the development of hierarchy items in proper ascending order of fearfulness, in timing correctly the presentation of the feared scene with the presentation of relaxation exercises, and in troubleshooting the problems that may arise in the desensitization process.

4.3.3. Assertiveness Training

Definition. Assertiveness training is a set of counterconditioning procedures that has as its goal teaching the client to distinguish between the three different modes of interpersonal behavior—nonassertive, assertive, and aggressive behavior—to recognize his or her interpersonal rights, and to learn alternative assertive responses for dealing with the violation of these rights.

There are a variety of methods and tacts for behaving assertively. The following is a list of some of these procedures.

1. *Simple assertion* involves saying "no" or denying a request without any excuse.

2. *Empathetic assertion* is based on the recognition of others' feelings or opinion but calmly continuing to make the assertive request or refusal.

3. *Feedback/behavior change request* is a more elaborate assertive response in the following form: "I feel _____ (state the feeling) when you _____ (describe the offensive behavior) because _____ (effect on the person). I would prefer that _____ (make the request for behavior change from the individual).

4. *Confrontation assertion* involves making a predetermined appointment to behave assertively with another individual, typically one in a position of authority, which will probably cause a confrontation.

5. *Humorous assertion* is a method of responding with light humor (without sarcasm) to a derogatory remark.

6. *Listening skills* is a set of facilitative responses used to increase the amount of information given by or shared with another.

7. *Broken record* is a method in which the assertive response is repeatedly and persistently given in a calm and neutral tone of voice to an individual making a similarly persistent request.

8. *Free information* involves helping another individual or the client to give freely information regarding one's background, feelings, and attitudes. This method teaches the client to use "what," "who," "when," and "how" questions.

9. *Self-disclosure* is used in conjunction with the free information procedure and is, in response to another's self-disclosure, a statement of feelings, attitudes, and opinions on the part of the listener.

10. *Calm disagreement* is simply the recognition of someone's position on an issue while calmly maintaining one's own position.

11. *Fogging* is a method whereby a person copes with criticism by not denying the accusations, by avoiding behaving defensively, or not counterattacking, but by agreeing with the portion of the criticism that is true, by agreeing with the probability of the truthfulness of the critical statement, or by agreeing in principle with the critical position.

12. *Negative inquiry* is a method in which the assertive response involves the inquiry and active prompting of criticism in order to gain information from another. Such a response helps the critic become more assertive, use a less defensive posture, and improve communication between the two individuals.

13. *Negative assertion* involves verbally shaped acknowledgment of errors by others as merely a statement of error in thinking or action without guilt or defensiveness.

14. *Positive assertion* is the statement to another individual of verbally stated praise that includes a positive feeling toward the person or toward the behavior demonstrated by the person.

15. *Other basic types of assertive messages* include "I want" statements, "I feel" statements, "I think" statements, mixed feelings statements, paraphrasing, listening without fear, nonverbal messages, probing or questioning, asking for a reaction, asking for what was heard, or asking for an explanation from an individual based on his or her body language.

Treatment considerations. Teaching a client to behave assertively is often one of the first procedures used in therapy with a client who is behaving nonassertively or aggressively. These procedures many times offer immediate success in a previously unsuccessful environment because the rationale and skills are easily acquired. However, a client may misuse these methods and misunderstand the difference between assertive responses and aggressive ones. Second, the client may become "assertive neurotic" in attempting to use these newly acquired skill in *every* situation in which there is even a slim chance that the individual's rights have been abused. Finally, some clients demonstrate extremes of nonassertive or aggressive behavior and may, therefore, have much difficulty learning new and more facilitative interpersonal responses.

4.3.4. Covert Sensitization

Definition. When a maladaptive behavior is maintained by very powerful reinforcers, procedures that are aversive in nature can be used to reduce the intrinsically reinforcing behavior. Covert sensitization involves the therapist's generating an aversive scene to be counterposed with a scene of the client's performing the maladaptive behavior. The rationale of this procedure is that by this association of an aversive scene with the image of the maladaptive behavior, the maladaptive behavior will be reduced in its frequency of occurrence. This procedure is used with such problem behaviors as pedophilia, alcoholism, substance abuse, smoking, and obesity.

Treatment considerations. In the development of the aversive scenes, the therapist must ensure that the scenes are indeed aversive. The client may be asked to visualize scenes that promote nausea, embarrassment, or fear of bodily harm as a means of determining stimulus aversiveness suitable for treatment. There are certainly ethical concerns that the therapist needs to consider, such as the amount of discomfort to the client and the need for alternative reinforcement procedures used in tandem for the client's appropriate behavior. Other procedures may need to be used prior to the use of this more restrictive procedure.

4.3.5. Covert Conditioning Procedures: Covert Reinforcement

Definition. In this procedure, the client is asked to imagine that he or she is engaging in some alternative and appropriate behavior. As the client reports having developed the image of engaging in the more appropriate behavior, he or she is next asked to imagine some highly desired event occurring immediately after the image of appropriate behavior as a reinforcing consequence of the behavior. It is assumed that this covert reinforcement serves to increase the occurrence of the desired behavior.

4.3.5.1. *Covert Extinction*

Definition. This procedure requires that the client imagine that he is engaging in some inappropriate behavior, and, once the client reports holding that image clearly, he is asked to imagine that none of the reinforcement that previously accompanied the maladaptive behavior follows the behavior. In this manner, the response probability is assumed to decrease in a manner similar to traditional extinction.

Treatment considerations. Like all coverant procedures, covert reinforcement and extinction require that the client develop the image clearly and maintain that image so as to provide reinforcement or extinction following the scene. If the client has intrusive thoughts or other extraneous images, then the effectiveness of these procedures is limited. Also, as in the considerations for the use of deep muscle relaxation, fear of losing control or failure may interfere with procedural effectiveness.

4.3.6. Flooding, Response Prevention, and Implosion

Definition. These procedures have many similarities. All of these methods of extinction via a classical conditioning model involve exposing the client to anxiety-provoking stimuli while preventing the client from escape or avoidance of the aversive properties of the feared situation. Usually, these methods are presented for an extended period of time at maximum intensity. However, in implosion, the scenes can be presented in a hierarchical fashion from least-to-most anxiety provoking, similar to desensitization.

Treatment considerations. One of the major concerns in the use of these procedures is that, without proper analysis of the client's problems or due consideration given to the client's capability to tolerate rather graphic descriptions of the fear-evoking stimuli or behavior, the therapist might inadvertently sensitize rather than extinguish the anxiety verbalized by the client. Thus, the anxiety might be further exacerbated through the use of these procedures. The therapist must do a very careful behavioral assessment and choose the least restrictive methods for dealing with the clinical problems presented rather than selecting these procedures as the first treatment of choice.

4.3.7. Aversion Relief

Definition. This procedure is defined as an escape-avoidance procedure. Essentially, the client views inappropriate stimuli or is asked to engage in some maladaptive behavior. Then contingent negative stimuli are imposed immediately upon the occurrence of this inappropriate behavior. When the client stops engaging in the maladaptive behavior or stops viewing the inappropriate stimuli, the contingent negative stimuli is turned off (e.g., "relief"). Thus, the client first learns to escape the unpleasant and sometimes painfully negative consequences and then learns to avoid the disruptive behavior altogether.

Treatment considerations. Electric shock as well as offensive drugs are usually used in these procedures as the contingent negative consequences, especially if the response is rather discrete and has a fairly discrete onset and offset. Use of proper medical precautions is essential when using such noxious stimuli.

4.4. SOCIAL LEARNING AND SELF-CONTROL PROCEDURES

4.4.1. Imitation and Modeling

Definition. These procedures involve teaching a client new and more functional behaviors through the use of a model demonstrating the appropriate behavior. This modeled behavior is then reinforced while the observer, the client, attends to the model's behavior as it occurs and is reinforced. Then the client is requested to engage in the same behavior while the therapist gives prompts to assist the client in the acquisition of this new behavior. There are different variations of this approach that have been used also for the reduction of fear and anxiety to some conditioned aversive stimulus. These include the following.

4.4.1.1. *Graduated Modeling, Guided Modeling, and Guided Modeling with Reinforcement*

These are defined as a group of methods in which the client is exposed to models who demonstrate gradually more fearful behaviors based on some hierarchy devised by the client and the therapist. These procedures involve some degree of gradual movement toward the most fearful situation perceived by the client.

4.4.1.2. *Participant Modeling, Modeling with Guided Performance, and Contact Desensitization*

With these procedures, the client is required not only to observe the desired behavior but also, to some degree depending on which of the procedures are used, engage in the desired behavior in the new or fearful setting. Essentially, the client must participate to some increasing level in how much he or she engages in the previously modeled behavior.

Treatment considerations. In each of these modeling procedures, there are basic assumptions that must be met if the client is to learn the modeled and observed behaviors. The principles of vicarious reinforcement and extinction operate to increase the probability that the client will engage in the new facilitative behavior and reduce the likelihood of avoiding some previously feared stimulus. Also, the therapist must insure that the behavior to be modeled is not too complex to prevent modeling and acquisition. In addition, there should be some similarity or common relationship between the model and the observer; those reinforcers delivered to the model should in fact be reinforcers desired by the observer/client.

4.4.2. Self-Control Methods

Definition. There are a variety of methods in the area of self-control that are effective in developing and maintaining appropriate behavior desired by clients. These procedures involve the application of behavior modification and cognitive techniques and are applied by the clients themselves under the direction of the therapist. Included in these methods are the following.

4.4.2.1. *Self-Reinforcement*

This involves the client's providing some highly desired reinforcer contingent on the completion of some task or performance of some appropriate behavior, sometimes specified within a predetermined period of time. Contingency contracting with oneself would be an example of such an arrangement.

4.4.2.2. *Self-Monitoring*

This is merely the client's keeping track of the frequency, rate, intensity, duration, or topography of some desired or undesired behavior. Self-monitoring can often result in temporary or more stable change in some desired direction of the occurrence of the targeted behavior. As a maintenance and generalization procedure, it is effective in continuing the desired changes obtained in the formal treatment program.

4.4.2.3. *Environmental Restriction*

This is another self-control method that allows the client to gradually provide for increased stimulus control over some undesired behavior toward the purpose of its significant reduction or elimination. The client would begin by specifying the various situations in which the maladaptive behavior would have an opportunity to occur. Then the client would agree to gradually limit the number of situations and the amount of time in which the behavior can be permitted to occur.

4.4.2.4. *Covert Positive and Negative Self-Statements*

This set of procedures is based somewhat on the cognitive approaches but also incorporates prompting as a means of the client's engaging in some appropriate behavior or avoiding the occurrence of some inappropriate behavior. This is accomplished by the client's regularly reading a set of written statements, often developed by the client, and reading or reciting these phrases regularly or in crucial situations in which the behavior is likely to occur. These techniques are also part of what may be termed *self-instruction*.

4.4.2.5. *Goal Setting, Time Management, and Activity Scheduling*

This procedure involves the client and the therapist setting long-term and short-term goals not only for therapy but also week to week in the client's daily life. In addition, clients who experience depression, social withdrawal, or procrastination profit from managing their time schedules better and planning more life activities as a means of generating greater continuity of appropriate behavior.

Treatment considerations. A very important consideration in the use of these self-control methods involves the reliability of whether the behavior actually occurs as is reported by the client and the reliability and validity of the data taken by the client. In addition, the therapist is unsure as to the proper implementation of these treatment procedures. Some therapists will enlist the aid of significant others in the client's environment to unobtrusively or even openly monitor the client's behavior and to provide some information regarding the treatment implementation with the client's verbal report and data collection.

4.5. COGNITIVE RESTRUCTURING PROCEDURES

4.5.1. Rational Emotive Therapy (RET)

Definition. This approach developed by Albert Ellis assumes that an individual's emotions and behavior are not based on or caused by events in the external environment but rather by the individual's interpretation of those environmental events. At the core of Ellis's system is the issue of rational and irrational beliefs by which people interpret these events. If one's belief system is based largely on such irrational beliefs as "awfulizing" and "catastrophizing," "I can't stand its," perfectionism, self- and other damnation, then such a belief system will lead to irrational and intensely negative emotional reactions and behavior.

Treatment considerations. Although it is often very easy to teach the client these RET concepts, intellectualization is not naturally followed by application and new rational response patterns. The therapist may find that the client will verbalize these concepts in the office but in stressful situations the client will engage in those former well-established inappropriate responses. Therefore, it is the responsibility of the therapist to help the client challenge these old emotional beliefs and practice replacing them with new, more facilitative rational responses. Using the Rational Self-Help Form (Ellis, 1976), available from the Institute of Rational Living, is very helpful in teaching the client to understand the A(ctivating events), B(eliefs), C(onsequences), D(isputing or challenging), and E(motional and behavioral consequences resulting from disputing) of irrational beliefs. Ellis has a variety of methods for teaching these concepts and their application to emotional and behavioral problems.

4.5.2. Cognitive Therapy

Definition. Aaron Beck is the prime developer of this cognitive approach to the treatment of emotional and behavioral difficulties. The underlying rationale of this approach is that an individual's affect and behavior are based, largely, on the way he or she structures the world. Beck postulates that a person's cognitions are based on assumptions— referred to as "schemas"—that are developed from a person's previous experience. This therapeutic approach attempts to help the client identify and test the faulty assumptions that are the distorted conceptualizations of the world and then teach the client to think and behave more realistically and adaptatively. There are many cognitive and behavioral techniques that Beck and his associates employ in this therapy endeavor. Some of these techniques are mastery and pleasure techniques, graded task assignments, cognitive rehearsal, assertiveness training, detection and testing automatic thoughts, reattribution, recording of dysfunctional thoughts, and substituting functional thoughts.

Treatment considerations. There are a number of technical problems that can arise in the use of this approach. These include the client's (a) attempting to manipulate the therapist; (b) intellectualizing but not applying the prescribed methods; (c) holding a belief that emotional and behavioral change is not possible; (d) deemphasizing the importance of the cognitive approach of therapy; (e) refusing to speak in the therapeutic session; (f) tangential discussion; and (g) generalization of one negative event to all aspects of the client's life.

4.5.3. Thought Stopping

Definition. This procedure is especially helpful for the client with persistent worry or obsessive thoughts. Thought stopping involves having the client think of the disturbing thought for a brief period after which the therapist suddenly yells "stop" or makes a loud noise. This will obviously disrupt the ongoing worrisome thought of the client. After repeated pairings of the client's thinking with the disruption by the therapist, the control is then shifted to the client. The client is then required to yell "stop" once he or she has the disturbing thought in mind. As the client disrupts this dysfunctional thinking with the shouting aloud, he is then asked to "yell" to himself when his thoughts become disturbing.

Treatment considerations. At times the client will report good success with this procedure but will complain that the disturbing thoughts will soon return after using it. The client is to be informed that there will be times when the thought will be persistent in its occurrence, but it is at these times that the client must be encouraged to yell "stop" repeatedly as frequently as the thought occurs, or even to yell "stop" aloud when possible under these extreme circumstances.

4.5.4. Stress Inoculation Training

Definition. This procedure developed largely by Meichenbaum and his associates involves three phases in teaching clients to cope more effectively with stressful situations. These three phases involve the (a) *educational phase* in which the client is given a conceptual framework for understanding the nature of his or her stressful response; (b) *rehearsal phase* which provides the client with a variety of coping strategies during the stressful events; and (c) *application training* which is the point at which the client uses these new strategies in actual stressful events.

Treatment considerations. Above all, it is very important that the client understand *in lay terms* how stress affects one emotionally and behaviorally. The client and therapist need to work together in a collaborative fashion to develop coping self-statements, control negative thinking, differentiate between the reality of the stressful situation versus how much arousal on the part of the client is additionally interfering, and to provide the needed self-reinforcement after coping successfully with the stressors.

4.5.5. Problem Solving and Impulse Control Training

Definition. In situations in which a child or adult has difficulties making decisions or behaves impulsively, the treatment of choice is often to teach problem solving and impulse control. These methods involve teaching the client to define the problem, think of all possible alternatives without regard for the goodness or badness of the alternative, analyze each alternative in terms of the risks and benefits of each, and then to make a decision based on that analysis. With impulsive children, this problem-solving technique is taught in a role-playing, rehearsal, corrective feedback, and reinforcement model that also uses increasingly difficult situations in which to apply these methods. For example, teaching a child to figure out how to locate places on a map is much less of a difficult task than is deciding what to do when he observes his best friend cheating on a test. Positive practice and a shift from a concrete to a conceptual model of problem solving are also features of these approaches.

Treatment considerations. The therapist must ensure that the client learns the steps in decision making and commits them to memory. When this is done, the client is first given situations that are straightforward applications of these methods and later more difficult ones that require the client to make decisions on emotional as well as practical issues. Making the jump from concrete to conceptual must be done gradually and in small steps in order for the client to apply them correctly and successfully in daily living. Relaxation training may need to be taught as well to facilitate a calm physical status by which clearer decision making can be accomplished.

4.6. BIOFEEDBACK AND PHYSIOLOGICAL RECONDITIONING METHODS

4.6.1. Electromyographic Training, Alpha Wave Training, Thermal Training, Electrodermal Training, and Blood Pressure and Heart Rate Training

Definition. Biofeedback procedures have been a very helpful adjunct to therapy. Relaxation training has been facilitated through the use of electromyographic training as well as alpha wave and thermal training. Electrodermal training enables the therapist to objectify levels of anxiety reported by the client and to use this information in the clinical interview as well as in the development of desensitization hierarchies. Blood pressure and heart rate training are used largely with medically referred clients in tandem with these other biofeedback procedures. All of these procedures allow the client to get a rather objective view of how stress influences their mental and physical well-being through these various windows into the autonomic nervous system, or "fight-or-flight" system.

Treatment considerations. It is a mistake to use biofeedback alone because research and clinical practice indicate that biofeedback, when used with other techniques, is of greater benefit to the client and increases maintenance and generalization of the effects of treatment than is biofeedback alone. The therapist must also be sensitive to the medical history of the client so as to avoid altering the client's physical state when doing so would prove hazardous to that client's health. The therapist using biofeedback would do well to keep in contact with the client's physician when there is possible physical danger to the client. Fuller (1977) discusses some possible dangers associated with biofeedback therapy.

4.6.2. Sensory Awareness and Autogenic Training

Definition. As a means of augmenting the biofeedback-assisted relaxation response, sensory awareness and autogenic training help the client obtain a deeper sense of calmness and awareness of the true muscle sense. Basically, these procedures involve teaching the client to become aware of such sensations as warmth, heaviness, numbness, floating, and a clear, calm mind. Images of pleasant scenes that promote these sensations are also taught and enhanced.

Treatment considerations. As in relaxation training, the therapist must be aware of client fears and other problems previously discussed that would inhibit the acquisition and maintenance of the relaxation response. The therapist must also be sensitive to the fact that one client's pleasant scenes may not necessarily be pleasant for another client or might actually be unpleasant to the next client.

4.7. CONCLUDING COMMENTS

As seen in this chapter, there are a variety of procedures at the disposal of the behavior therapist. Maintaining a broad-spectrum behavior therapy approach to treatment requires that the therapist select from all of these areas those procedures that appear to offer the client the highest probability of relief from suffering and that are the least restrictive. Therefore, there are many different combinations of procedures that can be used for the variety of clinical problems presented to the behavior therapist. Referencing the books and journals, some of which are listed and described in Chapter 7, will enable the therapist to obtain a perspective of which procedures are most applicable in terms of potential effectiveness for a client's problems.

5

Professional Standards and Ethical Issues for Private Practice

The practice of behavior therapy is, first and foremost, the practice of psychology. It is vital for the practitioner to design his or her clinical practice in accordance with the available guidelines and standards for establishing and maintaining a private practice. By adhering to such standards, not only is the client protected, but the therapist is also safeguarded from legal liability. Sheldon-Wildgen (1982) points out that legal liability can arise out of a client's lack of knowledge of fully informed consent, what is to be done in therapy, anticipated results, duration of therapy, costs of services, confidentiality, the qualifications of the professional, and the appropriateness of treatment.

There are a variety of sources to use as references for formulating one's guidelines for private practice. These guides discuss issues of ethics, standards and specialty guidelines for service providers, and, for the behavior therapist, standards governing the application of behavior therapy.

5.1. ETHICAL PRINCIPLES OF PSYCHOLOGISTS (APA, 1981)*

The American Psychological Association (APA) has continued to revise and update its tenets of ethical practices of psychologists (APA, 1981). This manual is an essential part of establishing a private practice

*This article appeared in the *American Psychologist, 36,* 1981. Copyright 1981 by the American Psychological Association. Reprinted by permission.

as it sets strict limitations as to the qualifications and boundaries of competence of the professional, how psychological services may be provided, and what safeguards have been taken to protect the client. The psychologist as well as those working in the office of the psychologist (e.g., secretary, biofeedback technician, mental health counselor) should ensure they are complying to the APA's ethical code. Regular yearly review of staff compliance to these standards is advised to update practice procedures and to "troubleshoot" when the ethical conduct by any staff member may be in question. In addition, staff should be made aware that a major condition of employment is this strict adherence to these ethical guidelines.

PREAMBLE

Psychologists respect the dignity and worth of the individual and strive for the preservation and protection of fundamental human rights. They are committed to increasing knowledge of human behavior and of people's understanding of themselves and others and to the utilization of such knowledge for the promotion of human welfare. While pursuing these objectives, they make every effort to protect the welfare of those who seek their services and of the research participants that may be the object of study. They use their skills only for purposes consistent with these values and do not knowingly permit their

---

This version of the Ethical Principles of Psychologists (formerly entitled Ethical Standards of Psychologists) was adopted by the American Psychological Association's Council of Representatives on January 24, 1981. The revised Ethical Principles contain both substantive and grammatical changes in each of the nine ethical principles constituting the Ethical Standards of Psychologists previously adopted by the Council of Representatives in 1979, plus a new tenth principle entitled Care and Use of Animals. Inquiries concerning the Ethical Principles of Psychologists should be addressed to the Administrative Officer for Ethics, American Psychological Association, 1200 Seventeenth Street, N.W., Washington, D.C. 20036.

These revised Ethical Principles apply to psychologists, to students of psychology, and to others who do work of a psychological nature under the supervision of a psychologist. They are also intended for the guidance of nonmembers of the Association who are engaged in psychological research or practice.

Any complaints of unethical conduct filed after January 24, 1981, shall be governed by this 1981 revision. However, conduct (a) complained about after January 24, 1981, but which occurred prior to that date, and (b) not considered unethical under prior versions of the principles but considered unethical under the 1981 revision, shall not be deemed a violation of ethical principles. Any complaints pending as of January 24, 1981, shall be governed either by the 1979 or by the 1981 version of the Ethical Principles, at the sound discretion of the Committee on Scientific and Professional Ethics and Conduct.

misuse by others. While demanding for themselves freedom of inquiry and communication, psychologists accept the responsibility this freedom requires: competence, objectivity in the application of skills, and concern for the best interests of clients, colleagues, students, research participants, and society. In the pursuit of these ideals, psychologists subscribe to principles in the following areas: 1. Responsibility, 2. Competence, 3. Moral and Legal Standards, 4. Public Statements, 5. Confidentiality, 6. Welfare of the Consumer, 7. Professional Relationships, 8. Assessment Techniques, 9. Research With Human Participants, and 10. Care and Use of Animals.

Acceptance of membership in the American Psychological Association commits the member to adherence to these principles.

Psychologists cooperate with duly constituted committees of the American Psychological Association, in particular, the Committee on Scientific and Professional Ethics and Conduct, by responding to inquiries promptly and completely. Members also respond promptly and completely to inquiries from duly constituted state association ethics committees and professional standards review committees.

Principle 1

RESPONSIBILITY

In providing services, psychologists maintain the highest standards of their profession. They accept responsibility for the consequences of their acts and make every effort to ensure that their services are used appropriately.

a. As scientists, psychologists accept responsibility for the selection of their research topics and the methods used in investigation, analysis, and reporting. They plan their research in ways to minimize the possibility that their findings will be misleading. They provide thorough discussion of the limitations of their data, especially where their work touches on social policy or might be construed to the detriment of persons in specific age, sex, ethnic, socioeconomic, or other social groups. In publishing reports of their work, they never suppress disconfirming data, and they acknowledge the existence of alternative hypotheses and explanations of their findings. Psychologists take credit only for work they have actually done.

b. Psychologists clarify in advance with all appropriate persons and agencies the expectations for sharing and utilizing research data. They avoid relationships that may limit their objectivity or create a conflict of interest. Interference with the milieu in which data are collected is kept to a minimum.

c. Psychologists have the responsibility to attempt to prevent distortion, misuse, or suppression of psychological findings by the institution or agency of which they are employees.

d. As members of governmental or other organizational bodies, psychologists remain accountable as individuals to the highest standards of their profession.

e. As teachers, psychologists recognize their primary obligation to help others acquire knowledge and skill. They maintain high standards of scholarship by presenting psychological information objectively, fully, and accurately.

f. As practitioners, psychologists know that they bear a heavy social responsibility because their recommendations and professional actions may alter the lives of others. They are alert to personal, social, organizational, financial, or political situations and pressures that might lead to misuse of their influence.

Principle 2

COMPETENCE

The maintenance of high standards of competence is a responsibility shared by all psychologists in the interest of the public and the profession as a whole. Psychologists recognize the boundaries of their competence and the limitations of their techniques. They only provide services and only use techniques for which they are qualified by training and experience. In those areas in which recognized standards do not yet exist, psychologists take whatever precautions are necessary to protect the welfare of their clients. They maintain knowledge of current scientific and professional information related to the services they render.

a. Psychologists accurately represent their competence, education, training, and experience. They claim as evidence of educational qualifications only those degrees obtained from institutions acceptable under the Bylaws and Rules of Council of the American Psychological Association.

b. As teachers, psychologists perform their duties on the basis of careful preparation so that their instruction is accurate, current, and scholarly.

c. Psychologists recognize the need for continuing education and are open to new procedures and changes in expectations and values over time.

d. Psychologists recognize differences among people, such as those that may be associated with age, sex, socioeconomic, and ethnic backgrounds. When necessary, they obtain training, experience, or counsel to assure competent service or research relating to such persons.

e. Psychologists responsible for decisions involving individuals or policies based on test results have an understanding of psychological or educational measurement, validation problems, and test research.

f. Psychologists recognize that personal problems and conflicts may interfere with professional effectiveness. Accordingly, they refrain from undertaking any activity in which their personal problems are likely to lead to inadequate performance or harm to a client, colleague, student, or research participant. If engaged in such activity when they become aware of their personal problems, they seek competent professional assistance to determine whether they should suspend, terminate, or limit the scope of their professional and/or scientific activities.

Principle 3

MORAL AND LEGAL STANDARDS

Psychologists' moral and ethical standards of behavior are a personal matter to the same degree as they are for any other citizen, except as these may compromise the fulfillment of their professional responsibilities or reduce the public trust in psychology and psychologists. Regarding their own behavior, psychologists are sensitive to prevailing community standards and to the possible impact that conformity to or deviation from these standards may have upon the quality of their performance as psychologists. Psychologists are also aware of the possible impact of their public behavior upon the ability of colleagues to perform their professional duties.

a. As teachers, psychologists are aware of the fact that their personal values may affect the selection and presentation of instructional materials. When dealing with topics that may give offense, they recognize and respect the diverse attitudes that students may have toward such materials.

b. As employees or employers, psychologists do not engage in or condone practices that are inhumane or that result in illegal or unjustifiable actions. Such practices include, but are not limited to, those based on considerations of race, handicap, age, gender, sexual preference, religion, or national origin in hiring, promotion, or training.

c. In their professional roles, psychologists avoid any action that will violate or diminish the legal and civil rights of clients or of others who may be affected by their actions.

d. As practitioners and researchers, psychologists act in accord with Association standards and guidelines related to practice and to the conduct of research with human beings and animals. In the ordinary course of events, psychologists adhere to relevant governmental laws and institutional regulations. When federal, state, provincial, organizational, or institutional laws, regulations, or practices are in conflict with Association standards and guidelines, psychologists make known their commitment to Association standards and guidelines and, wherever possible, work toward a resolution of the conflict. Both practitioners and researchers are concerned with the development of such legal and quasi-legal regulations as best serve the public interest, and they work toward changing existing regulations that are not beneficial to the public interest.

Principle 4

PUBLIC STATEMENTS

Public statements, announcements of services, advertising, and promotional activities of psychologists serve the purpose of helping the public make informed judgments and choices. Psychologists represent accurately and objectively their professional qualifications, affiliations, and functions, as well as those of the institutions or organizations with which they or the statements may be associated. In public statements providing psychological information or professional opinions or providing information about the availability of psychological products, publications, and services, psychologists base their statements on scientifically acceptable psychological findings and techniques with full recognition of the limits and uncertainties of such evidence.

a. When announcing or advertising professional services, psychologists may list the following information to describe the provider and services provided: name, highest relevant academic degree earned from a regionally accredited institution, date, type, and level of certification or licensure, diplomate status, APA membership status, address, telephone number, office hours, a brief listing of the type of psychological services offered, an appropriate presentation of fee information, foreign languages spoken, and policy with regard to third-party payments. Additional relevant or important consumer information may be included if not prohibited by other sections of these Ethical Principles.

b. In announcing or advertising the availability of psychological products, publications, or services, psychologists do not present their affiliation with any organization in a manner that falsely implies sponsorship or certification by that organization. In particular and for example, psychologists do not state APA membership or fellow status in a way to suggest that such status implies specialized professional competence or qualifications. Public statements include, but are not limited to, communication by means of periodical, book, list, directory, television, radio, or motion picture. They do not contain (i) a false, fraudulent, misleading, deceptive, or unfair statement; (ii) a misinterpretation of fact or a statement likely to mislead or deceive because in context it makes only a partial disclosure of relevant facts; (iii) a testimonial from a patient regarding the quality of a psychologists' services or products; (iv) a statement intended or likely to create false or unjustified expectations of favorable results; (v) a statement implying unusual, unique, or one-of-a-kind abilities; (vi) a statement intended or likely to appeal to a client's fear, anxieties, or emotions concerning the possible results of failure to obtain the offered services; (vii) a statement concerning the comparative desirability of offered services; (viii) a statement of direct solicitation of individual clients.

c. Psychologists do not compensate or give anything of value to a representative of the press, radio, television, or other communication medium in anticipation of or in return for professional publicity in a news item. A paid advertisement must be identified as such, unless it is apparent from the context that it is a paid advertisement. If communicated to the public by use of radio or television, an advertisement is prerecorded and approved for broadcast by the psychologist, and a recording of the actual transmission is retained by the psychologist.

d. Announcements or advertisements of "personal growth groups," clinics, and agencies give a clear statement of purpose and a clear description of the experiences to be provided. The education, training, and experience of the staff members are appropriately specified.

e. Psychologists associated with the development or promotion of psychological devices, books, or other products offered for commercial sale make reasonable efforts to ensure that announcements and advertisements are presented in a professional, scientifically acceptable, and factually informative manner.

f. Psychologists do not participate for personal gain in commercial announcements or advertisements recommending to the public the purchase or use of proprietary or single-source products or services when that participation is based solely upon their identification as psychologists.

g. Psychologists present the science of psychology and offer their services, products, and publications fairly and accurately, avoiding misrepresentation through sensationalism, exaggeration, or superficiality.

Psychologists are guided by the primary obligation to aid the public in developing informed judgments, opinions, and choices.

h. As teachers, psychologists ensure that statements in catalogs and course outlines are accurate and not misleading, particularly in terms of subject matter to be covered, bases for evaluating progress, and the nature of course experiences. Announcements, brochures, or advertisements describing workshops, seminars, or other educational programs accurately describe the audience for which the program is intended as well as eligibility requirements, educational objectives, and nature of the materials to be covered. These announcements also accurately represent the education, training, and experience of the psychologists presenting the programs and any fees involved.

i. Public announcements or advertisements soliciting research participants in which clinical services or other professional services are offered as an inducement make clear the nature of the services as well as the costs and other obligations to be accepted by participants in the research.

j. A psychologist accepts the obligation to correct others who represent the psychologist's professional qualifications, or associations with products or services, in a manner incompatible with these guidelines.

k. Individual diagnostic and therapeutic services are provided only in the context of a professional psychological relationship. When personal advice is given by means of public lectures or demonstrations, newspaper or magazine articles, radio or television programs, mail, or similar media, the psychologist utilizes the most current relevant data and exercises the highest level of professional judgment.

l. Products that are described or presented by means of public lectures or demonstrations, newspaper or magazine articles, radio or television programs, or similar media meet the same recognized standards as exist for products used in the context of a professional relationship.

Principle 5

CONFIDENTIALITY

Psychologists have a primary obligation to respect the confidentiality of information obtained from persons in the course of their work as psychologists. They reveal such information to others only with the consent of the person or the person's legal representative, except in those unusual circumstances in which not to do so would result in clear danger to the person or to others. Where appropriate, psychologists inform their clients of the legal limits of confidentiality.

a. Information obtained in clinical or consulting relationships, or evaluative data concerning children, students, employees, and others, is discussed only for professional purposes and only with persons clearly concerned with the case. Written and oral reports present only data germane to the purposes of the evaluation, and every effort is made to avoid undue invasion of privacy.

b. Psychologists who present personal information obtained during the course of professional work in writings, lectures, or other public forums either obtain adequate prior consent to do so or adequately disguise all identifying information.

c. Psychologists make provisions for maintaining confidentiality in the storage and disposal of records.

d. When working with minors or other persons who are unable to give voluntary, informed consent, psychologists take special care to protect these persons' best interests.

Principle 6

WELFARE OF THE CONSUMER

Psychologists respect the integrity and protect the welfare of the people and groups with whom they work. When conflicts of interest arise between clients and psychologists' employing institutions, psychologists clarify the nature and direction of their loyalties and responsibilities and keep all parties informed of their commitments. Psychologists fully inform consumers as to the purpose and nature of an evaluative, treatment, educational, or training procedure, and they freely acknowledge that clients, students, or participants in research have freedom of choice with regard to participation.

a. Psychologists are continually cognizant of their own needs and of their potentially influential position vis-à-vis persons such as clients, students, and subordinates. They avoid exploiting the trust and dependency of such persons. Psychologists make every effort to avoid dual relationships that could impair their professional judgment or increase the risk of exploitation. Examples of such dual relationships include, but are not limited to, research with and treatment of employees, students, supervisees, close friends, or relatives. Sexual intimacies with clients are unethical.

b. When a psychologist agrees to provide services to a client at the request of a third party, the psychologist assumes the responsibility of clarifying the nature of the relationships to all parties concerned.

c. Where the demands of an organization require psychologists to violate these Ethical Principles, psychologists clarify the nature of the conflict between the demands and these principles. They inform all parties of psychologists' ethical responsibilities and take appropriate action.

d. Psychologists make advance financial arrangements that safeguard the best interests of and are clearly understood by their clients. They neither give nor receive any remuneration for referring clients for professional services. They contribute a portion of their services to work for which they receive little or no financial return.

e. Psychologists terminate a clinical or consulting relationship when it is reasonably clear that the consumer is not benefiting from it. They offer to help the consumer locate alternative sources of assistance.

Principle 7

PROFESSIONAL RELATIONSHIPS

Psychologists act with due regard for the needs, special competencies, and obligations of their colleagues in psychology and other professions. They respect the prerogatives and obligations of the institutions or organizations with which these other colleagues are associated.

a. Psychologists understand the areas of competence of related professions. They make full use of all the professional, technical, and administrative resources that serve the best interests of consumers. The absence of formal relationships with other professional workers does not relieve psychologists of the responsibility of securing for their clients the best possible professional service, nor does it relieve them of the obligation to exercise foresight, diligence, and tact in obtaining the complementary or alternative assistance needed by clients.

b. Psychologists know and take into account the traditions and practices of other professional groups with whom they work and cooperate fully with such groups. If a person is receiving similar services from another professional, psychologists do not offer their own services directly to such a person. If a psychologist is contacted by a person who is already receiving similar services from another professional, the psychologist carefully considers that professional relationship and proceeds with caution and sensitivity to the therapeutic issues as well as the client's welfare. The psychologist discusses these issues with the client so as to minimize the risk of confusion and conflict.

c. Psychologists who employ or supervise other professionals or professionals in training accept the obligation to facilitate the further professional development of these individuals. They provide appropriate working conditions, timely evaluations, constructive consultation, and experience opportunities.

d. Psychologists do not exploit their professional relationships with clients, supervisees, students, employees, or research participants sexually or otherwise. Psychologists do not condone or engage in sexual harassment. Sexual harassment is defined as deliberate or repeated comments, gestures, or physical contacts of a sexual nature that are unwanted by the recipient.

e. In conducting research in institutions or organizations, psychologists secure appropriate authorization to conduct such research. They are aware of their obligations to future research workers and ensure that host institutions receive adequate information about the research and proper acknowledgment of their contributions.

f. Publication credit is assigned to those who have contributed to a publication in proportion to their professional contributions. Major contributions of a professional character made by several persons to a common project are recognized by joint authorship, with the individual who made the principal contribution listed first. Minor contributions of a professional character and extensive clerical or similar nonprofessional assistance may be acknowledged in footnotes or in an introductory statement. Acknowledgment through specific citations is made for unpublished as well as published material that has directly influenced the research or writing. Psychologists who compile and edit material of others for publication publish the material in the name of the originating group, if appropriate, with their own name appearing as chairperson or editor. All contributors are to be acknowledged and named.

g. When psychologists know of an ethical violation by another psychologist, and it seems appropriate, they informally attempt to resolve the issue by bringing the behavior to the attention of the psychologist. If the misconduct is of a minor nature and/or appears to be due to lack of sensitivity, knowledge, or experience, such an informal solution is usually appropriate. Such informal corrective efforts are made with sensitivity to any rights to confidentiality involved. If the violation does not seem amenable to an informal solution, or is of a more serious nature, psychologists bring it to the attention of the appropriate local, state, and/or national committee on professional ethics and conduct.

Principle 8

ASSESSMENT TECHNIQUES

In the development, publication, and utilization of psychological assessment techniques, psychologists make every effort to promote the welfare and best interests of the client. They guard against the misuse of assessment results. They respect the client's right to know the results, the interpretations made, and the bases for their conclusions and recommendations. Psychologists make every effort to maintain the security of tests and other assessment techniques within limits of legal mandates. They strive to ensure the appropriate use of assessment techniques by others.

a. In using assessment techniques, psychologists respect the right of clients to have full explanations of the nature and purpose of the techniques in language the clients can understand, unless an explicit exception to this right has been agreed upon in advance. When the explanations are to be provided by others, psychologists establish procedures for ensuring the adequacy of these explanations.

b. Psychologists responsible for the development and standardization of psychological tests and other assessment techniques utilize established scientific procedures and observe the relevant APA standards.

c. In reporting assessment results, psychologists indicate any reservations that exist regarding validity or reliability because of the circumstances of the assessment or the inappropriateness of the norms for the person tested. Psychologists strive to ensure that the results of assessments and their interpretations are not misused by others.

d. Psychologists recognize that assessment results may become obsolete. They make every effort to avoid and prevent the misuse of obsolete measures.

e. Psychologists offering scoring and interpretation services are able to produce appropriate evidence for the validity of the programs and procedures used in arriving at interpretations. The public offering of an automated interpretation service is considered a professional-to-professional consultation. Psychologists make every effort to avoid misuse of assessment reports.

f. Psychologists do not encourage or promote the use of psychological assessment techniques by inappropriately trained or otherwise unqualified persons through teaching, sponsorship, or supervision.

Principle 9

RESEARCH WITH HUMAN PARTICIPANTS

The decision to undertake research rests upon a considered judgment by the individual psychologist about how best to contribute to psychological science and human welfare. Having made the decision to conduct research, the psychologist considers alternative directions in which research energies and resources might be invested. On the basis of this consideration, the psychologist carries out the investigation with respect and concern for the dignity and welfare of the people who participate and with cognizance of federal and state regulations and professional standards governing the conduct of research with human participants.

a. In planning a study, the investigator has the responsibility to make a careful evaluation of its ethical acceptability. To the extent that the weighing of scientific and human values suggests a compromise of any principle, the investigator incurs a correspondingly serious obligation to seek ethical advice, and to observe stringent safeguards to protect the rights of human participants.

b. Considering whether a participant in a planned study will be a "subject at risk" or a "subject at minimal risk," according to recognized standards, is of primary ethical concern to the investigator.

c. The investigator always retains the responsibility for ensuring ethical practice in research. The investigator is also responsible for the ethical treatment of research participants by collaborators, assistants, students, and employees, all of whom, however, incur similar obligations.

d. Except in minimal-risk research, the investigator establishes a clear and fair agreement with research participants, prior to their participation, that clarifies the obligations and responsibilities of each. The investigator has the obligation to honor all promises and commitments included in that agreement. The investigator informs the participants of all aspects of the research that might reasonably be expected to influence willingness to participate and explains all other aspects of the research about which the participants inquire. Failure to make full disclosure prior to obtaining informed consent requires additional safeguards to protect the welfare and dignity of the research participants. Research with children or with participants who have impairments that would limit understanding and/or communication requires special safe-guarding procedures.

e. Methodological requirements of a study may make the use of concealment or deception necessary. Before conducting such a study, the investigator has a special responsibility to (i) determine whether the use of such techniques is justified by the study's prospective scientific, educational, or applied value; (ii) determine whether alternative procedures are available that do not use concealment or deception; and (iii) ensure that the participants are provided with sufficient explanation as soon as possible.

f. The investigator respects the individual's freedom to decline to participate in or to withdraw from the research at any time. The obligation to protect this freedom requires careful thought and consideration when the investigator is in a position of authority or influence over the participant. Such positions of authority include, but are not limited to, situations in which research participation is required as part of employment or in which the participant is a student, client, or employee of the investigator.

g. The investigator protects the participant from physical and mental discomfort, harm, and danger that may arise from research procedures. If risks of such consequences exist, the investigator informs the participant of that fact. Research procedures likely to cause serious or lasting harm to a participant are not used unless the failure to use these procedures might expose the participant to risk of greater harm, or unless the research has great potential benefit and fully informed and voluntary consent is obtained from each participant. The participant should be informed of procedures for contacting the investigator within a reasonable time period following participation should stress, potential harm, or related questions or concerns arise.

h. After the data are collected, the investigator provides the participant with information about the nature of the study and attempts to remove any misconceptions that may have arisen. Where scientific or humane values justify delaying or withholding this information, the investigator incurs a special responsibility to monitor the research and to ensure that there are no damaging consequences for the participant.

i. Where research procedures result in undesirable consequences for the individual participant, the investigator has the responsibility to detect and remove or correct these consequences, including long-term effects.

j. Information obtained about a research participant during the course of an investigation is confidential unless otherwise agreed upon in advance. When the possibility exists that others may obtain access to such information, this possibility, together with the plans for protecting confidentiality, is explained to the participant as part of the procedure for obtaining informed consent.

Principle 10

CARE AND USE OF ANIMALS

An investigator of animal behavior strives to advance understanding of basic behavior principles and/or to contribute to the improvement of human health and welfare. In seeking these ends, the investigator ensures the welfare of animals and treats them humanely. Laws and regulations notwithstanding, an animal's immediate protection depends upon the scientist's own conscience.

a. The acquisition, care, use, and disposal of all animals are in compliance with current federal, state or provincial, and local laws and regulations.

b. A psychologist trained in research methods and experienced in the care of laboratory animals closely supervises all procedures involving animals and is responsible for ensuring appropriate consideration of their comfort, health, and humane treatment.

c. Psychologists ensure that all individuals using animals under their supervision have received explicit instruction in experimental methods and in the care, maintenance, and handling of the species being used. Responsibilities and activities of individuals participating in a research project are consistent with their respective competencies.

d. Psychologists make every effort to minimize discomfort, illness, and pain of animals. A procedure subjecting animals to pain, stress, or privation is used only when an alternative procedure is unavailable and the goal is justified by its prospective scientific, educational, or applied value. Surgical procedures are performed under appropriate anesthesia; techniques to avoid infection and minimize pain are followed during and after surgery.

e. When it is appropriate that the animal's life be terminated, it is done rapidly and painlessly.

5.2. STANDARDS FOR PROVIDERS OF PSYCHOLOGICAL SERVICES (APA, 1977)*

In January of 1977, APA adopted the *Standards for Providers of Psychological Services*. The intent of these standards is to provide a set of national guidelines upon which psychological services could be provided uniformly and efficiently. These standards cover almost every aspect of proper client care and treatment by psychologists. Issues such as accountability to the client and to the public, direct management of programs and staff, regular review of services, and methods to ensure confidentiality are defined. Uniform procedures for carrying out these needed services in an efficient manner are given. It is extremely important that the practitioner contemplating private practice write a set of procedures detailing an overall plan for the delivery of services to be rendered by the office. This written service plan should be readily available for public and peer review. Also a service delivery plan as outlined and discussed in Chapter 3 should be written for each and every client.

The Standards that follow are the first revision of the national Standards for Providers of Psychological Services originally adopted by the American Psychological Association (APA) on September 4, 1974.[1]

In January 1975, the APA Council of Representatives created the original Committee on Standards for Providers of Psychological Services. The Committee was charged with updating and revising the Standards adopted in September 1974. Members of the Committee were Jacqueline C. Bouhoutsos, Leon Hall, Marian D. Hall, Mary Henle, Durand F. Jacobs (Chair), Abel Ossorio, and Wayne Sorenson. Task Force liaison was Jerry H. Clark, and Central Office liaison was Arthur Centor.

In January 1976, Council further charged the Committee to review the Standards and recommend revisions needed to reflect the varying needs of only those psychologists engaged in the activities of clinical, counseling, industrial-organizational, and school psychology. The Committee was reconstituted with one member representing each of the four applied activities, plus one member representing institutional practice and one representing the public interest.

Members were Jules Barron, clinical; Barbara A. Kirk, counseling; Frank Friedlander, industrial-organizational (replacing Virginia Schein); Durand F. Jacobs (Chair), institutional practice; M. Brewster Smith, public interest; Marian D. Hall, school; Arthur Centor was Central office liaison.

[1]Members of the Task Force on Standards for Service Facilities that submitted the original Standards in September 1974 were Milton L. Blum, Jacqueline C. Bouhoutsos, Jerry H. Clark, Harold A. Edgerton, Marian D. Hall, Durand F. Jacobs (Chair, 1972–1974), Floyd H. Martinez, John E. Muthard, Asher R. Pacht, William D. Pierce, Sue A. Warren, and Alfred M. Wellner (Chair, 1970–1971). Staff liaisons from the APA Office of Professional Affairs were John J. McMillan (1970–1971), Gottlieb C. Simon (1971–1973), and Arthur Centor (1973–1974).

The intent of these Standards is to improve the quality, effectiveness, and accessibility of psychological services to all who require them.[2]

These Standards represent the attainment of a goal for which the Association has striven for over 20 years, namely, to codify a uniform set of standards for psychological practice that would serve the respective needs of users, providers, and third-party purchasers and sanctioners of psychological services. In addition, the Association has established a standing committee charged with keeping the Standards responsive to the needs of these groups and with upgrading and extending them progressively as the profession and science of psychology continue to develop new knowledge, improved methods, and additional modes of psychological service. These Standards have been established by organized psychology as a means of self-regulation to protect the public interest.

While these revised Standards contain a number of important changes, they differ from the original Standards in two major respects:

1. They uniformly specify the *minimally acceptable levels* of quality assurance and performance that providers of those psychological services covered by the Standards must reach or exceed. Care has been taken to assure that each standard is clearly stated, readily measurable, realistic, and implementable.

2. The revised Standards apply to a more limited range of services than the original Standards. The present Standards have been restricted to applications in "human services" with the goal of facilitating more effective human functioning. The kinds of psychological services covered by the present Standards are those ordinarily involved in the practice of specialists in clinical, counseling, industrial-organizational, and school psychology. However, it is important to note that these Standards cover psychological *functions* and not classes of practitioners.

Any persons representing themselves as psychologists, when providing any of the covered psychological service functions at any time and in any setting, whether public or private, profit or nonprofit, are required to observe these standards of practice in order to promote the best interests and welfare of the users of such services. It is to be understood that fulfillment of the requirements to meet these Standards shall be judged by peers in relation to the capabilities for evaluation and the circumstances that prevail in the setting at the time the program or service is evaluated.

---

[2]The footnotes appended to these Standards represent an attempt to provide a coherent context of other policy statements of the Association regarding professional practice. The Standards extend these previous policy statements where necessary to reflect current concerns of the public and the profession.

Standards covering other psychological service functions may be added from time to time to those already listed. However, functions and activities related to the teaching of psychology, the writing or editing of scholarly or scientific manuscripts, and the conduct of scientific research do not fall within the purview of the present Standards.

Historical Background

Early in 1970, acting at the direction of the Association's Council of Representatives, the Board of Professional Affairs appointed a Task Force composed of practicing psychologists with specialized knowledge in at least one of every major class of human service facility and with experience relevant to the setting of standards. Its charge was to develop a set of standards for psychological practice. Soon thereafter, partial support for this activity was obtained through a grant from the National Institute of Mental Health.[3]

First, the Task Force established liaison with national groups already active in standard setting and accreditation. It was therefore able to influence the adoption of certain basic principles and wording contained in standards for psychological services published by the Joint Commission on Accreditation of Hospitals (JCAH), Accreditation Council for Facilities for the Mentally Retarded (1971), and by the Accreditation Council for Psychiatric Facilities (JCAH, 1972). It also contributed substantially to the "constitutionally required minimum standards for adequate treatment of the mentally ill" ordered by the U.S. District Court in Alabama (*Wyatt v. Stickney*, 1972). In concert with other APA committees, the Task Force also represented the Association in national-level deliberations with governmental groups and insurance carriers that defined the qualifications necessary for psychologists involved in providing health services.

These interim outcomes involved influence by the Association on actions by groups of nonpsychologists that directly affected the manner in which psychological services were employed, particularly in health and rehabilitation settings. However, these measures did not relieve the Association from exercising its responsibility to speak out directly and authoritatively on what standards for psychological practice should be throughout a broad range of human service settings. It was also the responsibility of the Association to determine how psychologists would be held accountable should their practice fail to meet quality standards.

[3]NIMH Grant MH 21696.

In September 1974, after more than 4 years of study and broad consultations, the Task Force proposed a set of standards, which the Association's Council of Representatives adopted and voted to publish in order to meet urgent needs of the public and the profession. Members of Council had various reservations about the scope and wording of the Standards as initially adopted. By establishing a continuing Committee on Standards, Council took the first step in what would be an ongoing process of review and revision.

The task of collecting, analyzing, and synthesizing reactions to the original Standards fell to two successive committees. They were charged similarly to review and revise the Standards and to suggest means to implement them, including their acceptance by relevant governmental and private accreditation groups. The dedicated work of the psychologists who served on both those communities is gratefully acknowledged. Also recognized with thanks are the several hundred comments received from scores of interested persons representing professional, academic, and scientific psychology, consumer groups, administrators of facilities, and others. This input from those directly affected by the original Standards provided the major stimulus and much of the content for the changes that appear in this revision.

Principles and Implications of Standards

A few basic principles have guided the development of these Standards:

1. There should be a single set of standards that governs psychological service functions offered by psychologists, regardless of their specialty, setting, or form of remuneration. All psychologists in professional practice should be guided by a uniform set of standards just as they are guided by a common code of ethics.

2. Standards should clearly establish minimally acceptable levels of quality for covered psychological service functions, regardless of the character of the users, purchasers, or sanctioners of such covered services.

3. All persons providing psychological services shall meet minimally acceptable levels of training and experience, which are consistent and appropriate with the functions they perform. However, final responsibility and accountability for services provided must rest with psychologists who have earned a doctoral degree in a program that is primarily psychological at a regionally accredited university or professional school. Those providing psychological services who have lesser (or other) levels of training shall be supervised by a psychologist with

the above training. This level of qualification is necessary to assure that the public receives services of high quality.

4. There should be a uniform set of standards governing the quality of services to all users of psychological services in both the private and public sectors. There is no justification for maintaining the double standard presently embedded in most state legislation whereby providers of private fee-based psychological services are subject to statutory regulation, while those providing similar psychological services under governmental auspices are usually exempt from such regulations. This circumstance tends to afford greater protection under the law for those receiving privately delivered psychological services. On the other hand, those receiving privately delivered psychological services currently lack many of the safeguards that are available in governmental settings; these include peer review, consultation, record review, and staff supervision.

5. While assuring the user of the psychologist's accountability for the nature and quality of services rendered, standards must not constrain the psychologist from employing new methods or making flexible use of support personnel in staffing the delivery of services.

The Standards here presented have broad implications both for the public who use psychological services and for providers of such services:

1. Standards provide a firmer basis for a mutual understanding between provider and user and facilitate more effective evaluation of services provided and outcomes achieved.

2. Standards are an important step toward greater uniformity in legislative and regulatory actions involving providers of psychological services, and Standards provide the basis for the development of accreditation procedures for service facilities.

3. Standards give specific content to the profession's concept of ethical practice.

4. Standards have significant impact on tomorrow's training models for both professional and support personnel in psychology.

5. Standards for the provision of psychological services in human service facilities influence what is considered acceptable structure, budgeting, and staffing patterns in these facilities.

6. Standards are living documents that require continual review and revision.

The Standards illuminate weaknesses in the delivery of psychological services and point to their correction. Some settings are known to require additional and/or higher standards for specific areas of service delivery than those herein proposed. There is no intent to diminish the scope or quality of psychological services that exceed these Standards.

Systematically applied, these Standards serve to establish uniformly the *minimally acceptable levels* of psychological services. They serve to establish a more effective and consistent basis for evaluating the performance of individual service providers, and they serve to guide the organizing of psychological service units in human service settings.

Definitions

Providers of psychological services refers to the following persons:

A. Professional psychologists.[4] Professional psychologists have a doctoral degree from a regionally accredited university or professional school in a program that is primarily psychological[5] and appropriate training and experience in the area of service offered.[6]

[4]For the purpose of transition, persons who met the following criteria on or before the date of adoption of the original Standards on September 4, 1974, shall also be considered professional psychologists: (a) a master's degree from a program primarily psychological in content from a regionally accredited university or professional school; (b) appropriate education, training, and experience in the area of service offered; (c) a license or certificate in the state in which they practice, conferred by a state board of psychological examiners, or the endorsement of the state psychological association through voluntary certification, or, for practice in primary and secondary schools, a state department of education certificate as a school psychologist provided that the certificate required at least two graduate years.

[5]Minutes of the Board of Professional Affairs meeting, Washington, D.C., March 8–9, 1974.

[6]This definition is less restrictive than Recommendation 4 of the APA (1967) policy statement setting forth model state legislation affecting the practice of psychology (hereinafter referred to as State Guidelines), proposing one level for state license or certificate and "requiring the doctoral degree from an accredited university or college in a program that is primarily psychological, and no less than 2 years of supervised experience, one of which is subsequent to the granting of the doctoral degree. This level should be designated by the title of 'psychologist' " (p. 1099).

The 1972 APA "Guidelines for Conditions of Employment of Psychologists" (hereinafter referred to as CEP Guidelines) introduces slightly different shadings of meaning in its section on "Standards for Entry into the Profession" as follows: "Persons are properly identified as psychologists when they have completed the training and experience recognized as necessary to perform functions consistent with one of the several levels in a career in psychology. This training includes possession of a degree earned in a program primarily psychological in content. In the case of psychological practice, it involves services for a fee, appropriate registration, certification, or licensing as provided by laws of the state in which the practices will apply" (APA, 1972, p. 331).

In some situations, specialty designations and standards may be relevant, *The National Register of Health Service Providers in Psychology,* which based its criteria on this standard, identifies qualified psychologists in the health services field.

B. All other persons who offer psychological services under the supervision of a professional psychologist.

Psychological services refers to one or more of the following:[7]

A. Evaluation, diagnosis, and assessment of the functioning of individuals and groups in a variety of settings and activities.

B. Interventions to facilitate the functioning of individuals and groups. Such interventions may include psychological counseling, psychotherapy, and process consultation.

C. Consultation relating to A and B above.

D. Program development services in the areas of A, B, and C above.[8]

E. Supervision of psychological services.

A *psychological service unit* is the functional unit through which psychological services are provided:

A. A psychological service unit is a unit that provides predominantly psychological services and is composed of one or more professional psychologists and supporting staff.

[7]As noted in the opening section of these Standards, functions and activities of psychologists relating to the teaching of psychology, the writing or editing of scholarly or scientific manuscripts, and the conduct of scientific research do not fall within the purview of these Standards.

[8]These definitions should be compared to the State Guidelines, which include definitions of *psychologist* and the *practice of psychology* as follows: "A person represents himself to be a psychologist when he holds himself out to the public by any title or description of services incorporating the words 'psychology,' 'psychological,' 'psychologist,' and/or offers to render or renders services as defined below to individuals, groups, organizations, or the public for a fee, monetary or otherwise.

"The practice of psychology within the meaning of this act is defined as rendering to individuals, groups or organizations, or the public any psychological service involving the application of principles, methods, and procedures of understanding, predicting, and influencing behavior, such as the principles pertaining to learning, perception, motivation, thinking, emotions, and interpersonal relationships; the methods and procedures of interviewing, counseling, and psychotherapy; of constructing, administering, and interpreting tests of mental abilities, aptitudes, interests, attitudes, personality characteristics, emotion, and motivation; and of assessing public opinion.

"The application of said principles and methods includes but is not restricted to: diagnosis, prevention, and amelioration of adjustment problems and emotional and mental disorders of individuals and groups; hypnosis; educational and vocational counseling; personnel selection and management; the evaluation and planning for effective work and learning situations; advertising and market research; and the resolution of interpersonal and social conflicts.

"Psychotherapy within the meaning of this act means the use of learning, conditioning methods, and emotional reactions, in a professional relationship, to assist a person or persons to modify feelings, attitudes, and behavior which are intellectually, socially, or emotionally maladjustive or ineffectual.

"The practice of psychology shall be as defined above, any existing statute in the state of _____to the contrary notwithstanding" (APA, 1967, pp. 1098–1099).

B. A psychological service unit may operate as a professional service or as a functional or geographic component of a larger governmental, educational, correction[al], health, training, industrial, or commercial organizational unit.[9]

C. A psychologist providing professional services in a multioccupational setting is regarded as a psychological service unit.

D. A psychological service unit also may be an individual or group of individuals in a private practice or a psychological consulting firm.

User includes:

A. Direct users or recipients of psychological services.

B. Public and private institutions, facilities, or organizations receiving psychological services.

C. Third-party purchasers—those who pay for the delivery of services but who are not the recipients of services.

Sanctioners refers to those users and nonusers who have a legitimate concern with the accessibility, timeliness, efficacy, and standards of quality attending the provision of psychological services. In addition to the users, sanctioners may include members of the user's family, the court, the probation officer, the school administrator, the employer, the union representative, the facility director, etc. Another class of sanctioners is represented by various governmental, peer review, and accreditation bodies concerned with the assurance of quality.

Standard 1. Providers

1.1. *Each psychological service unit offering psychological services shall have available at least one professional psychologist and as many more professional psychologists as are necessary to assure the quality of services offered.*

INTERPRETATION: The intent of this Standard is that one or more providers of psychological services in any psychological service unit shall meet the levels of training and experience of the professional psychologist as specified in the preceding definitions.[10]

---

[9]The relation of a psychological service unit to a larger facility or institution is also addressed indirectly in the CEP Guidelines, which emphasize the roles, responsibilities, and prerogatives of the psychologist when he or she is employed by or provides services for another agency, institution, or business.

[10]This Standard replaces earlier recommendations in the 1967 State Guidelines concerning exemption of psychologists from licensure. Recommendations 8 and 9 of those Guidelines read as follows: "8. Persons employed as psychologists by accredited academic institutions, governmental agencies, research laboratories, and business corporations should be exempted, provided such employees are performing those duties for which they are employed by such organizations, and within the confines of such organizations."

When a professional psychologist is not available on a full-time basis, the facility shall retain the services of one or more professional psychologists on a regular part-time basis to supervise the psychological services provided. The psychologist(s) so retained shall have authority and participate sufficiently to enable him or her to assess the needs for services, review the content of services provided, and assume professional responsibility and accountability for them.

1.2. *Providers of psychological services who do not meet the requirements for the professional psychologist shall be supervised by a professional psychologist who shall assume professional responsibility and accountability for the services provided. The level and extent of supervision may vary from task to task so long as the supervising psychologist retains a sufficiently close supervisory relationship to meet this standard.*

1.3. *Wherever a psychological service unit exists, a professional psychologist shall be responsible for planning, directing, and reviewing the provision of psychological services.*

INTERPRETATION: This psychologist shall coordinate the activities of the psychological service unit with other professional, administrative, and technical groups, both within and outside the facility. This psychologist, who may be the director, chief, or coordinator of the psychological service unit, has related responsibilities including, but not limited to, recruiting qualified staff, directing training and research activities of the service, maintaining a high level of professional and ethical practice, and assuring that staff members function only within the areas of their competency.

In order to facilitate the effectiveness of services by increasing the level of staff sensitivity and professional skills, the psychologist designated as director shall be responsible for participating in the selection

---

"9. Persons employed as psychologists by accredited academic institutions, governmental agencies, research laboratories, and business corporations consulting or offering their research findings or providing scientific information to like organizations for a fee should be exempted" (APA, 1967, p. 1100).

On the other hand, the 1967 State Guidelines specifically denied exemptions under certain conditions, as noted in Recommendations 10 and 11: "10. Persons employed as psychologists who offer or provide psychological services to the public for a fee, over and above the salary that they receive for the performance of their regular duties, should not be exempted.

"11. Persons employed as psychologists by organizations that sell psychological services to the public should not be exempted" (APA, 1967, pp. 1100–1101).

The present APA policy, as reflected in this Standard, establishes a single code of practice for psychologists providing covered services to users in any setting. The present minimum requirement is that a psychologist providing any covered service must meet local statutory requirements for licensure or certification. See the section Principles and Implications of the Standards for an elaboration of this position.

of the staff and supporting personnel whose qualifications and skills (e.g., language, cultural and experiential background, race, and sex) are directly relevant to the needs and characteristics of the users served.

1.4. *When functioning as part of an organizational setting, professional psychologists shall bring their background and skills to bear whenever appropriate upon the goals of the organization by participating in the planning and development of overall services.*[11]

INTERPRETATION: Professional psychologists shall participate in the maintenance of high professional standards by representation on committees concerned with service delivery.

As appropriate to the setting, these activities may include active participation, as voting and as office-holding members on the facility's executive, planning, and evaluation boards and committees.

1.5. *Psychologists shall maintain current knowledge of scientific and professional developments that are directly related to the services they render.*

INTERPRETATION: Methods through which knowledge of scientific and professional development may be gained include, but are not limited to, continuing education, attendance at workshops, participation in staff development, and reading scientific publications.[12]

The psychologist shall have ready access to reference material related to the provision of psychological services.

Psychologists must be prepared to show evidence periodically that they are staying abreast of current knowledge and practices through continuing education.

1.6. *Psychologists shall limit their practice to their demonstrated areas of professional competence.*

INTERPRETATION: Psychological services will be offered in accordance with the provider's areas of competence as defined by verifiable

---

[11]A closely related principle is found in the APA (1972) CEP Guidelines: "It is the policy of APA that psychology as an independent profession is entitled to parity with other health and human service professions in institutional practices and before the law. Psychologists in interdisciplinary settings such as colleges and universities, medical schools, clinics, private practice groups, and other agencies expect parity with other professions in such matters as academic rank, board status, salaries, fringe benefits, fees, participation in administrative decisions, and all other conditions of employment, private contractual arrangements, and status before the law and legal institutions" (APA, 1972, p. 333).

[12]See CEP Guidelines (section entitled "Career Development") for a closely related statement: "Psychologists are expected to encourage institutions and agencies which employ them to sponsor or conduct career development programs. The purpose of these programs would be to enable psychologists to engage in study for professional advancement and to keep abreast of developments in their field" (APA, 1972, p. 332).

training and experience. When extending services beyond the range of their usual practice, psychologists shall obtain pertinent training or appropriate professional supervision.

1.7. Psychologists who wish to change their service specialty or to add an additional area of applied specialization must meet the same requirements with respect to subject matter and professional skills that apply to doctoral training in the new specialty.[13]

INTERPRETATION: Training of doctoral-level psychologists to quality them for change in specialty will be under the auspices of accredited university departments or professional schools that offer the doctoral degree in that specialty. Such training should be individualized, due credit being given for relevant coursework or requirements that have previously been satisfied. Merely taking an internship or acquiring experience in a practicum setting is not considered adequate preparation for becoming a clinical, counseling, industrial-organizational, or school psychologist when prior training has not been in the relevant area. Fulfillment of such an individualized training program is attested to by the award of a certificate by the supervising department or professional school indicating the successful completion of preparation in the particular specialty.

Standard 2. Programs

2.1. Composition and organization of a psychological service unit:

2.1.1. The composition and programs of a psychological service unit shall be responsive to the needs of the persons or settings served.

INTERPRETATION: A psychological service unit shall be so structured as to facilitate effective and economical delivery of services. For example, a psychological service unit serving a predominantly low-income, ethnic, or racial minority group should have a staffing pattern and service program that is adapted to the linguistic, experiential, and attitudinal characteristics of the users.

2.1.2. A description of the organization of the psychological service unit and its lines of responsibility and accountability for the delivery of psychological

---

[13]This Standard follows closely the statement regarding "Policy on Training for Psychologists Wishing to Change Their Specialty" adopted by the APA Council of Representatives in January 1976. Included therein was the implementing provision that "this policy statement shall be incorporated in the guidelines of the Committee on Accreditation so that appropriate sanctions can be brought to bear on university and internship training programs which violate [it]."

services shall be available in written form to staff of the unit and to users and sanctioners upon request.

INTERPRETATION: The description should include lines of responsibility, supervisory relationships, and the level and extent of accountability for each person who provides psychological services.

2.1.3. A psychological service unit shall include sufficient numbers of professional and support personnel to achieve its goals, objectives, and purposes.

INTERPRETATION: The workload and diversity of psychological services required and the specific goals and objectives of the setting will determine the numbers and qualifications of professional and support personnel in the psychological service unit. Where shortages in personnel exist so that psychological services cannot be rendered in a professional manner, the director of the psychological service unit shall initiate action to modify appropriately the specific goals and objectives of the service.

2.2. Policies:

2.2.1. When the psychological service unit is composed of more than one person wherein a supervisory relationship exists or is a component of a larger organization, a written statement of its objectives and scope of services shall be developed and maintained.

INTERPRETATION: The psychological service unit shall review its objectives and scope of services annually and revise them as necessary to insure that the psychological services offered are consistent with staff competencies and current psychological knowledge and practice. This statement should be distributed to staff and, where appropriate, to users and sanctioners upon request.

2.2.2. All providers within a psychological service unit shall support the legal and civil rights of the user.[14]

INTERPRETATION: Providers of psychological services shall safeguard the interests of the user with regard to personal, legal, and civil rights. They shall continually be sensitive to the issue of confidentiality of information, the short-term and long-term impact of their decisions and recommendations, and other matters pertaining to individual, legal, and civil rights. Concerns regarding the safeguarding of individual rights of

[14]See also APA's (1977) *Ethical Standards of Psychologists*, especially Principles 5 (Confidentiality), 6 (Welfare of the Consumer), and 9 (Pursuit of Research Activities); and see *Ethical Principles in the Conduct of Research with Human Participants* (APA, 1973a).

users include, but are not limited to, problems of self-incrimination in judicial proceedings, involuntary commitment to hospitals, protection of minors or legal incompetents, discriminatory practices in employment selection procedures, recommendations for special education provisions, information relative to adverse personnel actions in the armed services, and the adjudication of domestic relations disputes in divorce and custodial proceedings. Providers of psychological services should take affirmative action by making themselves available for local committees, review boards, and similar advisory groups established to safeguard the human, civil, and legal rights of service users.

2.2.3. *All providers within a psychological service unit shall be familiar with and adhere to the American Psychological Association's* Ethical Standards of Psychologists, Psychology as a Profession, Standards for Educational and Psychological Tests, *and other official policy statements relevant to standards for professional services issued by the Association.*

INTERPRETATION: Providers of psychological services, users, and sanctioners may order copies of these documents from the American Psychological Association.

2.2.4. *All providers within a psychological service unit shall conform to relevant statutes established by federal, state, and local governments.*

INTERPRETATION: All providers of psychological services shall be familiar with appropriate statutes regulating the practice of psychology. They shall also be informed about agency regulations that have the force of law and that relate to the delivery of psychological services (e.g., evaluation for disability retirement and special education placements). In addition, all providers shall be cognizant that federal agencies such as the Veterans Administration and the Department of Health, Education, and Welfare have policy statements regarding psychological services. Providers of psychological services shall be familiar with other statutes and regulations, including those addressed to the civil and legal rights of users (e.g., those promulgated by the federal Equal Employment Opportunity Commission) that are pertinent to their scope of practice.

It shall be the responsibility of the American Psychological Association to publish periodically those federal policies, statutes, and regulations relating to this section. The state psychological associations are similarly urged to publish and distribute periodically appropriate state statutes and regulations.

2.2.5. All providers within a psychological service unit shall, where appropriate, inform themselves about and use the network of human services in their communities in order to link users with relevant services and resources.

INTERPRETATION: It is incumbent upon psychologists and supporting staff to be sensitive to the broader context of human needs. In recognizing the matrix of personal and societal problems, providers shall, where appropriate, make available information regarding human services such as legal aid societies, social services, employment agencies, health resources, and educational and recreational facilities. The provider of psychological services shall refer to such community resources and, when indicated, actively intervene on behalf of the user.

2.2.6. In the delivery of psychological services, the providers shall maintain a continuing cooperative relationship with colleagues and co-workers whenever in the best interest of the user.[15]

INTERPRETATION: It shall be the responsibility of the psychologist to recognize the areas of special competence of other psychologists and of other professionals for either consultation or referral purposes. Providers of psychological services shall make appropriate use of other professional, technical, and administrative resources whenever these serve the best interests of the user, and shall establish and maintain cooperative arrangements with such other resources as required to meet the needs of users.

2.3. Procedures:

2.3.1. Where appropriate, each psychological service unit shall be guided by a set of procedural guidelines for the delivery of psychological services. If appropriate to the setting, these guidelines shall be in written form.

INTERPRETATION: Depending on the nature of the setting, and whenever feasible, providers should be prepared to provide a statement of procedural guidelines in either oral or written form that can be understood by users as well as sanctioners. This statement may describe the current methods, forms, procedures, and techniques being used to achieve the objectives and goals for psychological services.

---

[15]Support for this position is found in the section in *Psychology as a Profession* on relations with other professions: "Professional persons have an obligation to know and take into account the traditions and practices of other professional groups with whom they work and to cooperate fully with members of such groups with whom research, service, and other functions are shared" (APA, 1968, p. 5).

This statement shall be communicated to staff and, when appropriate, to users and sanctioners. The psychological service unit shall provide for the annual review of its procedures for the delivery of psychological services.

2.3.2. *Providers shall develop a plan appropriate to the provider's professional strategy of practice and to the problems presented by the user.*

INTERPRETATION: Whenever appropriate or mandated in the setting, this plan shall be in written form as a means of providing a basis for establishing accountability, obtaining informed consent, and providing a mechanism for subsequent peer review. Regardless of the type of setting or users involved, it is desirable that a plan be developed that describes the psychological services indicated and the manner in which they will be provided.[16]

A psychologist who provides services as one member of a collaborative effort shall participate in the development and implementation of the overall service plan and provide for its periodic review.

2.3.3. *There shall be a mutually acceptable understanding between the provider and user or responsible agent regarding the delivery of service.*

INTERPRETATION: Varying service settings call for understandings differing in explicitness and formality. For instance, a psychologist providing services within a user organization may operate within a broad framework of understanding with this organization as a condition of employment. As another example, psychologists providing professional services to individuals in clinical, counseling, or school settings require an open-ended agreement, which specifies procedures and their known

---

[16]One example of a specific application of this principle is found in Guideline 2 in APA's (1973b) "Guidelines for Psychologists Conducting Growth Groups":

The following information should be made available *in writing* [italics added] to all prospective participants:

(a) An explicit statement of the purpose of the group;

(b) Types of techniques that may be employed;

(c) The education, training, and experience of the leader or leaders;

(d) The fee and any additional expense that may be incurred;

(e) A statement as to whether or not a follow-up service is included in the fee;

(f) Goals of the group experience and techniques to be used;

(g) Amounts and kinds of responsibility to be assumed by the leader and by the participants. For example, (i) the degree to which a participant is free not to follow suggestions and prescriptions of the group leader and other group members; (ii) any restrictions on a participant's freedom to leave the group at any time; and,

(h) Issues of confidentiality. (p. 933)

risks (if any), costs, and respective responsibilities of provider and user for achieving the agreed-upon objectives.

2.3.4. Accurate, current, and pertinent documentation shall be made of essential psychological services provided.

INTERPRETATION: Records kept of psychological services may include, but not be limited to, identifying data, dates of services, types of services, and significant actions taken. Providers of psychological services shall insure that essential information concerning services rendered is appropriately recorded within a reasonable time of their completion.

2.3.5. Providers of psychological services shall establish a system to protect confidentiality of their records.[17]

INTERPRETATION: Psychologists are responsible for maintaining the confidentiality of information about users of services whether obtained by themselves or by those they supervise. All persons supervised by psychologists, including nonprofessional personnel and students, who have access to records of psychological services shall be required to maintain this confidentiality as a condition of employment.

The psychologist shall not release confidential information, except with the written consent of the user directly involved or his or her legal representative. Even after the consent has been obtained for release, the psychologist should clearly identify such information as confidential to the recipient of the information.[18] If directed otherwise by statute or regulations with the force of law or by court order, the psychologist shall seek a resolution to the conflict that is both ethically and legally feasible and appropriate.

Users shall be informed in advance of any limits in the setting for maintenance of confidentiality of psychological information. For instance, psychologists in hospital settings shall inform their patients that psychological information in a patient's clinical record may be available

[17]See again Principle 5 (Confidentiality) in *Ethical Standards of Psychologists* (APA, 1977).
[18]Support for the principle of privileged communication is found in at least two policy statements of the Association: "In the interest of both the public and the client and in accordance with the requirements of good professional practice, the profession of psychology seeks recognition of the privileged nature of confidential communications with clients, preferably through statutory enactment or by administrative policy where more appropriate" (APA, 1968, p. 8).
   "25. Wherever possible, a clause protecting the privileged nature of the psychologist–client relationship be included."
   "26. When appropriate, psychologists assist in obtaining general 'across the board' legislation for such privileged communications" (APA, 1967, p. 1103).

without the patient's written consent to other members of the profes-sional staff associated with the patient's treatment or rehabilitation. Sim-ilar limitations on confidentiality of psychological information may be present in certain school, industrial, or military settings, or in instances where the user has waived confidentiality for purposes of third-party payment.

When the user intends to waive confidentiality, the psychologist should discuss the implications of releasing psychological information, and assist the user in limiting disclosure only to information required by the present circumstance.

Raw psychological data (e.g., test protocols, therapy or interview notes, or questionnaire returns) in which a user is identified shall be released only with the written consent of the user or legal representative and released only to a person recognized by the psychologist as com-petent to use the data.

Any use made of psychological reports, records, or data for research or training purposes shall be consistent with this Standard. Additionally, providers of psychological services shall comply with statutory confi-dentiality requirements and those embodied in the American Psycho-logical Association's *Ethical Standards of Psychologists* (APA, 1977).

Providers of psychological services should remain sensitive to both the benefits and the possible misuse of information regarding individuals that is stored in large computerized data banks. Providers should use their influence to ensure that such information is used in a socially responsible manner.

Standard 3. Accountability

3.1. Psychologists' professional activity shall be primarily guided by the principle of promoting human welfare.

INTERPRETATION: Psychologists shall provide services to users in a manner that is considerate, effective, and economical.

Psychologists are responsible for making their services readily accessible to users in a manner that facilitates the user's freedom of choice.

Psychologists shall be mindful of their accountability to the sanc-tioners of psychological services and to the general public, provided that appropriate steps are taken to protect the confidentiality of the service relationship. In the pursuit of their professional activities they shall aid in the conservation of human, material, and financial resources.

The psychological service unit will not withhold services to a poten-tial client on the basis of that user's race, color, religion, sex, age, or

· national origin. Recognition is given, however, to the following considerations: The professional right of psychologists to limit their practice
to a specific category of user (e.g., children, adolescents, women); the
right and responsibility of psychologists to withold an assessment procedure when not validly applicable; the right and responsibility of psychologists to withhold evaluative, psychotherapeutic, counseling, or other
services in specific instances where considerations of race, religion, color,
sex, or any other difference between psychologist and client might impair
the effectiveness of the relationship.[19]

Psychologists who find that psychological services are being provided in a manner that is discriminatory or exploitative to users and/or
contrary to these Standards or to state or federal statutes shall take
appropriate corrective action, which may include the refusal to provide
services. When conflicts of interest arise, the psychologist shall be guided
in the resolution of differences by the principles set forth in the *Ethical
Standards of Psychologists* of the American Psychological Association and
by the Guidelines for Conditions of Employment of Psychologists (1972).[20]

3.2. *Psychologists shall pursue their activities as members of an independent, autonomous profession.*[21]

[19]This paragraph is drawn directly from the CEP Guidelines (APA, 1972, p. 333).
[20]"It is recognized that under certain circumstances, the interests and goals of a particular
community or segment of interest in the population may be in conflict with the general
welfare. Under such circumstances, the psychologist's professional activity must be primarily guided by the principle of promoting human welfare" (APA, 1972, p. 334).
[21]Support for the principle of the independence of psychology as a profession is found in
the following: "As a member of an autonomous profession, a psychologist rejects limitations upon his freedom of thought and action other than those imposed by his moral,
legal, and social responsibilities. The Association is always prepared to provide appropriate assistance to any responsible member who becomes subjected to unreasonable
limitations upon his opportunity to function as a practitioner, teacher, researcher, administrator, or consultant. The Association is always prepared to cooperate with any responsible professional organization in opposing any unreasonable limitations on the professional
functions of the members of that organization."
"This insistence upon professional autonomy has been upheld over the years by the
affirmative actions of the courts and other public and private bodies in support of the
right of the psychologist—and other professionals—to pursue those functions for which
he is trained and qualified to perform" (APA, 1968, p. 9).
"Organized psychology has the responsibility to define and develop its own profes-
son, consistent with the general canons of science and with the public welfare.
"Psychologists recognize that other professions and other groups will, from time to
time, seek to define the roles and responsibilities of psychologists. The APA opposes
such developments on the same principles that it is opposed to the psychological profession taking positions which would define the work and scope of responsibility of other
duly recognized professions" (APA, 1972, p. 333).

INTERPRETATION: Psychologists shall be aware of the implications of their activities for the profession as a whole. They shall seek to eliminate discriminatory practices instituted for self-serving purposes that are not in the interest of the user (e.g., arbitrary requirements for referral and supervision by another profession). They shall be cognizant of their responsibilities for the development of the profession, participate where possible in the training and career development of students and other providers, participate as appropriate in the training of paraprofessionals, and integrate and supervise their contributions within the structure established for delivering psychological services. Where appropriate, they shall facilitate the development of, and participate in, professional standards review mechanisms.[22]

Psychologists shall seek to work with other professionals in a cooperative manner for the good of the user and the benefit of the general public. Psychologists associated with multidisciplinary settings shall support the principle that members of each participating profession shall have equal rights and opportunities to share all privileges and responsibilities of full membership in the human service facility, and to administer service programs in their respective areas of competence.

3.3. *There shall be periodic, systematic, and effective evaluations of psychological services.*[23]

---

[22]APA support for peer review is detailed in the following excerpt from the APA (1971) statement entitled "Psychology and National Health Care": "All professions participating in a national health plan should be directed to establish review mechanisms (or performance evaluations) that include not only peer review but active participation by persons representing the consumer. In situations where there are fiscal agents, they should also have representation when appropriate" (p. 1026).

[23]This Standard on program evaluation is based directly on the following excerpts of two APA position papers: "The quality and availability of health services should be evaluated continuously by both consumers and health professionals. Research into the efficiency and effectiveness of the system should be conducted both internally and under independent auspices" (APA, 1971, p. 1025).

"The comprehensive community mental health center should devote an explicit portion of its budget to program evaluation. All centers should inculcate in their staff attention to and respect for research findings; the larger centers have an obligation to set a high priority on basic research and to give formal recognition to research as a legitimate part of the duties of staff members.

. . . Only through explicit appraisal of program effects can worthy approaches be retained and refined, ineffective ones dropped. Evaluative monitoring of program achievements may vary, of course, from the relatively informal to the systematic and quantitative, depending on the importance of the issue, the availability of resources, and the willingness of those responsible to take the risks of substituting informed judgment for evidence" (Smith & Hobbs, 1966, pp. 21–22).

INTERPRETATION:When the psychological service unit is a component of a larger organization, regular assessment of progress in achieving goals shall be provided in the service delivery plan, including consideration of the effectiveness of psychological services relative to costs in terms of time, money, and the availability of professional and support personnel.

Evaluation of the efficiency and effectiveness of the psychological service delivery system should be conducted internally and, when possible, under independent auspices.

It is highly desirable that there be a periodic reexamination of review mechanisms to ensure that these attempts at public safeguards are effective and cost-efficient and do not place unnecessary encumbrances on the provider or unnecessary additional expense to users or sanctioners for services rendered.

3.4. *Psychologists are accountable for all aspects of the services they provide and shall be responsive to those concerned with these services.*[24]

INTERPRETATION: In recognizing their responsibilities to users, sanctioners, third-party purchasers, and other providers, wherever appropriate and consistent with the user's legal rights and privileged communications, psychologists shall make available information about, and opportunity to participate in, decisions concerning such issues as initiation, termination, continuation, modification, and evaluation of psychological services. Additional copies of these *Standards for Providers of Psychological Services* can be ordered from the American Psychological Association.

Depending upon the settings, accurate and full information shall be made available to prospective individual or organization users regarding the qualifications of providers, the nature and extent of services offered, and, where appropriate, financial and social costs.

Where appropriate, psychologists shall inform users of their payment policies and their willingness to assist in obtaining reimbursement. Those who accept reimbursement from a third party should be acquainted with the appropriate statutes and regulations and should instruct their users on proper procedures for submitting claims and limits on confidentiality of claims information, in accordance with pertinent statutes.

[24]See also the CEP Guidelines for the following statement: "A psychologist recognizes that . . . he alone is accountable for the consequences and effects of his services, whether as teacher, researcher, or practitioner. This responsibility cannot be shared, delegated, or reduced" (APA, 1972, p. 334).

Standard 4. Environment

4.1. *Providers of psychological services shall promote the development in the service setting of a physical, organizational, and social environment that facilitates optimal human functioning.*

INTERPRETATION: Federal, state, and local requirements for safety, health, and sanitation must be observed. Attention shall be given to the comfort and, where relevant, to the privacy of providers and users.

As providers of services, psychologists have the responsibility to be concerned with the environment of their service unit, especially as it affects the quality of service, but also as it impinges on human functioning in the larger unit or organization when the service unit is included in such a larger context. Physical arrangements and organizational policies and procedures should be conducive to the human dignity, self-respect, and optimal functioning of users, and to the effective delivery of service. The atmosphere in which psychological services are rendered should be appropriate to the service and to the users, whether in office, clinic, school, or industrial organization.

REFERENCES

Accreditation Council for Facilities for the Mentally Retarded. *Standards for residential facilities for the mentally retarded.* Chicago, Ill.: Joint Commission on Accreditation of Hospitals, 1971.

American Psychological Association, Committee on Legislation. A model for state legislation affecting the practice of psychology 1967. *American Psychologist, 1967, 22,* 1095–1103.

American Psychological Association. *Psychology as a profession.* Washington, D.C.: Author, 1968.

American Psychological Association. Guidelines for conditions of employment of psychologists. *American Psychologist, 1972, 27,* 331–334.

American Psychological Association. *Ethical principles in the conduct of research with human participants.* Washington, D.C.: Author, 1973. (a)

American Psychological Association. Guidelines for psychologists conducting growth groups. *American Psychologist, 1973, 28,* 933. (b)

American Psychological Association. *Standards for educational and psychological tests.* Washington, D.C.: Author, 1974.

American Psychological Association. *Ethical standards of psychologists* (Rev. ed.). Washington, D.C.: Author, 1977.

Joint Commission on Accreditation of Hospitals. *Accreditation manual for psychiatric facilities 1972.* Chicago, Ill.: Author, 1972.

Smith, M. B., & Hobbs, N. *The community and the community mental health center.* Washington, D.C.: American Psychological Association, 1966.

5.3. SPECIALTY GUIDELINES FOR THE DELIVERY OF SERVICES (APA, 1980)*

In January 1980, the APA Committee on Professional Standards responsible for the *Standards for Providers of Psychological Services* also formulated the *Specialty Guidelines for the Delivery of Services* for four specialty areas of psychology: clinical, counseling, industrial/organizational, and school psychology. These specialty guidelines describe thoroughly the procedures for providing psychological services and differentiates each specialty area as to a professonal's qualifications, procedures, and guidelines governing the specialty practice. These specialty guidelines supplement the standards written by APA. The following are specialty guidelines for the delivery of services by Clinical Psychologists, whereas *Specialty Guidelines for Counseling, School, and Industrial Psychologists* can be purchased from the APA Order Department, P.O. Box 2710, Hyattsville, Maryland 20784.

COMMITTEE ON PROFESSIONAL STANDARDS

In September 1976, the APA Council of Representatives reviewed and commented on the draft revisions of the *Standards for Providers of Psychological Services* prepared by the Committee on Standards for Providers of Psychological Services. During that discussion, the Council acknowledged the need for standards in certain specialty areas in addition to the generic *Standards* covered by the draft revision. The Council authorized the committee to hold additional meetings to develop multiple standards in all specialty areas of psychology.

Following the adoption of the revised generic *Standards* in January 1977, the committee, working with psychologists in the four recognized specialty areas of psychology, spent the next three years modifying the generic *Standards* to meet the needs of clinical, counseling, industrial/ organizational, and school psychologists. The four documents produced

---

*This article appeared in the *American Psychologist, 36*, 1981. Copyright 1981 by the American Psychological Association. Reprinted by permission. These Specialty Guidelines were prepared through the cooperative efforts of the APA Committee on Standards for Providers of Psychological Services (COSPOPS) and many professional clinical psychologists from the divisions of APA, including those involved in education and training programs and in public and private practice. Jules Barron, succeeded by Morris Goodman, served as the clinical psychology representative on COSPOPS. The committee was chaired by Durand F. Jacobs; the Central Office liaisons were Arthur Centor and Richard Kilburg.

by the committee went through extensive revisions. Convention programs discussing these developments were held every year. Comments were solicitated from all major constituencies in psychology and from thousands of individuals. The comments received and reviewed by the committee were varied and numerous.

In January 1980, following this extensive process and after making several additional modifications, the Council of Representatives adopted as APA policy the *Specialty Guidelines for the Delivery of Services by Clinical (Counseling, Industrial/Organizational, School) Psychologists.* As stated in the introductions of these four documents, the intent of the *Specialty Guidelines* is "to educate the public, the profession, and other interested parties regarding specialty professional practices . . . and to facilitate the continued systematic development of the profession."

At the same meeting, the Council also approved a reorganization of the Board of Professional Affairs' committee structure, which included the establishment of the Committee on Professional Standards to succeed the Committee on Standards for Providers of Psychological Services. The Committee on Professional Standards has been directed to review all comments on the *Specialty Guidelines* when considering its revisions. APA members and other interested individuals or groups with comments or suggestions are requested to send them to the American Psychological Association, Committee on Professional Standards, 1200 Seventeenth Street, N.W., Washington, D.C. 20036.

The members of the Committee on Standards for Providers of Psychological Services (1977–1980) who developed the *Specialty Guidelines* were Jack I. Bardon, school; Jules Barron, clinical; Frank Friedlander, industrial/organizational; Morris Goodman, clinical; Durand F. Jacobs (Chair), institutional practice; Barbara A. Kirk, counseling; Nadine M. Lambert, school; Virginia Ellen Schein, industrial/organizational; and Milton Schwebel, counseling. Arthur Centor and Richard Kilburg were the Central Office liaisons.

The members of the Committee on Professional Standards (1980–1981) who made the final changes to the *Specialty Guidelines* and were charged with future revisions were Juanita Braddock, public member; Lorraine Eyde, industrial/organizational; Morris Goodman, clinical; Judy Hall, experimental/mental retardation; John H. Jackson, school; Nadine M. Lambert, school; Dave Mills (1981 Chair, partial), clinical/counseling; Milton Schwebel, counseling; Gilfred Tanabe (1980 Chair), clinical; and Murphy Thomas (1981 Chair, partial), clinical. The Central Office liaisons were Joy Burke, Sharon A. Shueman, and Pam Arnold.

The Specialty Guidelines that follow are based on the generic *Standards for Providers of Psychological Services* originally adopted by the

American Psychological Association (APA) in September 1974 and revised in January 1977 (APA, 1974b, 1977b). Together with the generic *Standards*, these Specialty Guidelines state the official policy of the Association regarding delivery of services by clinical psychologists. Admission to the practice of psychology is regulated by state statute. It is the position of the Association that licensing be based on generic, and not on specialty, qualifications. Specialty guidelines serve the additional purpose of providing potential users and other interested groups with essential information about particular services available from the several specialties in professional psychology.

Professional psychology specialties have evolved from generic practice in psychology and are supported by university training programs. There are now at least four recognized professional specialties—clinical, counseling, school, and industrial/organizational psychology.

The knowledge base in each of these specialty areas has increased, refining the state of the art to the point that a set of uniform specialty guidelines is now possible and desirable. The present Guidelines are intended to educate the public, the profession, and other interested parties regarding specialty professional practices. They are also intended to facilitate the continued systematic development of the profession.

The content of each Specialty Guideline reflects a consensus of university faculty and public and private practitioners regarding the knowledge base, services provided, problems addressed, and clients served.

Traditionally, all learned disciplines have treated the designation of specialty practice as a reflection of preparation in greater depth in a particular subject matter, together with a voluntary limiting of focus to a more restricted area of practice by the professional. Lack of specialty designation does not preclude general providers of psychological services from using the methods or dealing with the populations of any specialty, except insofar as psychologists voluntarily refrain from providing services they are not trained to render. It is the intent of these Guidelines, however, that after the grandparenting period, psychologists not put themselves forward as *specialists* in a given area of practice unless they meet the qualifications noted in the Guidelines (see Definitions). Therefore, these Guidelines are meant to apply only to those psychologists who voluntarily wish to be designated as *clinical psychologists*. They do not apply to other psychologists.

These Guidelines represent the profession's best judgment of the conditions, credentials, and experience that contribute to competent professional practice. The APA strongly encourages, and plans to participate in, efforts to identify professional practitioner behaviors and job functions and to validate the relation between these and desired client outcomes. Thus, future revisions of these Guidelines will increasingly reflect the results of such efforts.

These Guidelines follow the format and, wherever applicable, the wording of the generic *Standards*.[1] (Note: Footnotes appear at the end of the Specialty Guidelines. See pp. 648–651). The intent of these Guidelines is to improve the quality, effectiveness, and accessibility of psychological services. They are meant to provide guidance to providers, users, and sanctioners regarding the best judgment of the profession on these matters. Although the Specialty Guidelines have been derived from and are consistent with the generic *Standards,* they may be used as separate documents. However, *Standards for Providers of Psychological Services* (APA, 1977b) shall remain the basic policy statement and shall take precedence where there are questions of interpretation.

Professional psychology in general and clinical psychology as a specialty have labored long and diligently to codify a uniform set of guidelines for the delivery of services by clinical psychologists that would serve the respective needs of users, providers, third-party purchasers, and sanctioners of psychological services.

The Committee on Professonal Standards, established by the APA in January 1980, is charged with keeping the generic *Standards* and the Specialty Guidelines responsive to the needs of the public and the profession. It is also charged with continually reviewing, modifying, and extending them progressively as the profession and the science of psychology develop new knowledge, improved methods, and additional modes of psychological services.

The Specialty Guidelines for the Delivery of Services by Clinical Psychologists that follow have been established by the APA as a means of self-regulation to protect the public interest. They guide the specialty practice of clinical psychology by specifying important areas of quality assurance and performance that contribute to the goal of facilitating more effective human functioning.

Principles and Implications of the Specialty Guidelines

These Specialty Guidelines have emerged from and reaffirm the same basic principles that guided the development of the generic *Standards for Providers of Psychological Services* (APA, 1977b):

[1]The footnotes appended to these Specialty Guidelines represent an attempt to provide a coherent context of other policy statements of the Association regarding professional practice. The Guidelines extend these previous policy statements where necessary to reflect current concerns of the public and the profession.

1. These Guidelines recognize that admission to the practice of psychology is regulated by state statute.

2. It is the intention of the APA that the generic *Standards* provide appropriate guidelines for statutory licensing of psychologists. In addition, although it is the position of the APA that licensing be generic and not in specialty areas, these Specialty Guidelines in clinical psychology provide an authoritative reference for use in credentialing specialty providers of clinical psychological services by such groups as divisions of the APA and state associations and by boards and agencies that find such criteria useful for quality assurance.

3. A uniform set of Specialty Guidelines governs the quality of services to all users of clinical psychological services in both the private and the public sectors. Those receiving clinical psychological services are protected by the same kinds of safeguards, irrespective of sector; these include constitutional guarantees, statutory regulation, peer review, consultation, record review, and supervision.

4. A uniform set of Specialty Guidelines governs clinical psychological service functions offered by clinical psychologists, regardless of setting or form of remuneration. All clinical psychologists in professional practice recognize and are responsive to a uniform set of Specialty Guidelines, just as they are guided by a common code of ethics.

5. Clinical psychology Guidelines establish clearly articulated levels of quality for covered clinical psychological service functions, regardless of the nature of the users, purchasers, or sanctioners of such covered services.

6. All persons providing clinical psychological services meet specified levels of training and experience that are consistent with, and appropriate to, the functions they perform. Clinical psychological services provided by persons who do not meet the APA qualifications for a professional clinical psychologist (see Definitions) are supervised by a professional clinical psychologist. Final responsibility and accountability for services provided rest with professional clinical psychologists.

7. When providing any of the covered clinical psychological service functions at any time and in any setting, whether public or private, profit or nonprofit, clinical psychologists observe these Guidelines in order to promote the best interest and welfare of the users of such services. The extent to which clinical psychologists observe these Guidelines is judged by peers.

8. These Guidelines, while assuring the user of the clinical psychologist's accountability for the nature and quality of services specified in this document, do not preclude the clinical psychologist from using new methods or developing innovative procedures in the delivery of clinical services.

These Specialty Guidelines have broad implications both for users of clinical psychological services and for providers of such services:

1. Guidelines for clinical psychological services provide a foundation for mutual understanding between provider and user and facilitate more effective evaluation of services provided and outcomes achieved.

2. Guidelines for clinical psychologists are essential for uniformity in specialty credentialing of clinical psychologists.

3. Guidelines give specific content to the profession's concept of ethical practice as it applies to the functions of clinical psychologists.

4. Guidelines for clinical psychological services may have significant impact on tomorrow's education and training models for both professional and support personnel in clinical psychology.

5. Guidelines for the provision of clinical psychological services in human service facilities influence the determination of acceptable structure, budgeting, and staffing patterns in these facilities.

6. Guidelines for clinical psychological services require continual review and revision.

The Specialty Guidelines here presented are intended to improve the quality and delivery of clinical psychological services by specifying criteria for key aspects of the practice setting. Some settings may require additional and/or more stringent criteria for specific areas of service delivery.

Systematically applied, these Guidelines serve to establish a more effective and consistent basis for evaluating the performance of individual service providers as well as to guide the organization of clinical psychological service units in human service settings.

Definitions

Providers of clinical psychological services refers to two categories of persons who provide clinical psychological services:

A. Professional clinical psychologists.[2] Professional clinical psychologists have a doctoral degree from a regionally accredited university

---

[2]The following two categories of professional psychologists who met the criteria indicated below on or before the adoption of these Specialty Guidelines on January 31, 1980, are also considered clinical psychologists: Category 1—persons who completed (a) a doctoral degree program primarily psychological in content at a regionally accredited university or professional school and (b) 3 postdoctoral years of appropriate education, training, and experience in providing clinical psychological services as defined herein, including a minimum of 1 year in a clinical setting; Category 2—persons who on or before September 4,

or professional school providing an organized, sequential clinical psychology program in a department of psychology in a university or college, or in an appropriate department or unit of a professional school. Clinical psychology programs that are accredited by the American Psychological Association are recognized as meeting the definition of a clinical psychology program. Clinical psychology programs that are not accredited by the American Psychological Association meet the definition of a clinical psychology program if they satisfy the following criteria:

1. The program is primarily psychological in nature and stands as a recognizable, coherent organizational entity within the institution.

2. The program provides an integrated, organized sequence of study.

3. The program has an identifiable body of students who are matriculated in that program for a degree.

4. There is a clear authority with primary responsibility for the core and specialty areas, whether or not the program cuts across administrative lines.

5. There is an identifiable psychology faculty, and a psychologist is responsible for the program.

In addition to a doctoral education, clinical psychologists acquire doctoral and postdoctoral training. Patterns of education and training in clinical psychology[3] are consistent with the functions to be performed

---

1974, (a) completed a master's degree from a program primarily psychological in content at a regionally accredited university or professional school and (b) held a license or certificate in the state in which they practiced, conferred by a state board of psychological examiners, or the endorsement of the state psychological association through voluntary certification, and who, in addition, prior to January 31, 1980, (c) obtained 5 post-master's years of appropriate education, training, and experience in providing clinical psychological services as defined herein, including a minimum of 2 years in a clinical setting.

After January 31, 1980, professional psychologists who wish to be recognized as professional clinical psychologists are referred to Guideline 1.7.

The definition of the professional clinical psychologist in these Guidelines does not contradict or supersede in any way the broader definition accorded the term *clinical psychologist* in the Federal Employees Health Benefits Program (see *Access to Psychologists and Optometrists Under Federal Health Benefits Program*, U.S. Senate Report No. 93–961, June 25, 1974).

[3]The areas of knowledge and training that are a part of the educational program for all professional psychologists have been presented in two APA documents, *Education and Credentialing in Psychology II* (APA, 1977a) and *Criteria for Accreditation of Doctoral Training Programs and Internships in Professional Psychology* (APA, 1979). There is consistency in the presentation of core areas in the education and training of all professional psychologists. The description of education and training in these Guidelines is based primarily on the document *Education and Credentialing in Psychology II*. It is intended to indicate broad areas of required curriculum, with the expectation that training programs will undoubtedly want to interpret the specific content of these areas in different ways depending on the nature, philosophy, and intent of the programs.

and the services to be provided, in accordance with the ages, populations, and problems encountered in various settings.

B. All other persons who are not professional clinical psychologists and who participate in the delivery of clinical psychological services under the supervision of a professional clinical psychologist. Although there may be variations in the titles of such persons, they are not referred to as clinical psychologists. Their functions may be indicated by use of the adjective *psychological* preceding the noun, for example, *psychological associate, psychological assistant, psychological technician,* or *psychological aide.* Their services are rendered under the supervision of a professional clinical psychologist, who is responsible for the designation given them and for quality control. To be assigned such a designation, a person has the background, training, or experience that is appropriate to the functions performed.

Clinical psychological services refers to the application of principles, methods, and procedures for understanding, predicting, and alleviating intellectual, emotional, psychological, and behavioral disability and discomfort. Direct services are provided in a variety of health settings, and direct and supportive services are provided in the entire range of social, organizational, and academic institutions and agencies.[4] Clinical psychological services include the following:[5]

---

[4]Functions and activities of psychologists relating to the teaching of psychology, the writing or editing of scholarly or scientific manuscripts, and the conduct of scientific research do not fall within the purview of these Guidelines.

[5]The definitions should be compared with the APA (1967) guidelines for state legislation (hereinafter referred to as state guidelines), which define *psychologist* and the *practice of psychology* as follows: "A person represents himself [or herself] to be a psychologist when he [or she] holds himself [or herself] out to the public by any title or description of services incorporating the words 'psychology,' 'psychological,' 'psychologist,' and/or offers to render or renders services as defined below to individuals, groups, organizations, or the public for a fee, monetary or otherwise.

"The practice of psychology within the meaning of this act is defined as rendering to individuals, groups, organizations, or the public any psychological service involving the application of principles, methods, and procedures of understanding, predicting, and influencing behavior, such as the principles pertaining to learning, perception, motivation, thinking, emotions, and interpersonal relationships; the methods and procedures of interviewing, counseling, and psychotherapy; of constructing, administering, and interpreting tests of mental abilities, aptitudes, interests, attitudes, personality characteristics, emotion, and motivation; and of assessing public opinion.

"The application of said principles and methods includes, but is not restricted to: diagnosis, prevention, and amelioration of adjustment problems and emotional and mental disorders of individuals and groups; hypnosis, educational and vocational counseling, personnel selection and management; the evaluation and planning for effective work and learning situations; advertising and market research; and the resolution of interpersonal and social conflicts.

A. Assessment directed toward diagnosing the nature and causes, and predicting the effects, of subjective distress; of personal, social, and work dysfunction; and of the psychological and emotional factors involved in, and consequent to, physical disease and disability. Procedures may include, but are not limited to, interviewing, and administering and interpreting tests of intellectual abilities, attitudes, emotions, motivations, personality characteristics, psychoneurological status, and other aspects of human experience and behavior relevant to the disturbance.

B. Interventions directed at identifying and correcting the emotional conflicts, personality disturbances, and skill deficits underlying a person's distress and/or dysfunction. Interventions may reflect a variety of theoretical orientations, techniques, and modalities. These may include, but are not limited to, psychotherapy, psychoanalysis, behavior therapy, marital and family therapy, group psychotherapy, hypnotherapy, social-learning approaches, biofeedback techniques, and environmental consultation and design.

C. Professional consultation in relation to A and B above.

D. Program development services in the areas of A, B, and C above.

E. Supervision of clinical psychological services.

F. Evaluation of all services noted in A through E above.

A *clinical psychological service unit* is the functional unit through which clinical psychological services are provided; such a unit may be part of a larger psychological service organization comprising psychologists of more than one specialty and headed by a professional psychologist.

A. A clinical psychological service unit provides predominantly clinical psychological services and is composed of one or more professional clinical psychologists and supporting staff.

B. A clinical psychological service unit may operate as a professional service or as a functional or geographic component of a larger multipsychological service unit or of a governmental, educational, correctional, health, training, industrial, or commercial organizational unit.[6]

"Psychotherapy within the meaning of this act means the use of learning, conditioning methods, and emotional reactions, in a professional relationship, to assist a person or persons to modify feelings, attitudes, and behavior which are intellectually, socially, or emotionally maladjustive or ineffectual.

"The practice of psychology shall be as defined above, any existing statute in the state of _____ to the contrary notwithstanding" (APA, 1967, pp. 1098–1099).

[6]The relation of a psychological service unit to a larger facility or institution is also addressed indirectly in the APA (1972) "Guidelines for Conditions of Employment of Psychologists"

C. One or more clinical psychologists providing professional services in a multidisciplinary setting constitute a clinical psychological service unit.

D. A clinical psychological service unit may also be one or more clinical psychologists in a private practice or a psychological consulting firm.

Users of clinical psychological services include:

A. Direct users or recipients of clinical psychological services.

B. Public and private institutions, facilities, or organizations receiving clinical psychological services.

C. Third-party purchasers—those who pay for the delivery of services but who are not the recipients of services.

D. Sanctioners—those who have a legitimate concern with the accessibility, timeliness, efficacy, and standards of quality attending the provision of clinical psychological services. Sanctioners may include members of the user's family, the court, the probation officer, the school administrator, the employer, the union representative, the facility director, and so on. Sanctioners may also include various governmental, peer review, and accreditation bodies concerned with the assurance of quality.

Guideline 1

PROVIDERS

1.1. *Each clinical psychological service unit offering psychological services has available at least one professional clinical psychologist and as many more professional clinical psychologists as are necessary to assure the adequacy and quality of services offered.*

INTERPRETATION: The intent of this Guideline is that one or more providers of psychological services in any clinical psychological service unit meet the levels of training and experience of the professional clinical psychologist as specified in the preceding definitions.[7]

(hereinafter referred to as CEP Guidelines), which emphasizes the roles, responsibilities, and prerogatives of the psychologist when he or she is employed by or provides services for another agency, institution, or business.

[7]This Guideline replaces earlier recommendations in the 1967 state guidelines concerning exemption of psychologists from licensure. Recommendations 8 and 9 of those guidelines read as follows: "Persons employed as psychologists by accredited academic institutions, governmental agencies, research laboratories, and business corporations should be

When a facility offering clinical psychological services does not have a full-time professional clinical psychologist available, the facility retains the services of one or more professional clinical psychologists on a regular part-time basis. The clinical psychologist so retained directs and supervises the psychological services provided, participates sufficiently to be able to assess the need for services, reviews the content of services provided, and has the authority to assume professional responsibility and accountability for them.

The psychologist directing the service unit is responsible for determining and justifying appropriate ratios of psychologists to users and psychologists to support staff, in order to ensure proper scope, accessibility, and quality of services provided in that setting.

1.2. Providers of clinical psychological services who do not meet the requirements for the professional clinical psychologist are supervised directly by a professional clinical psychologist who assumes professional responsibility and accountability for the services provided. The level and extent of supervision may vary from task to task so long as the supervising psychologist retains a sufficiently close supervisory relationship to meet this Guideline. Special proficiency training or supervision may be provided by a professional psychologist of another specialty or by a professional from another discipline whose competence in the given area has been demonstrated by previous training and experience.

INTERPRETATION: In each clinical psychological service unit there may be varying levels of responsibility with respect to the nature and quality of services provided. Support personnel are considered to be

---

exempted, provided such employees are performing those duties for which they are employed by such organizations, and within the confines of such organizations.

"Persons employed as psychologists by accredited academic institutions, governmental agencies, research laboratories, and business corporations consulting or offering their research findings or providing scientific information to like organizations for a fee should be exempted" (APA, 1967, p. 1100).

On the other hand, the 1967 state guidelines specifically denied exemptions under certain conditions, as noted in Recommendations 10 and 11: "Persons employed as psychologists who offer or provide psychological services to the public for a fee, over and above the salary that they receive for the performance of their regular duties, should not be exempted.

"Persons employed as psychologists by organizations that sell psychological services to the public should not be exempted" (APA, 1967, pp. 1100–1101).

The present APA policy, as reflected in this Guideline, establishes a single code of practice for psychologists providing covered services to users in any setting. The present position is that a psychologist providing any covered service meets local statutory requirements for licensure or certification. See the section entitled Principles and Implications of the Specialty Guidelines for an elaboration of this position.

responsible for their functions and behavior when assisting in the provision of clinical psychological services and are accountable to the professional clinical psychologist. Ultimate professional responsibility and accountability for the services provided require that the supervisor review and approve reports and test protocols, review and approve intervention plans and strategies, and review outcomes. Therefore, the supervision of all clinical psychological services is provided directly by a professional clinical psychologist in individual and/or group face-to-face meetings.

In order to meet this Guideline, an appropriate number of hours per week are devoted to direct face-to-face supervision of each clinical psychological service unit staff member. In no event is such supervision less than 1 hour per week. The more comprehensive the psychological services are, the more supervision is needed. A plan or formula for relating increasing amounts of supervisory time to the complexity of professional responsibilities is to be developed. The amount and nature of supervision is made known to all parties concerned.

Such communications are in writing and describe and delineate the duties of the employee with respect to range and type of services to be provided. The limits of independent action and decision making are defined. The description of responsibility also specifies the means by which the employee will contact the professional clinical psychologist in the event of emergency or crisis situations.

1.3. *Wherever a clinical psychological service unit exists, a professional clinical psychologist is responsible for planning, directing, and reviewing the provision of clinical psychological services. Whenever the clinical psychological service unit is part of a larger professional psychological service encompassing various psychological specialties, a professional psychologist is the administrative head of the service.*

INTERPRETATION: The clinical psychologist coordinates the activities of the clinical psychological service unit with other professional, administrative, and technical groups, both within and outside the facility. This clinical psychologist, who may be the director, chief, or coordinator of the clinical psychologist service unit, has related responsibilities including, but not limited to, recruiting qualified staff, directing training and research activities of the service, maintaining a high level of professional and ethical practice, and ensuring that staff members function only within the areas of their competency.

To facilitate the effectiveness of clinical services by raising the level of staff sensitivity and professional skills, the clinical psychologist designated as director is responsible for participating in the selection of staff and support personnel whose qualifications and skills (e.g., language, cultural and experiential background, race, sex, and age) are directly relevant to the needs and characteristics of the users served.

1.4. *When functioning as part of an organizational setting, professional clinical psychologists bring their backgrounds and skills to bear on the goals of the organization, whenever appropriate, by participation in the planning and development of overall services.*[8]

INTERPRETATION: Professional clinical psychologists participate in the maintenance of high professional standards by representation on committees concerned with service delivery.

As appropriate to the setting, their activities may include active participation, as voting and as office-holding members, on the professional staffs of hospitals and other facilities and on other executive, planning, and evalution boards and committees.

1.5. *Clinical psychologists maintain current knowledge of scientific and professional developments to preserve and enhance their professional competence.*[9]

INTERPRETATION: Methods through which knowledge of scientific and professional developments may be gained include, but are not limited to, reading scientific and professional publications, attendance at workshops, participation in staff development programs, and other forms of continuing education. The clinical psychologist has ready access to reference material related to the provision of psychological services. Clinical psychologists are prepared to show evidence periodically that they are staying abreast of current knowledge and practices in the field of clinical psychology through continuing education.

1.6. *Clinical psychologists limit their practice to their demonstrated areas of professional competence.*

[8]A closely related principle is found in the APA (1972) CEP Guidelines: "It is the policy of APA that psychology as an independent profession is entitled to parity with other health and human service professions in institutional practices and before the law. Psychologists in interdisciplinary settings such as colleges and universities, medical schools, clinics, private practice groups, and other agencies expect parity with other professions in such matters as academic rank, board status, salaries, fringe benefits, fees, participation in administrative decisions, and all other conditions of employment, private contractual arrangements, and status before the law and legal institutions" (APA, 1972, p. 333).

[9]See CEP Guidelines (section entitled Career Development) for a closely related statement: "Psychologists are expected to encourage institutions and agencies which employ them to sponsor or conduct career development programs. The purpose to these programs would be to enable psychologists to engage in study for professional advancement and to keep abreast of developments in their field" (APA, 1972, p. 332).

INTERPRETATION: Clinical psychological services are offered in accordance with the providers' areas of competence as defined by verifiable training and experience. When extending services beyond the range of their usual practice, psychologists obtain pertinent training or appropriate professional supervision. Such training or supervision is consistent with the extension of functions performed and services provided. An extension of services may involve a change in the theoretical orientation of the clinical psychologist, a change in modality or technique, or a change in the type of client and/or the kinds of problems or disorders for which services are to be provided (e.g., children, elderly persons, mental retardation, neurological impairment).

1.7. *Professional psychologists who wish to qualify as clinical psychologists meet the same requirements with respect to subject matter and professional skills that apply to doctoral and postdoctoral education and training in clinical psychology.*[10]

INTERPRETATION: Education of doctoral-level psychologists to qualify them for specialty practice in clinical psychology is under the auspices of a department in a regionally accredited university or of a professional school that offers the doctoral degree in clinical psychology. Such education is individualized, with due credit being given for relevant course work and other requirements that have previously been satisfied. In addition, doctoral-level training plus 1 year of postdoctoral experience supervised by a clinical psychologist is required. Merely taking an internship in clinical psychology or acquiring experience in a practicum setting is not adequate preparation for becoming a clinical psychologist when prior education has not been in that area. Fulfillment of such an individualized educational program is attested to by the awarding of a certificate by the supervising department or professional school that indicates the successful completion of preparation in clinical psychology.

1.8. *Professional clinical psychologists are encouraged to develop innovative theories and procedures and to provide appropriate theoretical and/or empirical support for their innovations.*

INTERPRETATION: A specialty of a profession rooted in a science intends continually to explore and experiment with a view to developing

---

[10]This Guideline follows closely the statement regarding "Policy on Training for Psychologists Wishing to Change Their Specialty" adopted by the APA Council of Representatives in January 1976. Included therein was the implementing provision that "this policy statement shall be incorporated in the guidelines of the Committee on Accreditation so that appropriate sanctions can be brought to bear on university and internship training programs that violate [it]" (Conger, 1976, p. 424).

and verifying new and improved methods of serving the public in ways that can be documented.

Guideline 2

PROGRAMS

2.1. *Composition and organization of a clinical psychological service unit:*

2.1.1. *The composition and programs of a clinical psychological service unit are responsive to the needs of the persons or settings served.*

INTERPRETATION: A clinical psychological service unit is structured so as to facilitate effective and economical delivery of services. For example, a clinical psychological service unit serving predominantly a low-income, ethnic, or racial minority group has a staffing pattern and service programs that are adapted to the linguistic, experiential, and attitudinal characteristics of the users.

2.1.2. *A description of the organization of the clinical psychological service unit and its lines of responsibility and accountability for the delivery of psychological services is available in written form to staff of the unit and to users and sanctioners upon request.*

INTERPRETATION: The description includes lines of responsibility, supervisory relationships, and the level and extent of accountability for each person who provides psychological services.

2.1.3. *A clinical psychological service unit includes sufficient numbers of professional and support personnel to achieve its goals, objectives, and purposes.*

INTERPRETATION: The work load and diversity of psychological services required and the specific goals and objectives of the setting determine the numbers and qualifications of professional and support personnel in the clinical psychological service unit. Where shortages in personnel exist, so that psychological services cannot be rendered in a professional manner, the director of the clinical psychological service unit initiates action to remedy such shortages. When this fails, the director appropriately modifies the scope or work load of the unit to maintain the quality of the services rendered.

2.2. *Policies:*

2.2.1. *When the clinical psychological service unit is composed of more than one person or is a component of a larger organization, a written statement of its objectives and scope of services is developed, maintained, and reviewed.*

INTERPRETATION: The clinical psychological service unit reviews its objectives and scope of services annually and revises them as necessary to ensure that the psychological services offered are consistent with staff competencies and current psychological knowledge and practice. This statement is discussed with staff, reviewed with the apppropriate administrator, and distributed to users and sanctioners upon request, whenever appropriate.

2.2.2. *All providers within a clinical psychological service unit support the legal and civil rights of the users.*[11]

INTERPRETATION: Providers of clinical psychological services safeguard the interests of the users with regard to personal, legal, and civil rights. They are continually sensitive to the issue of confidentiality of information, the short-term and long-term impacts of their decisions and recommendations, and other matters pertaining to individual, legal, and civil rights. Concerns regarding the safeguarding of individual rights of users include, but are not limited to, problems of self-incrimination in judicial proceedings, involuntary commitment to hospitals, protection of minors or legal incompetents, discriminatory practices in employment selection procedures, recommendation for special education provisions, information relative to adverse personnel actions in the armed services, and adjudication of domestic relations disputes in divorce and custodial proceedings. Providers of clinical psychological services take affirmative action by making themselves available to local committees, review boards, and similar advisory groups established to safeguard the human, civil, and legal rights of service users.

2.2.3. *All providers within a clinical psychological service unit are familiar with and adhere to the American Psychological Association's* Standards for Providers of Psychological Services, Ethical Principles of Psychologists, Standards for Educational and Psychological Tests, Ethical Principles in the Conduct of Research With Human Participants, *and other official policy statements relevant to standards for professional services issued by the Association.*

---

[11]See also APA's (1981b) *Ethical Principles of Psychologists,* especially Principles 5 (Confidentiality), 6 (Welfare of the Consumer), and 9 (Research with Human Participants); and see *Ethical Principles in the Conduct of Research With Human Participants* (APA, 1973a). Also, in 1978 Division 17 approved in principle a statement on "Principles for Counseling and Psychotherapy With Women," which was designed to protect the interests of female users of clinical psychological services.

INTERPRETATON: Providers of clinical psychological services maintain up-to-date knowledge of the relevant standards of the American Psychological Association.

2.2.4. *All providers within a clinical psychological service unit conform to relevant statutes established by federal, state, and local governments.*

INTERPRETATION: All providers of clinical psychological services are familiar with appropriate statutes regulating the practice of psychology. They observe agency regulations that have the force of law and that relate to the delivery of psychological services (e.g., evaluation for disability retirement and special education placements). In addition, all providers are cognizant that federal agencies such as the Veterans Administration, the Department of Education, and the Department of Health and Human Services have policy statements regarding psychological services, and where relevant, providers conform to them. Providers of clinical psychological services are also familiar with other statutes and regulations, including those addressed to the civil and legal rights of users (e.g., those promulgated by the federal Equal Employment Opportunity Commission), that are pertinent to their scope of practice.

It is the responsibility of the American Psychological Association to maintain current files of those federal policies, statutes, and regulations relating to this section and to assist its members in obtaining them. The state psychological associations and the state licensing boards periodically publish and distribute appropriate state statutes and regulations.

2.2.5. *All providers within a clinical psychological service unit inform themselves about and use the network of human services in their communities in order to link users with relevant services and resources.*

INTERPRETATION: Clinical psychologists and support staff are sensitive to the broader context of human needs. In recognizing the matrix of personal and societal problems, providers make available to users information regarding human services such as legal aid societies, social services, employment agencies, health resources, and educational and recreational facilities. Providers of clinical psychological services refer to such community resources and, when indicated, actively intervene on behalf of the users.

Community resources include the private as well as the public sectors. Private resources include private agencies and centers and psychologists in independent private practice. Consultation is sought or referral made within the public or private network of services whenever required in the best interest of the users. Clinical psychologists, in either the private or the public setting, utilize other resources in the community whenever indicated because of limitations within the psychological service unit providing the services. Professional clinical psychologists in private practice are familiar with the types of services offered through local community mental health clinics and centers, including alternatives to hospitalization, and know the costs and eligibility requirements for those services.

2.2.6. *In the delivery of clinical psychological services, the providers maintain a cooperative relationship with colleagues and co-workers in the best interest of the users.*[12]

INTERPRETATION: Clinical psychologists recognize the areas of special competence of other professional psychologists and of professionals in other fields for either consultation or referral purposes. Providers of clinical psychological services make appropriate use of other professional, research, technical, and administrative resources to serve the best interests of users and establish and maintain cooperative arrangements with such other resources as required to meet the needs of users.

2.3. *Procedures:*

2.3.1. *Each clinical psychological service unit follows a set of procedural guidelines for the delivery of psychological services.*

INTERPRETATION: Providers are prepared to provide a statement of procedural guidelines, in either oral or written form, in terms that can be understood by users, including sanctioners and local administrators. This statement describes the current methods, forms, procedures, and techniques being used to achieve the objectives and goals for psychological services.

2.3.2. *Providers of clinical psychological services develop plans appropriate to the providers' professional practices and to the problems presented by the users.*

INTERPRETATION: A clinical psychologist develops a plan that describes the psychological services, their objectives, and the manner

---

[12]Support for this position is found in *Psychology as a Profession* in the section on relations with other professions: "Professional persons have an obligation to know and take into account the traditions and practices of other professional groups with whom they work and to cooperate fully with members of such groups with whom research, service, and other functions are shared" (APA, 1968, p. 5).

in which they will be provided.[13,14] This plan is in written form; it serves as a basis for obtaining understanding and concurrence from the user and provides a mechanism for subsequent peer review. This plan is, of course, modified as new needs or information develops.

A clinical psychologist who provides services as one member of a collaborative effort participates in the development and implementation of the overall service plan and provides for its periodic review.

2.3.3. *Accurate, current, and pertinent documentation of essential clinical psychological services provided is maintained.*

INTERPRETATION: Records kept of clinical psychological services may include, but are not limited to, identifying data, dates of services, types of services, significant actions taken, and outcome at termination. Providers of clinical psychological services ensure that essential information concerning services rendered is recorded within a reasonable time following their completion.

2.3.4. *Each clinical psychological service unit follows an established record retention and disposition policy.*

INTERPRETATION: The policy on record retention and disposition conforms to federal or state statutes or administrative regulations where such are applicable. In the absence of such regulations, the policy is (a) that the full record be retained intact for 3 years after the completion of planned services or after the date of last contact with the user, whichever is later; (b) that a full record or summary of the record be maintained for an additional 12 years; and (c) that the record may be disposed of no sooner than 15 years after the completion of planned services or after

---

[13]One example of a specific application of this principle is found in Guideline 2 in APA's (1973b) "Guidelines for Psychologists Conducting Growth Groups":

The following information should be made available in *writing* [italics added] to all prospective participants:
    (a) An explicit statement of the purpose of the group;
    (b) Types of techniques that may be employed;
    (c) The education, training, and experience of the leader or leaders;
    (d) The fee and any additional expense that may be incurred;
    (e) A statement as to whether or not a follow-up service is included in the fee;
    (f) Goals of the group experience and techniques to be used;
    (g) Amounts and kinds of responsibility to be assumed by the leader and by the participants. For example, (i) the degree to which a participant is free not to follow suggestions and prescriptions of the group leader and other group members; (ii) any restrictions on a participant's freedom to leave the group at any time; and
    (h) Issues of confidentiality. (p. 933)
[14]See APA's (1981a) APA/CHAMPUS *Outpatient Psychological Provider Manual.*

the date of the last contact, whichever is later. These temporal guides are consistent with procedures currently in use by federal record centers.

In the event of the death or incapacity of a clinical psychologist in independent practice, special procedures are necessary to ensure the continuity of active services to users and the proper safeguarding of inactive records being retained to meet this Guideline. Following approval by the affected user, it is appropriate for another clinical psychologist, acting under the auspices of the local professional standards review committee (PSRC), to review the records with the user and recommend a course of action for continuing professional service, if needed. Depending on local circumstances, the reviewing psychologist may also recommend appropriate arrangements for the balance of the record retention and disposition period.

This Guideline has been designed to meet a variety of circumstances that may arise, often years after a set of psychological services has been completed. More and more records are being used in forensic matters, for peer review, and in response to requests from users, other professionals, or other legitimate parties requiring accurate information about the exact dates, nature, course, and outcome of a set of psychological services. These record retention procedures also provide valuable baseline data for the original psychologist—provider when a previous user returns for additional services.

2.3.5. Providers of clinical psychological services maintain a system to protect confidentiality of their records.[15]

INTERPRETATION: Clinical psychologists are responsible for maintaining the confidentiality of information about users of services, from whatever source derived. All persons supervised by clinical psychologists, including nonprofessional personnel and students, who have access to records of psychological services are required to maintain this confidentiality as a condition of employment.

The clinical psychologist does not release confidential information, except with the written consent of the user directly involved or his or her legal representative. Even after consent for release has been obtained, the clinical psychologist clearly identifies such information as confidential to the recipient of the information.[16] If directed otherwise by statute

---

[15]See Principle 5 (Confidentiality) in *Ethical Principles of Psychologists* (APA, 1981b).
[16]Support for the principle of privileged communication is found in at least two policy statements of the Association: "In the interest of both the public and the client and in accordance with the requirements of good professional practice, the profession of psychology seeks recognition of the privileged nature of confidential communications with

or regulations with the force of law or by court order, the psychologist may seek a resolution to the conflict that is both ethically and legally feasible and appropriate.

Users are informed in advance of any limits in the setting for maintenance of confidentiality of psychological information. For instance, clinical psychologists in hospital, clinic, or agency settings inform their patients that psychological information in a patient's clinical record may be available without the patient's written consent to other members of the professional staff associated with the patient's treatment or rehabilitation. Similar limitations on confidentiality of psychological information may be present in certain school, industrial, military, or other institutional settings, or in instances in which the user has waived confidentiality for purposes of third-party payment.

Users have the right to obtain information from their psychological records. However, the records are the property of the psychologist or the facility in which the psychologist works and are, therefore, the responsibility of the psychologist and subject to his or her control.

When the user's intention to waive confidentiality is judged by the professional clinical psychologist to be contrary to the user's best interests or to be in conflict with the user's civil and legal rights, it is the responsibility of the clinical psychologist to discuss the implications of releasing psychological information and to assist the user in limiting disclosure only to information required by the present circumstance.

Raw psychological data (e.g., questionnnaire returns or test protocols) in which a user is identified are released only with the written consent of the user or his or her legal representative and released only to a person recognized by the clinical psychologist as qualified and competent to use the data.

Any use made of psychological reports, records, or data for research or training purposes is consistent with this Guideline. Additionally, providers of clinical psychological services comply with statutory confidentiality requirements and those embodied in the American Psychological Association's *Ethical Principles of Psychologists* (APA, 1981b).

Providers of clinical psychological services remain sensitive to both the benefits and the possible misuse of information regarding individuals that is stored in large computerized data banks. Providers use their

---

clients, preferably through statutory enactment or by administrative policy where more appropriate (APA, 1968, p. 8).

"Wherever possible, a clause protecting the privileged nature of the psychologist–client relationship be included.

"When appropriate, psychologists assist in obtaining general 'across the board' legislation for such privileged communications" (APA, 1967, p. 1103).

influence to ensure that such information is used in a socially responsible manner.

Guideline 3

ACCOUNTABILITY

3.1. The clinical psychologist's professional activity is guided primarily by the principle of promoting human welfare.

INTERPRETATION: Clinical psychologists provide services to users in a manner that is considerate, effective, economical, and humane. Clinical psychologists make their services readily accessible to users in a manner that facilitates the users' freedom of choice.

Clinical psychologists are mindful of their accountability to the sanctioneers of clinical psychological services and to the general public, provided that appropriate steps are taken to protect the confidentiality of the service relationship. In the pursuit of their professional activities, they aid in the conservation of human, material, and financial resources.

The clinical psychological service unit does not withhold services to a potential client on the basis of that user's race, color, religion, gender, sexual orientation, age, or national origin. Recognition is given, however, to the following considerations: the professional right of clinical psychologists to limit their practice to a specific category of users (e.g., children, adolescents, women); the right and responsibility of clinical psychologists to withhold an assessment procedure when not validly applicable; and the right and responsibility of clinical psychologists to withhold evaluative, psychotherapeutic, counseling, or other services in specific instances in which their own limitations or client characteristics might impair the effectiveness of the relationship.[17,18] Clinical psychologists seek to ameliorate through peer review, consultation, or other personal therapeutic procedures those factors that inhibit the provision of services to particular users. When indicated services are not available, clinical psychologists take whatever action is appropriate to inform responsible persons and agencies of the lack of such services.

[17]This paragraph is directly adapted from the CEP Guidelines (APA, 1972, p. 333).
[18]The CEP Guidelines also include the following: "It is recognized that under certain circumstances, the interests and goals of a particular community or segment of interest in the population may be in conflict with the general welfare. Under such circumstances, the psychologist's professional activity must be primarily guided by the principle of 'promoting human welfare' " (APA, 1972, p. 334).

Clinical psychologists who find that psychological services are being provided in a manner that is discriminatory or exploitative to users and/or contrary to these Guidelines or to state or federal statutes take appropriate corrective action, which may include the refusal to provide services. When conflicts of interest arise, the clinical psychologist is guided in the resolution of differences by the principles set forth in the American Psychological Association's *Ethical Principles of Psychologists* (APA, 1981b) and "Guidelines for Conditions of Employment of Psychologists" (APA, 1972).

3.2. *Clinical psychologists pursue their activities as members of the independent, autonomous profession of psychology.*[19]

INTERPRETATION: Clinical psychologists, as members of an independent profession, are responsible both to the public and to their peers through established review mechanisms. Clinical psychologists are aware of the implications of their activities for the profession as a whole. They seek to eliminate discriminatory practices instituted for self-serving purposes that are not in the interest of the users (e.g., arbitrary requirements for referral and supervision by another profession). They are cognizant of their responsibilities for the development of the profession. They participate where possible in the training and career development of students and other providers, participate as appropriate in the training of paraprofessionals or other professionals, and integrate and supervise the implementation of their contributions with the structure established

---

[19]Support for the principle of the independence of psychology as a profession is found in the followiing: "As a member of an autonomous profession, a psychologist rejects limitations upon his [or her] freedom of thought and action other than those imposed by his [or her] moral, legal, and social responsibilities. The Association is always prepared to provide appropriate assistance to any responsible member who becomes subjected to unreasonable limitations upon his [or her] opportunity to function as a practitioner, teacher, researcher, administrator, or consultant. The Association is always prepared to cooperate with any responsible professional organization in opposing any unreasonable limitations on the professional functions of the members of that organization.

"This insistence upon professional autonomy has been upheld over the years by the affirmative actions of the courts and other public and private bodies in support of the right of the psychologist—and other professionals—to pursue those functions for which he [or she] is trained and qualified to perform" (APA, 1968, p. 9).

"Organized psychology has the responsibility to define and develop its own profession, consistent with the general canons of science and with the public welfare.

"Psychologists recognize that other professions and other groups will, from time to time, seek to define the roles and responsibilities of psychologists. The APA opposes such developments on the same principle that it is opposed to the psychological profession taking positions which would define the work and scope of responsibility of other duly recognized professions" (APA, 1972, p. 333).

for delivering psychological services. Clinical psychologists facilitate the development of, and participate in, professional standards review mechanisms.[20]

Clinical psychologists seek to work with other professionals in a cooperative manner for the good of the users and the benefit of the general public. Clinical psychologists associated with multidisciplinary settings support the principle that members of each participating profession have equal rights and opportunities to share all privileges and responsibilities of full membership in hospital facilities or other human service facilities and to administer service programs in their respective areas of competence.

3.3. *There are periodic, systematic, and effective evaluations of clinical psychological services.*[21]

INTERPRETATION: When the clinical psychological service unit is a component of a larger organization, regular evaluation of progress in achieving goals is provided for in the service delivery plan, including consideration of the effectiveness of clinical psychological services relative to costs in terms of use of time and money and the availability of professional and support personnel.

Evaluation of the clinical psychological service delivery system is conducted internally and, when possible, under independent auspices as well. This evaluation includes an assessment of effectiveness (to determine what the service unit accomplished), efficiency (to determine the

[20]APA support for peer review is detailed in the following excerpt from the APA (1971) statement entitled "Psychology and National Health Care": "All professions participating in a national health plan should be directed to establish review mechanisms (or performance evaluations) that include not only peer review but active participation by persons representing the consumer. In situations where there are fiscal agents, they should also have representation when appropriate" (p. 1026).

[21]This Guideline on program evaluation is based directly on the following excerpts from two APA position papers: "The quality and availability of health services should be evaluated continuously by both consumers and health professionals. Research into the efficiency and effectiveness of the system should be conducted both internally and under independent auspices" (APA, 1971, p. 1025).

"The comprehensive community mental health center should devote an explicit portion of its budget to program evaluation. All centers should inculcate in their staff attention to and respect for research findings; the larger centers have an obligation to set a high priority on basic research and to give formal recognition to research as a legitimate part of the duties of staff members.

"Only through explicit appraisal of program effects can worthy approaches be retained and refined, ineffective ones dropped. Evaluative monitoring of program achievements may vary, of course, from the relatively informal to the systematic and quantitative, depending on the importance of the issue, the availability of resources, and the willingness of those responsible to take risks of substituting informed judgment for evidence" (Smith & Hobbs, 1966, pp. 21–22).

total costs of providing the services), continuity (to ensure that the services are appropriately linked to other human services), availability (to determine appropriate levels and distributions of services and personnel), accessibility (to ensure that the services are barrier free to users), and adequacy (to determine whether the services meet the identified needs for such services).

There is a periodic reexamination of review mechanisms to ensure that these attempts at public safeguards are effective and cost efficient and do not place unnecessary encumbrances on the providers or impose unnecessary additional expenses on users or sanctioners for services rendered.

3.4. *Clinical psychologists are accountable for all aspects of the services they provide and are responsive to those concerned with these services.*[22]

INTERPRETATION: In recognizing their responsibilities to users, and where appropriate and consistent with the users' legal rights and privileged communications, clinical psychologists make available information about, and provide opportunity to participate in, decisions concerning such issues as initiation, termination, continuation, modification, and evaluation of clinical psychological services.

Depending on the settings, accurate and full information is made available to prospective individual or organizational users regarding the qualifications of providers, the nature and extent of services offered, and where appropriate, financial and social costs.

Where appropriate, clinical psychologists inform users of their payment policies and their willingness to assist in obtaining reimbursement. Those who accept reimbursement from a third party are acquainted with the appropriate statutes and regulations and assist their users in understanding procedures for submitting claims and limits on confidentiality of claims information, in accordance with pertinent statutes.

Guideline 4

ENVIRONMENT

4.1. *Providers of clinical psychological services promote the development in the service setting of a physical, organizational, and social environment that facilitates optimal human functioning.*

[22]See also the CEP Guidelines for the following statement: "A psychologist recognizes that . . . he [or she] alone is accountable for the consequences and effects of his [or her] services, whether as teacher, researcher, or practitioner. This responsibility cannot be shared, delegated, or reduced" (APA, 1972, p. 334).

INTERPRETATION: Federal, state, and local requirements for safety, health, and sanitation are observed.

As providers of services, clinical psychologists are concerned with the environment of their service unit, especially as it affects the quality of service, but also as it impinges on human functioning when the service unit is included in a larger context. Physical arrangements and organizational policies and procedures are conducive to the human dignity, self-respect, and optimal functioning of users and to the effective delivery of service. Attention is given to the comfort and the privacy of users. The atmosphere in which clinical psychological services are rendered is appropriate to the service and to the users, whether in an office, clinic, school, industrial organization, or other institutional setting.

REFERENCES

American Psychological Association, Committee on Legislation. A model for state legislation affecting the practice of psychology, *American Psychologist*. 1967, 22, 1095–1103.

American Psychological Association. *Psychology as a profession*, Washington, D.C.: Author, 1968.

American Psychological Association. Psychology and national health care. *American Psychologist*, 1971, 26, 1025–1026.

American Psychological Association. Guideines for conditions of employment of psychologists. *American Psychologist*, 1972, 27, 331–334.

American Psychological Association. *Ethical principles in the conduct of research with human participants*. Washington, D.C.: Author, 1973. (a)

American Psychological Association. Guidelines for psychologists conducting growth groups. *American Psychologist*, 1973, 28, 933. (b)

American Psychological Association. *Standards for educational and psychological tests*. Washington, D.C.: Author, 1974. (a)

American Psychological Association. *Standards for providers of psychological services*. Washington, D.C.: Author, 1974. (b)

American Psychological Association. *Education and credentialing in psychology II*. Report of a meeting, June 4–5, 1977. Washington, D.C.: Author, 1977. (a)

American Psychological Association. *Standards for providers of psychological services* (Rev. ed.). Washington, D.C.: Author, 1977. (b)

American Psychological Association. *Criteria for accreditation of doctoral training programs and internships in professional psychology*. Washington, D.C.: Author, 1979 (amended 1980).

American Psychological Association. *APA/CHAMPUS outpatient psychological provider manual* (Rev. ed.). Washington, D.C.: Author, 1981. (a)

American Psychological Association. *Ethical principles of psychologists* (Rev. ed.). Washington, D.C.: Author, 1981. (b)

Conger, J. J. Proceedings of the American Psychological Association, Incorporated, for the year 1975. Minutes of the annual meeting of the Council of Representatives. *American Psychologist*, 1976, 31, 406–434.

Smith, M. B., & Hobbs, N. *The community and the community mental health center.* Washington, D.C.: American Psychological Association, 1966.

5.4. ETHICAL ISSUES FOR HUMAN SERVICES (AABT, 1977)*

On May 22, 1977, the Board of Directors of the Association for the Advancement of Behavior Therapy (AABT) adopted a set of standards governing the application of behavior therapy in all settings in which human services are provided. Issues involving the goals of treatment, the appropriate choice and evaluation of treatment methods, informed consent, confidentiality, and therapist responsibilities and qualifications are discussed. Such issues and concerns should be incorporated into the overall delivery of services plan and individual treatment plan for each client. In this manner, clients can be provided quality and professional human services.

The focus of this statement is on critical issues of central importance to human services. The statement is not a list of prescriptions and proscriptions.

On each of the issues described below, ideal interventions would have maximum involvement by the person whose behavior is to be changed, and the fullest possible consideration of societal pressures on that person, the therapist, and the therapist's employer. It is recognized that the practicalities of actual settings sometimes require exceptions, and that there certainly are occasions when exceptions can be consistent with ethical practice. Even though some exceptions may eventually be necessary, each of these issues should be explicitly considered.

In the list of issues, the term "client" is used to describe the person whose behavior is to be changed; "therapist" is used to describe the professional in charge of the intervention; "treatment" and "problem" although used in the singular, refer to any and all treatments and problems being formulated with this checklist. The issues are formulated so as to be relevant across as many settings and populations as possible. Thus, they need to be qualified when someone other than the person whose behavior is to be changed is paying the therapist, or when that person's competence or the voluntary nature of that person's consent is questioned. For example, if the therapist has found that the client does not understand the goals or methods being considered, the therapist should substitute the client's guardian or other responsible person for "client," when reviewing the issues below.

A. Have the goals of treatment been adequately considered?
   1. To insure that the goals are explicit, are they written?
   2. Has the client's understanding of the goals been assured by having the client restate them orally or in writing?
   3. Have the therapist and client agreed on the goals of therapy?
   4. Will serving the client's interests be contrary to the interests of other persons?
   5. Will serving the client's immediate interests be contrary to the client's long-term interest?
B. Has the choice of treatment methods been adequately considered?
   1. Does the published literature show the procedure to be the best one available for that problem?
   2. If no literature exists regarding the treatment method, is the method consistent with generally accepted practice?
   3. Has the client been told of alternative procedures that might be preferred by the client on the basis of significant differences in discomfort, treatment time, cost, or degree of demonstrated effectiveness?
   4. If a treatment procedure is publicly, legally, or professionally controversial, has formal professional consultation been obtained, has the reaction of the affected segment of the public been adequately considered, and have the alternative treatment methods been more closely reexamined and reconsidered?
C. Is the client's participation voluntary?
   1. Have possible sources of coercion on the client's participation been considered?
   2. If treatment is legally mandated, has the available range of treatments and therapists been offered?
   3. Can the client withdraw from treatment without a penalty or financial loss that exceeds actual clinical costs?
D. When another person or an agency is empowered to arrange for therapy, have the interests of the subordinated client been sufficiently considered?
   1. Has the subordinated client been informed of the treatment objectives and participated in the choice of treatment procedures?
   2. Where the subordinated client's competence to decide is limited, have the client as well as the guardian participated

in the treatment discussions to the extent that the client's abilities permit?
   3. If the interests of the subordinated person and the superordinate persons or agency conflict, have attempts been made to reduce the conflict by dealing with both interests?
 E. Has the adequacy of treatment been evaluated?
   1. Have quantitative measures of the problem and its progress been obtained?
   2. Have the measures of the problem and its progress been made available to the client during treatment?
 F. Has the confidentiality of the treatment relationship been protected?
   1. Has the client been told who has access to the records?
   2. Are records available only to authorized persons?
 G. Does the therapist refer the clients to other therapists when necessary?
   1. If treatment is unsuccessful, is the client referred to other therapists?
   2. Has the client been told that if dissatisfied with the treatment, referral will be made?
 H. Is the therapist qualified to provide treatment?
   1. Has the therapist had training or experience in treating problems like the client's?
   2. If deficits exist in the therapist's qualifications, has the client been informed?
   3. If the therapist is not adequately qualified, is the client referred to other therapists, or has supervision by a qualified therapist been provided? Is the client informed of the supervisory relation?
   4. If the treatment is administered by mediators, have the mediators been adequately supervised by a qualified therapist?

5.5. FORMULATING A WRITTEN SERVICE DELIVERY PLAN: PERTINENT PROFESSIONAL QUESTIONS

As emphasized earlier in this chapter, a psychologist/behavioral practitioner contemplating entering private practice should have a written service delivery plan that serves as the basis for the conduct of all aspects of the private practice: professional and ethical, technical, and business. Such a plan helps the practitioner define the limits and scope of his or her practice. This plan should be available for review by clients, peer review committees, and by staff.

The written service delivery plan should provide guidelines based on the following topics. These topical areas are listed in the form of questions and are a compilation of the recommended professional regulations discussed in the APA's *Ethical Standards of Psychologists, Standards for Providers of Psychological Services, Specialty Guidelines for the Delivery of Services,* and AABT's *Ethical Issues for Human Services.*

1. What services will be provided and excluded?
2. What population(s) will be served and excluded?
3. If employed elsewhere, what populations will one not serve to avoid conflict of interest?
4. Who is eligible for the services offered?
5. What are the procedures by which clients make appointments?
6. On what basis will waiting lists or time before services are provided to the new clients be determined?
7. Have procedures for seeing clients on an emergency basis been specified?
8. How will clients be referred to other professionals or agencies if therapy is deemed not appropriate for the client or when therapy has not been successful?
9. What agencies and individuals will be visited in order to establish referral sources and contracts?
10. How will the professional services of the office be announced?
11. What professional equipment, forms, and materials will be needed?
12. How will the office be laid out so that confidentiality of the client is assured through proper office placement and sound-proofing?
13. Has an easy filing system been developed that also protects the confidentiality of the client?
14. How will confidentiality be arranged through all other office procedures and by all staff?
15. What provisions have been made for ensuring ongoing client welfare?
16. Have the goals of treatment been adequately considered and has the client been educated toward a behavioral approach to the treatment of his or her difficulties?
17. Has the choice of treatment methods been adequately considered in terms of the risks and benefits, and according to the least restrictive alternative rule?

18. Has fully informed consent been obtained from the client or his or her representatives that includes a statement of the responsibilities of the therapist and client, the diagnosis of the client's problem(s), the nature of treatment and various treatment alternatives, risks and benefits of treatment to the client, estimate of frequency of sessions and duration of treatment, prospects for success, and prognosis of the problem being treated?
19. What activities will occur during the therapy hour?
20. Have the treatment procedures been evaluated properly by the therapist via the client's and/or others' data collection, paper/pencil questionnaires, self-reports, and direct observation?
21. Has client involvement in his or her own treatment been arranged and it is ongoing?
22. What will be the format and method for reporting the results of psychological services (e.g., behavioral evaluations, treatment plan formats, testing, etc.)?
23. What are the follow-up procedures for the services rendered and the clients served?
24. What is the schedule to review the client folders, procedures, and problems regularly as part of a weekly caseload review?
25. Is there a written delivery of services plan, and a flow chart detailing the preceding issues on file in the office and have all staff read this plan?
26. Has there been a review of the overall professional and office delivery of services plan to insure continued effectiveness and quality of services? On what regular schedule will this review be conducted?
27. What provisions are there for hiring and supervising other professionals in one's practice?
28. Have the guides referred to in this chapter been reviewed for additional information helpful in establishing and maintaining a private practice?

5.5.1. Flow Chart of Services

As part of the written service delivery plan, it is recommended that a flow chart be designed that follows the client through the delivery of services from the initial appointment to the termination of services. Figure 1 is a sample of such a flow chart for the delivery of services in a private practice. Provisions are made for prevention of dual services to the client, emergencies, testing, initial problem identification and

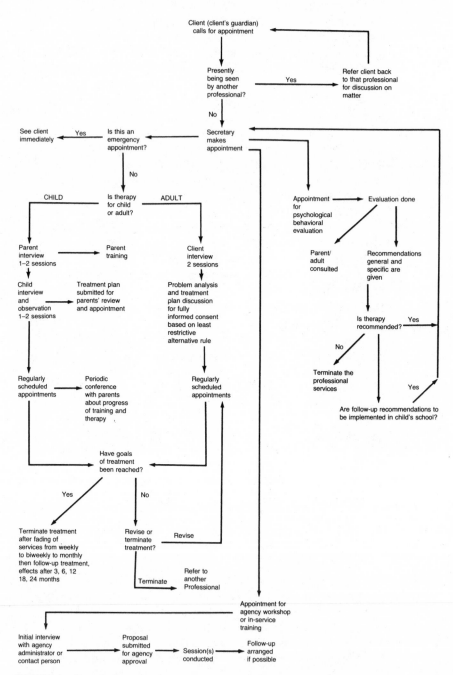

FIGURE 1.   Sample flowchart of the delivery of services in private practice.

evaluation over several sessions, submission and review of the treatment plan to the client, periodic adjunct consultations, and goals review during treatment and prior to termination. Agency consultations and the process of providing such services are also included.

5.5.2. Professional Liability

By following all of the principles covered by the *Ethical Principles of Psychologists* and the other related guides, the psychologist practitioner minimizes professional liability. Psychologists and other psychotherapists have been increasingly concerned with ethical and legal liability partly because of the accumulated evidence that psychotherapy is increasingly effective (Widiger & Rorer, 1984). The procedures such as those available to the behavior therapist that are effective in altering thoughts, feelings, and behavior may produce undesired effects that go beyond the stated goals or may result in undesired changes in the eco-system in which the client functions. In their article, Widiger and Rorer suggest that if the therapist is expected to behave ethically, then he or she must first behave responsibly as a psychologist, avoiding negative consequences to the client, and be accountable for treatment outcomes. These authors discuss the efficacy of contracts and informed consent as they apply to all forms of psychotherapy.

There are advantages and disadvantages of contracts and informed consent. Some advantages involve greater specificity of the formal clinical relationship and joint agreement of goals and of the methods to achieve these goals. Disadvantages involve giving up the role and influence of *benevolent controller* to other contingencies (i.e., the "whims" of the client), the inequity in understanding of the formal contract, the therapeutic process, and the resulting bargaining power between the client and the therapist, that is, patient capacity for responsible decisions in therapy. Another disadvantage involves the capacity of the therapist to assure the client of all the risks cited and that the treatment procedures will not adversely affect other behaviors, cognitions, or social relationships. In essence, one must be aware that contracting for outcome can establish a basis upon which prosecution can occur if the stated goal is not achieved in therapy. Widiger and Rorer suggest that different ethical standards may have to be placed on different therapeutic orientations. Further, because of the equivocal nature of the different forms of psychotherapy, the therapist's own professional ethics may need to be made available to each client (such as suggested via the earlier discussion covering written service delivery plans). Not only, then, would there be a general adherence to existing ethical standards, but there would also be compliance to specific therapist ethical guidelines.

The issues of legal liability and the rights of clients and professional ethics have been debated by many professionals in behavior therapy (Brown, Wienckowski, & Stolz, 1975; Goldiamond, 1975a, 1975b; Griffith, 1980; Reese, 1982; Schwitzgebel, 1975; Sheldon-Wildgen, 1982). This debate has arisen largely out of the misuses of behavior modification in prisons and institutions in the early 1970s and because of the Subcommittee on Constitutional Rights (1974) report entitled *Individual Rights and the Federal Role in Behavior Modification.* As a result, greater client care, fully informed consent, right to treatment, the least restrictive alternative rule, greater client involvement, and an emphasis on Eighth Amendment rights are now part of overall behavioral treatment programs in many public and private facilities and clinics.

Despite these higher standards of treatment, establishing ethical guidelines for behavior modification and therapy can be a difficult task. Brown, Wienckowski, and Stolz (1975) indicate that specifying, for example, informed consent for different problems and different populations (young children, handicapped adults, adolescents, prison inmates) would certainly vary from population to population. Other problems outlined by these authors include the difficulty a peer review committee may have in reaching some consensus as to the definition of risks and benefits for various populations and settings; how to ensure that programs are monitored by professionals with adequate training and experience who accept accountability for treatment outcomes; how to ensure that professionals are continually responsible for closely supervising, training, and monitoring the activities of direct care staff in the specific prescribed treatment; and that such direct care staff do not make major changes or decisions in the treatment of the client beyond the guidelines previously established for treatment.

Sheldon-Wildgen (1982) has discussed the rights and responsibilities of therapists with regard to their legal liability, using as a central focus the individual client–behavior therapist relationship, whereas Goldiamond, Griffith, Reese, and Schwitzgebel largely discuss the legal and ethical ramifications of institution populations. Sheldon-Wildgen contends that even the most cautious of therapists are subject to liability in day-to-day practice. Therefore, the therapist must plan treatment carefully and conform to the ethical and legal standards of practice in order to protect his or her practice and minimize the chance of ethical misconduct and/or malpractice suits. Sheldon-Wildgen provides a checklist of responsibilities for therapists and various considerations in providing therapy.

The first responsibility the therapist has is to provide specific information to the client and to obtain fully informed consent for the prescribed treatment. Sheldon-Wildgen suggests that a formal contract be written so that the therapist and client can understand and discuss each other's expectations in therapy. The following issues should be a part of pretreatment agreements between client and therapist:

1. *A description of the services that will be provided, the goals to be attained, and the procedures to be used.* Such a description should avoid technical jargon, and should specify the goals and procedures in therapy. Homework and outside therapy hour practice should also be described.

2. *The behavior required of the client.* The client's participation in therapy should be outlined very clearly.

3. *The anticipated results to include beneficial results and possible negative side effects.* There is, of course, no way to ensure attainment of goals, but the therapist can indicate what behaviors are to be expected as targets. In addition, Sheldon-Wildgen suggests that a list of any possible negative results of treatment be given to the client with the stipulation that the listed negative side effects do not constitute all the possible side effects that could result.

4. *The estimated duration and frequency of therapy sessions.* Clients may vary in the type of problems they present and may, therefore, require different lengths of treatment. However, clients should be given an estimate of how long the therapist projects therapy will last based on his or her prior knowledge of the prescribed treatment for the same or similar clinical problem.

5. *A timetable for reviewing progress of treatment.* The therapy should specify review dates to discuss the client's progress. However, at any of those review points, the client, if not satisfied with therapy, may terminate without cost or further explanation. The client should be informed of this fact in pretreatment discussions.

6. *Cost of services.* The therapist should specify the fees for the services to be provided. These fees should be itemized thoroughly (individual therapy, group therapy, testing or evaluation fees, phone consults, and emergency office visits) and the schedule by which payment is to be made by the client (e.g., in full when services are rendered, only the client's portion in third-party reimbursement situations, or billed monthly). However, if a therapist allows a client to accumulate fees and these fees are not collected until after therapy is concluded, this does constitute professional misconduct.

7. *A statement of confidentiality and privileged information.* The therapist should indicate what information is confidential and what information is not, as well as the bounds and limits of confidentiality. In the

initial session, the therapist insures the client of the confidential nature of any information the client shares except in cases where, by law, protection of society is imminently more important at the time than protection of the client's right to privacy. However, the therapists has a duty to warn the client about the issue of "privileged communication." That is, in some states, statutes permit a professional to refuse to testify if the client prohibits the professional from doing so on the basis of privileged information (the privilege belongs to the client).

8. *The therapist's acknowledgment of the client's informed consent.* There are three elements of a client's consent. These are *capacity*, which refers to the client's ability to think, act, and choose rationally; *information*, which is the content of the information as well as how it is conveyed; and *voluntariness*, or the ability of the person, free from coercion, duress, or force to exercise "free choice." Of course, if the client referred does not have the capacity to choose rationally, the client's representative should act on the client's behalf.

Once this information has been conveyed, it is imperative that the therapist provide the most appropriate therapy. First, the client's problem should be properly diagnosed, and second, the chosen techniques must be based on the available empirically tested procedures found in professional journals. The therapist should also discuss alternative procedures with the client. However, when a novel or controversial procedure has to be developed, the therapist should consult a peer review committee on human rights organization as an added protection for the client that minimizes legal liability for the therapist. All these treatment procedures should be described in written form so that treatment can proceed.

Sheldon-Wildgen indicates that therapists should determine the various areas of specialization in which they wish to practice. Because of the wide range of referrals that come to the behavior therapist, he or she may choose what problems will be dealt with in therapy and what problems will be referred elsewhere. However, if the therapist assumes the responsibility for a client's problems, he or she must have the necessary skills and qualifications to provide quality services to the client. Skills are obtained and maintained by keeping abreast of the current literature, attending conferences and workshops in the chosen areas of expertise, and consulting with one's colleagues. Negligence by a therapist can occur if that therapist treats a problem without having the complete knowledge, training, and experience equivalent to that of another professional expert in that clinical area. Thus, the therapist must know the limits and bounds of his or her expertise so as to refer the client to the appropriately trained and qualified professional. It is very important that the therapist inform clients when they are unable to provide adequate services. In addition, if there are problems that arise in a therapist–client relationship that inhibit or prevent therapy toward the stated goals, the therapist should inform the client that some other professional may be better able to provide services to the client and refer the client to the appropriate professional in such a way as to not abandon or mistreat the client in the transfer to the new therapist. Such recognition of the rights and welfare of the client can help avoid any malpractice or professional misconduct.

Liability is of major concern to the therapist in cases of potential suicide or homicide cases. The Tarasoff (1976) decision in California now requires that the therapist, who is responsible for determining if a client poses a danger to himself or others, bear the responsibility to exercise reasonable care in the protection of the foreseeable victims of that danger.

In light of this legal decision, Sheldon-Wildgen suggests that various precautions be taken by the therapist. First, it is the therapist's responsibility to clearly advise the client as to which information discussed in therapy is confidential (which the therapist will not reveal without client permission) and what information the therapist is required to reveal (in situations where he or she may harm others or when a court has ordered the evaluation of the client). Second, the therapist should base the belief of a danger to others on overt behaviors emitted by the client. Indications include repeated statements of the client's intention and/or plan to harm others, the client's having the means available to accomplish the plan, the client's past history of violent acts, and the absence of a history of refraining from harm to others. Finally, whenever these criteria are met, it is the therapist's responsibility to inform the victim and law enforcement officials. In this manner, therapists can put more emphasis on skills rather than having a constant fear of legal recourse. However, therapists must accept a certain responsibility to inform, protect, and care for clients.

In summary, the professional has a number of guides for setting up and regulating the ethical and professional conduct of his or her practice. Applying these ethical principles and professional standards with a regular review to ensure continued quality professional services enhances client care and therapist accountability. The therapist must be aware of the legal liability and reduce its occurrence by a written behavior agreement detailing therapeutic goals and fully informed consent, regarding issues of goal review points, confidentiality, fees, and duration of treatment. These responsibilities free the therapist, to some degree, to be concerned more with the quality of therapy than with legal liability.

6

Recording and Treatment Forms

After the initial intake questionnaires and assessment surveys, the assessment interviews, and written evaluation have all been completed, there are a variety of forms that can help the behavioral clinician organize, implement, monitor, track, and troubleshoot the treatment procedures planned. These forms have been developed by this author as well as by noted behaviorists in the clinical field and are categorized as either *recording forms*, those in which the clinician collects data or wants to track the progress of the client's behavior during therapy, or *treatment forms*, which the therapist uses to facilitate treatment. Summaries of treatment procedures pertinent to the client's problems or suggested homework assignments for the client to complete are two examples. In this chapter, many of the recording and treatment forms that a therapist can use are listed and discussed.

6.1. RECORDING FORMS

Recording is an important activity for the clinician for three reasons. First, such recording provides data that can be graphed and reviewed daily or weekly as a means of monitoring the client's progress during various phases of therapy. Second, recording anecdotal as well as more objective information provides the therapist with a basis for accountability. Finally, such recording provides written observations that, upon case review, may suggest reasons for treatment failure or suggestions for new treatment approaches.

6.1.1. Treatment Plan Form

After the assessment has been completed and the clinician is reviewing the problem areas presented by the client or deemed critical by the clinician, it is important to list these various maladaptive behaviors and the treatment strategies planned. The treatment plan form can be used before or after the written evaluation has been formulated and discussed with the client. Cautela's (1977) rather simple treatment plan form specifies the maladaptive behaviors targeted for treatment on the left side of the form with a provision for the treatment procedures to be used for each problem on the right side of the form. Figure 2 is a reproduction of Cautela's treatment plan form for use in therapy. This form can be a guide affixed to the opposite side of a client's folder for ready reference by the therapist.

6.1.2. Session-by-Session Treatment Tracking Form

A second very important form is adapted from a form used by Humphreys and Beiman (1975). In their research, these authors treated the multiple and complex behavioral problems presented by a client.

CLIENT _____	DATE _____
MALADAPTIVE BEHAVIORS	TREATMENT
1. _____	_____
2. _____	_____
3. _____	_____
4. _____	_____
5. _____	_____
6. _____	_____
7. _____	_____
8. _____	_____
9. _____	_____
10. _____	_____

FIGURE 2. Treatment plan. From *Behavior Analysis Forms for Clinical Intervention* (p. 23) by J. Cautela, 1977, Champaign, IL: Research Press. Copyright by Research Press. Reprinted by permission.

The number and variety of problems of this client prompted the authors to chart the session-by-session treatment for each of the client's problems as a means of monitoring progress and treatment. Figure 3 is the session-by-session treatment tracking form that has proven to be useful in the clinical practice of behavior therapy. Clients have this form in their file made easily accessible to the therapist for monitoring client treatment. This form is used in tandem with Cautela's treatment plan form to track the treatment of each client from intake through termination and follow-up.

6.1.3. Session Summary Form

As in any clinical practice, it is necessary to have a session summary form for each session conducted with a client. Thorough summary notes are vital for continuity of treatment from one session to the next, for personal notes of concern to pursue with the client in the next session, and for the therapist's accountability, as has been previously indicated. In my practice, a simple form is used that has the following headings and space for the therapist to make appropriate notes (Kaplan, 1983):

1. Session summary notes (what occurred in today's session?)
2. Progress and problems by area
   Behavior
      baseline level
      current level
      percentage change from baseline
      targeted goal
   Cognitions
   (Therapist's comments regarding frequency of irrational statements or degree of compliance to assignments involving cognitive restructuring)
   Affective
   (Therapist's comments regarding client's statements of physical sensations, disturbing imagery, or anxious feelings and/or therapist observations of client discomfort such as poor eye contact, cold hands, sweating, flushed face, or stuttering and stammering)
3. Further treatment suggestions and concerns for next session
   (Pertinent homework assignments, intuitive statements that might change the method of treatment being used, need for consults with other professional or with various members of the client's family)

Client's Name _____ TREATMENT PROCEDURES	DATE BY VISIT											
	1	2	3	4	5	6	7	8	9	10	11	12
Problem identification												
History												
School observation												
School consultation												
Evaluation												
Paper/pencil testing												
Written behavioral assessment												
Rational-emotive therapy												
Relaxation training												
Assertiveness training												
Biofeedback												
Baseline												
Psychophysiological profile												
Treatment												
Generalization												
Systematic desensitization												
Hierarchy construction												
Treatment												
Communication skills												
Couple/family/marital counseling												
Facilitative verbal responses												
Contracting												
Sexual therapy												
Social skills training												
Behavior modification/contingency management												
Aversion therapy												
Covert sensitization												
Aversion relief												
Implosion/flooding												

(Continued)

FIGURE 3. Session by session treatment tracking form. From "The Application of Multiple Behavioral Techniques to Multiple Problems of a Complex Case" by L. Humphreys and I. Beiman, 1975, *Journal of Behavior Therapy and Experimental Psychology, 6*, p. 313. Copyright 1975 by Pergamon Press. Adapted by permission.

FIGURE 3. (*Continued*)

Client's Name _____ TREATMENT PROCEDURES	DATE BY VISIT											
	1	2	3	4	5	6	7	8	9	10	11	12
Covert techniques and other methods of cognitive restructuring												
Modeling and imitation												
Self-control and self-effi-cacy training												
Impulse control and prob-lem-solving training												
Other treatment procedures												
Termination session												
Follow-up sessions												

6.1.4. Data Collection and Homework Assignment Sheets

There are other forms that are important to the organizational flow of treatment. Data collection sheets and homework assignments are standard sheets given to the client. Data collection sheets are designed for such diverse problems as childhood noncompliant behaviors and other disruptive behaviors, progress and problems of the client through systematic desensitization, covert sensitization, aversive conditioning, flooding/implosion, imitation and modeling, number and type of irrational beliefs held during therapy or between sessions, and level of electromyographic, thermal, or endodermal responses during biofeedback training. Of course, a common data collection form used by the therapist and/or the client is the graph. For clients who have demonstrated excellent treatment compliance, the therapist may give them the task of plotting their own data either exclusively or concurrently with the therapist for self-monitoring reasons. The graph is made as a permanent record to be placed in the client's folder as well.

The homework assignment sheet is a no-carbon-required form that the therapist uses to assign the client certain pertinent tasks between sessions. This sheet allows the therapist to retain a copy of assignments to review during the next session. These forms are a helpful part of evaluating client progress and compliance to the treatment regimen.

6.1.5. Motivation for Behavior Change Form

Cautela & Upper's (1975) Motivation for Behavior Change scale allows the client and therapist to evaluate periodically the client's behaviors that suggest continued cooperation with therapy and effort to continue to its completion. Figure 4 lists such areas to be rated by the therapist and the client as frequency of verbal behavior by the client involving wanting treatment, number of appointments missed, compliance to record keeping and treatment assignments, and behavior during the therapy session. This form can be completed every 4 to 6 weeks of treatment with the client.

6.1.6. Termination and Follow-Up Forms

Once treatment has been completed successfully or unsuccessfully, the therapist can evaluate treatment on the termination report. Figure 5 lists various topics similar to those on the Motivation for Behavior Change form. On this form, which is a modification of Cautela's (1977) Final Report and Motivation for Behavior Change form, the therapist answers questions regarding whether therapy was successful or not and the degree to which the client followed the treatment procedures (Kaplan & Kuhling, 1984). In this manner, the therapist can be provided feedback as to the variables that contributed to client success or failure in therapy.

Follow-up forms are simply those that the therapist sends to previous clients. On these forms, the former clients indicate the degree with which the success of therapy has been maintained. This form can be sent out to clients at the end of 6, 9, 12, 18, and 24 months. Follow-up may be accomplished by sending a letter to former clients that outlines the previously referred problem behavior, the treatment effectiveness, and the current level of the client's problem. Examples of some questions that could be asked of former clients are:

1. After treatment, my major problems for which I sought therapy are: significantly worse, slightly worse, at the same level, slightly improved, significantly improved?
2. The methods I learned to control or eliminate my problem helped me: none, little, some, greatly, significantly?

NAME _____ DATE _____

1. Frequency of verbal behavior indicating the client wants treatment:
   - (a) not at all ☐
   - (b) a little ☐
   - (c) a fair amount ☐
   - (d) much ☐
   - (e) very much ☐
2. Intensity of desire for treatment as expressed by verbal behavior:
   - (a) not at all: I really don't want to change ☐
   - (b) a little intensity: I don't want to change, but my (wife) (husband) (children) (parents) want me to, so I might as well try ☐
   - (c) a fair amount of intensity: I'm ambivalent about it; sometimes I want to change and stop and sometimes I don't ☐
   - (d) much intensity: I guess I really should change ☐
   - (e) very much intensity: I really want to change, believe me ☐

3. Number of appointments missed:
   - (a) cancels or fails to show up for appointments 60% of the time ☐
   - (b) cancels or fails to show up for appointments about 40% to 60% of the time ☐
   - (c) cancels or fails to show up for appointments about 20% to 40% of the time ☐
   - (d) cancels or fails to show up for appointments about 10% to 20% of the time ☐
   - (e) cancels or fails to show up for appointments about 5% to 10% of the time ☐
   - (f) rarely and then with good reason ☐

4. Record keeping:
   - (a) never keeps records as required ☐
   - (b) keeps records occasionally and omits some data ☐
   - (c) keeps records occasionally and includes all relevant data ☐
   - (d) keeps records consistently but omits some data ☐
   - (e) keeps records consistently and includes all relevant data ☐

5. Does homework assignments:
   - (a) not at all ☐
   - (b) occasionally and incomplete ☐
   - (c) regularly but does not complete assignment ☐
   - (d) regularly and completes assignment ☐

6. During the therapy session the client:
   - (a) refuses to answer any question ☐
   - (b) refuses to answer some of the questions with evasion ☐
   - (c) tries to answer some questions without evasion ☐
   - (d) tries to answer most of the questions without evasion ☐
   - (e) answers all of the questions without evasion ☐

7. Pays attention (looks at therapist, answers questions promptly, follows directions easily, etc.):
   - (a) not at all ☐
   - (b) a little ☐
   - (c) a fair amount of the time ☐
   - (d) most of the time ☐
   - (e) all of the time ☐

8. Scheduling of appointments (assuming work or school schedule permits):
   - (a) is available only on a particular hour during the week ☐
   - (b) is available on either a particular morning, afternoon, or evening ☐
   - (c) is available any time on a particular day ☐
   - (d) is available on any one of three days ☐
   - (e) is available any time the therapist has an opening ☐

FIGURE 4. Motivation for Behavior Change Scale (MBCS). From "The Process of Individual Behavior Therapy" (p. 293) by J. R. Cautela and D. Upper, in M. Hersen, R. M. Eisler, and P. M. Miller (Eds.), *Progress in Behavior Modification* (Vol. 1), 1975, New York: Academic Press. Copyright 1975 by Academic Press. Reprinted by permission.

NAME _____   DATE _____

1. Client is now deemed *inactive* for the following reasons:
    (a) Therapy completed successfully ☐
    (b) Therapy completed unsuccessfully and the client referred to other professional ☐
    (c) Client failed to keep appointments or call back for another appointment after a 3-month period of time ☐
    (d) Financial difficulties and client referred to public agency ☐
    (e) Other please specify

    _____
    _____

2. Evaluation of treatment
    (a) Number of appointments missed:
        (1) canceled or failed to show up for apointments over 60% of the time ☐
        (2) canceled or failed to show up for appointments above 40% to 60% of the time ☐
        (3) canceled or failed to show up for appointments above 20% to 40% of the time ☐
        (4) canceled or failed to show up for appointments above 10% or 20% of the time ☐
        (5) canceled or failed to show up for appointments above 5% to 10% of the time ☐
        (6) rarely and then with good reason ☐
    (b) During session and homework assignments were done:
        (1) not at all ☐
        (2) occasionally and incomplete ☐
        (3) regularly but did not complete assignments ☐
        (4) regularly and completed assignment ☐
    (c) Overall progress in therapy:
        Poor ☐ Fair ☐ Good ☐ Very Good ☐ Excellent ☐
3. Prognosis
        Poor ☐ Fair ☐ Good ☐ Very Good ☐ Excellent ☐
4. Other comments

    _____
    _____

FIGURE 5. Termination report. From *Behavior Analysis Forms for Clinical Intervention* (p. 39) by J. Cautela, 1977, Champaign, IL: Research Press. Copyright 1977 by Research Press. Adapted by permission.

3. How confident are you in handling your own problems at this time compared to when you initially sought therapy: poor, not confident, neutral, somewhat confident, very confident?

Follow-up could also be done by conducting observations of the client's behavior in the naturalistic setting such as in the classroom with a child's behavior, in the home with parent–child situations, in role-playing situations with children and adult social skills deficits, by bringing the client back to the clinician's office for a follow-up interview to review client knowledge and application of cognitive and rational emotive therapeutic principles, or by arranging for the client to return for baseline measures on various biofeedback equipment regarding muscle tension, thermal training, and endodermal responsivity.

6.2. TREATMENT FORMS

There are a variety of treatment forms and aids that can be helpful in the use of the treatment procedures common in behavior therapy. Treatment forms are useful to the clinician for several reasons. First, they outline various critical aspects of the treatment procedure the therapist has prescribed. By listing and reviewing the important ingredients in the myriad of behavioral procedures available to the clinician, he or she is able to ensure greater accountability of treatment effectiveness for the client's problem. Second, these forms assist the client in applying the therapeutic assignments given from one session to the next. Generalization exercises or other cuing methods in naturalistic situations pertinent to the client's problem are examples. Third, these forms assist the clinician in conducting therapy. Blank behavior contract forms and token economy charts for home and school are some treatment forms that are often used. Finally, these treatment forms serve to clarify further for the client the concepts and exercises used in therapy. Often when some behavioral or cognitive principles are explained and discussed in therapy, the client may show acquisition of such information in the session. However, between sessions he or she may not be able to recall the precise nature of the didactic material and, therefore, misapply or forget the critical elements of the procedures. By giving written information to the client, the therapist may speed both understanding and application of the prescribed approaches.

The following is a list by each area of behavior therapy of some of these resources available to the therapist. These forms have been developed by this author, whereas others are either commercially available from the publisher or from the behavioral clinicians who developed them.

6.2.1. Traditional Behavior Modification Procedures

1. *List of praise statements for parents* (Madsen & Madsen, 1972). Despite the fact that the therapist may recommend to the parents of a child with problem behavior to provide verbal praise in instances of

desired behavior, this alone does not insure that the parents will do so or will have the verbal repertoire to give such social reinforcement. By giving the parents a list of examples of praise statements and by practicing these statements in the office as well as the therapist's observing such practice at home in the naturalistic setting, the effects of praise and further programming may be more successful.

2. *Form for parents and teachers to count statements of praise and criticism.* A means of demonstrating to parents and teachers the effects of the amount of praise and criticism on childhood behavior, it is frequently recommended that they be asked to count the number of statements of praise and reprimands; then ask parents or teachers to alter their frequencies while continuing to record the amounts of praise and reprimands that they deliver. In this manner, these change agents can directly observe the effects of altering their own behavior on the behavior of the children referred.

3. *Instruction sheets for parents to use in planning responsibilities and privileges for their children and adolescents.* Parents often need direction in scheduling the occurrence of privileges in exchange for responsibilities assigned. In this case, it is helpful to the therapist to give written instructions to parents that specify the exact nature of these contingent relationships. The therapist should work closely with parents to survey reinforcers using available reinforcement menus, and then help them list the responsibilities a child has in the home. This process is facilitated by written instructions to the parents.

4. *Instruction sheet for parents to use correctly, time-out procedures for noncompliance and other disruptive behavior.* Time-out has been a well-researched procedure for the reduction of disruptive behavior (Forehand & McMahon, 1981). However, when a therapist is recommending the use of this technique, he or she must be careful to specify the parameters of this procedure. Type and maximum number of warnings given prior to the use of time-out, optimum amount of time for the time-out period, method of timing of the procedure, and a system for reinforcing appropriate and behavior by avoiding all yelling or talking to the child during time-out to avoid emotional behaviors should be specified in writing to parents.

5. *Blank behavior contract forms for use with adults, parents and children, teachers and children.* Behavioral contracting has long been recognized as an effective method for specifying contingencies. Contracting can be accomplished between the therapist and the adult client, the adult client with him- or herself as a means of self-management, between therapist and child with verification by the child's parents, and between the teacher and the child. The therapist can also benefit from a list of instructions

regarding the important ingredients in formulating a sound behavior contract (Homme, Csanyi, Gonzales, & Rechs, 1969).

6. *Nervous tics, weight control, smoking cessation, and other habit reversal instructions.* In the literature are many references describing techniques helpful in alleviating frequent tics, nail biting, persistent hair pulling, and other nervous habits. Also, there are a variety of procedures available to the clinician in planning treatment for such common difficulties as smoking, and weight loss and management. The therapist would benefit by developing a list or outline of treatment methods for minimizing these behaviors.

7. *Instructions to correct daytime and nighttime enuresis and encopresis.* When dealing with the behavioral and emotional difficulties of children, problems with enuresis and encopresis are not uncommon. Researchers in the field have provided the practitioner with a variety of procedures that, if tailored to the individual child's problem, can alleviate these difficulties in a short period of time with the parent's cooperation.

6.2.2. Pavlovian/Wolpean Procedures

1. *Instructions for relaxation training procedures* (Jacobson, 1938; Lazarus, 1971; Wolpe, 1973). Deep muscle relaxation training procedures have long been used in the therapy of clients with anxiety and phobic disorders. It is often advisable for the therapist to make a tape of the relaxation training instructional session for the client to listen to at home as a means of developing generalization and as daily practice. For the therapist, having a script from which to read various highly effective paragraphs that suggest to the client ways to relax various muscle groups will facilitate that client's learning this important skill.

2. *Sensory awareness training exercises* (Fishman, 1978). After establishing the relaxation response in a client, it is helpful to enhance this response by instructing the client to use autogenic phrases that represent very pleasant scenes that are familiar and relaxing to the client. These phrases refer not only to pleasant scenes but also to the client's bodily sensations of heaviness, warmth, numbness, and tingling, which are associated with such scenes. In this manner, the client can learn a variety of methods of relaxation to minimize excessive stress, fear, and anxiety.

3. *Systematic desensitization flowchart* (Craighead, Rogers, & Bauer, 1979). These authors have compiled an easy method for conducting systematic desensitization and one that can be tracked at any point during therapy. Headings that might appear on the tracking form are (a) scene number; (b) subjective units of disturbance (suds) level; (c)

anticipated length of treatment; (d) amount of time between scenes; and (e) duration of each scene presentation. Subsequent to each systematic desensitization session the therapist can give the client written instructions, to apply *in vivo,* and generalization exercises at each hierarchy item mastered during therapy.

4. *Assertiveness training instructions, role-playing vignettes, and recording forms.* When, in the practice of assertiveness training, it becomes necessary to arrange role-playing exercises to evaluate the newly acquired skills of the shy client, the therapist can refer to a list of areas of assertiveness training that might be pertinent to the client's problems. Areas such as modes of accepting and giving compliments, dealing with anger or criticism, and giving gradually more confrontive assertive requests are some examples that the therapist can refer to during the skills training/evaluation session. The therapist may then use recording forms to rate, for example, eye contact, voice inflection, body stance, and directness of the assertive response by the client.

5. *Stroebel's quieting reflex (QR) program forms for children and adults.* Stroebel has developed a variety of procedures for the development of the relaxation response via a simple but systematic program of teaching the client various breathing techniques, muscle relaxation, and warming strategies in a program he calls the "quieting reflex" (QR). This author also supplies the interested clinician with a manual together with appropriate forms for the maintenance and generalization of the QR response by the client (Stroebel, 1982; Stroebel & Sandweiss, 1979; Stroebel, Stroebel, & Holland, 1980).

6. *Examples of suggested scenes for covert sensitization.* When dealing with deviant behavior or behavior that has a long history of obtaining reinforcement via highly deviant behavior, the therapist may wish to explore with the client the rationale and examples of treatment using covert sensitization. These examples serve to inform the client of the method to be used in therapy. Examples of descriptive scenes are often instructive to the client (Rimm & Masters, 1974).

6.2.3. Bandura's Social Learning and Self-Control Methods

1. *Social skills training procedures, role-playing vignettes, and evaluation forms.* As in the training of assertive skills, the therapist should also maintain a set of standard procedures available for use with clients who experience social skills deficiencies. In addition, the therapist should, for evaluation and educational purposes, have a set of vignettes that best represent situations in which the client may have difficulty in engaging in effective social skills. In group settings, clients may benefit by evaluating the social skills performance of each other in such role-playing

situations on an evaluation form from which corrective and positive feedback can be given to the client by other group members.

2. *Recommendations to therapists, parents, and teachers for role-playing and the development of social skills and prosocial behaviors by adults and children.* Sometimes the therapist cannot see the adult, parent, adolescent, or child in therapy, but may see the client for an evaluation only with suitable recommendations. If the therapist maintains a list of recommendations to change agents or to the client himself, the client at least has a start regarding what skills need improvement and what one's social skills deficiencies are. Teachers are most receptive to establishing such social skills development methods as "the people game" or "making friends" and then playing a game in which the children learn to cooperate, give compliments, make requests, deny requests, disagree, and utilize other such social skills. Having an available list of procedures for the teacher to use and implement may, at the least, begin to have an impact on the development of prosocial skills.

3. *Procedures for the therapist to use behavioral rehearsal, modeling and imitation, and reinforcement in the development of heterosexual skills in sex therapy.* Not only might sex therapy involve some of Masters and Johnson's (1966) techniques, but as some researchers point out (Barlow, 1973), some heterosexual performance is due in part to poor heterosexual skills development. The therapist can work with this special form of social skills deficiencies (e.g., social, sexual, and emotional intimacy skills). The therapist can maintain a set of procedures to which he or she can occasionally refer, in order to teach the client to behave in more appropriate, intimate ways with his or her partner.

4. *Participant modeling instructions in fear reduction treatment.* The therapist may choose to use the participant modeling approach to desensitizing a client to some phobic stimulus or stimuli. In this case, it might be helpful for the therapist to retain a list of the documented steps for implementing this procedure as well as homework assignments for practice by the client in the developing generalization.

5. *Self-reinforcement, time management, and individual goal setting recommendations.* In these procedures, the client is his or her own therapist by learning goal setting, time and activity management, and self-reinforcement methods.

6.2.4. Cognitive Restructuring Procedures

1. *Rational emotive therapy explanation forms, self-analysis forms, and arguments against irrational beliefs forms* (Ellis, 1970). In educating the client in the theory and principles of rational emotive therapy, it is often helpful

to use the visual aids supplied by the Institute of Rational Living. These visual aids depict the anatomy of emotions, ways to challenge irrational beliefs, and the rational self-analysis form for analyzing one's actions in terms of antecedent or concommitant thoughts and feelings. The therapist may wish to use these materials to help the client analyze his or her irrational behavior, beliefs, thoughts, and feelings. Such activities in therapy are educative and help the client view the actions of others in more rational ways.

2. *Common Irrational Beliefs Chart* (Ellis, 1970). On this chart, Ellis has listed the 12 most common irrational beliefs clients hold to make themselves upset and behave in ways that are not cost-effective to the client. Having the client memorize and discuss these irrational beliefs and to otherwise become very familiar with them might certainly facilitate treatment. Another helpful list is entitled "Arguments against Irrational Beliefs" (Ellis, 1970). On this form, the client is given "disputing" statements that challenge those that are irrational and related to the inappropriate behavior. Homework assignments that involve learning these common irrational beliefs and their rational challenges ("disputing" statements) and citing examples in the client's daily life where these beliefs may be operating are most educative to the client and promotes generalization in naturalistic settings.

3. *Beck's (1978) Daily Log of Dysfunctional Thoughts.* Aaron Beck and his associates view the development of emotions in a somewhat different manner than does Ellis (Beck, 1976). Beck assists the client in reviewing and assessing the nature of the client's automatic thinking and the degree to which it generates discomfort. After the client evaluates his or her own automatic thoughts as to their degree of distortion, the client can then substitute a more rational or logical thought in its place. The dysfunctional thoughts form assists the client in this assessment. It is highly advisable that the therapist keep a supply of these forms for client use in cognitive therapy.

4. *Stress Inoculation List of Coping Responses* (Meichenbaum, 1977). As part of cognitive restructuring techniques, "stress inoculation training," as developed by Meichenbaum (1977), helps the client prepare for some stressors so that excessive anxiety, fear, and anger will be less likely to occur. The therapist can have available a list of coping statements for preparing for the stressor, confronting the stressor, and for after having successfully "coped" with the stressor. Such phrases as "If I remain as relaxed as I can before talking to my boss, I will probably do a better job of asking him for my raise" can be given as assignments to practice and for the client to use in actual situations between sessions.

5. *Compliment cards for use by children and adults.* In situations in which it is observed that the client, child or adult, engages in frequent

self-deprecatory statements, it is often useful for that client to complete a compliment card. On a 3 × 5 index card the client records several compliments he gives to himself during the course of a day, as well as his counting how many compliments he gives and receives from others during the same day. The client is given a weeks' supply of these cards to complete from session to session. When the client does return these cards, the therapist can go over them and determine the extent to which the client can give and receive compliments as well as his giving compliments to himself. Shaping, role playing, and corrective feedback can then be a follow-up activity to the completion of these cards (Phillips & Mordock, 1970).

6. *Covert conditioning recommendations (reinforcement, extinction, positive imagery, thought stopping, and covert sensitization).* At times, the therapist may wish to use the variety of covert conditioning procedures available in the literature. Having a set of procedures to which the therapist can refer for each of these therapeutic methods would assist in the implementation of each respective procedure. Also, reminders of certain nuances of each procedure can be instructive and corrective to the therapist.

7. *Knaus's (1974) procedures and forms for rational emotive education for parents, teachers, and children.* Knaus has published a manual that has various forms for children to learn the basics of rational emotive education and the principles of rational emotive therapy. These forms explore such issues as perfectionism, bullying, stereotypes, the role of thoughts, feelings, and behaviors in emotions, and other such emotional issues. The Happening, Thought, Feeling, Reaction (Knaus, 1974) form is one in which the client can analyze the thoughts that contributed to the occurrence of irrational behavior by that client. Other forms are assessment forms as well as treatment forms that help the therapist evaluate the degree to which the client can verbalize and use the rational methods presented.

6.2.5. Biofeedback and Physiological Reconditioning Forms

1. *Biofeedback recording and procedural forms and flowcharts* (Fuller, 1977; Hartje, 1981; Stroebel & Sandweiss, 1979). Autogenic Systems published a series of technical books, and other professionals have developed materials regarding biofeedback to use as a reference for the treatment of various stress-related disorders. These forms range from tension charts for helping the therapist locate the muscle-appropriate spots for electrode placement to flowcharts for the treatment of various disorders using biofeedback and stress management measures as the treatment of choice.

2. *Taped autogenic phrases for client home practice.* The therapist and the client develop a variety of assignments for the development of the relaxation response by the client. The therapist can have available a set of autogenic phrases that most often influence a physical release of tension as reported by the client and verified by instrumentation. The therapist can also develop other phrases that are more idiosyncratic of the client's own relaxation response and, then, record these phrases on a tape that the client can take home for home practice.

3. *Sex therapy recommendations.* The therapist may wish to retain a list of up-to-date procedures for the treatment of various sexual disorders. Treatment of nonorgasmic women or impotent men to treatment of sex offenders with such difficulties as pedophilia, exhibitionism, and voyeurism are populations and problems frequently addressed in this area.

7

Supplementary Tools for Behavioral Practice

Applied researchers and clinicians in the field of behavior therapy continue to upgrade the technology of the field and their own expertise. Since the early days of behavioral psychology in which devices such as the Skinner box, the cumulative recorder, and Mowrer's enuresis bell and pad alarm were developed, behavior therapists have been inventing new methods and machines to facilitate the measurement and treatment of behavior. In addition, the field of behavior therapy has seen a rise in the number of books and journals written on the various topics of concern to the clinician. In recent years also, state licensing and certification boards have seen fit to require mental health professionals to complete a specified number of continuing education hours as a means of ensuring continued professional training and competence. Also, with the advent of the microcomputer, the practitioner has greater capability to do research, handle and store data, and utilize various software in the development of behavioral treatment programs and plans. These tools for behavioral practice aid the therapist in researching clinical problems and their treatment, in applying various measurement techniques, and in implementing these treatment methods used for pertinent clinical problems. The purpose of this chapter is to review and discuss these tools of a behavioral practice—equipment, books, continuing education, and computers—so as to inform the clinician of these available resources.

7.1. EQUIPMENT

Devices that aid in the measurement and treatment of behavior and emotional disorders increase the efficiency of behavior therapy. The clinician who practices broad-spectrum or multiform behavior therapy has an assortment of electronic devices and other equipment to help implement the therapeutic procedures. The following is a list and discussion of each device or set of materials within each area of behavior therapy.

7.1.1. Traditional Behavior Modification

7.1.1.1. Reinforcers of All Forms

The therapist who works with such populations as retarded or psychotic children and adults, schoolchildren, and parents should maintain a supply of reinforcers or, at least, have a budgeted amount of overhead devoted to the purchase of such reinforcers. During sessions with children, tokens can be delivered for instances of appropriate behavior in the session or between sessions as measured and reported by the child's parents. These tokens can then be exchanged for tangible articles such as stickers, posters, or small toys, activities such as playing video games or card games at the end of the session, or privileges such as staying up 15 minutes later that night at home or other privileges as permitted by the parents.

7.1.1.2. Wrist Counters, Cue Beepers, and Other Timing Devices for Recording Behavior and Scheduling of Reinforcers

During and between sessions, the therapist needs to record the frequency, rate, duration, or intensity of the target behavior. Such devices can be used by the therapist or by the parent/trainers with ease. Use of such devices aids in the precise and reliable measurement of the problem behavior. The therapist may wish to train parent/trainers *in vivo* as a means of validating the data to be collected.

7.1.1.3. Videotaping Equipment for Role-Playing and Parent Training

In individual and group behavior therapy sessions involving, for example, parent training and social skills training, videotaping the practice and actual parent–child or social interactions can provide the client with helpful feedback on the nature of the problems he or she experiences. Further, such videotaping provides the therapist with a permanent product for evaluating behavior change and planning alternative treatment procedures to remediate the clinical problems.

7.1.1.4. *Remote Control Listening and Communication Devices for Monitoring and Undetected Instruction Giving*

The Farrall Instrument Company's (1983) "bug-in-the-ear" device can be used behind a two-way mirror in a room in which parent–child or social interactions are taking place. The therapist can give instructions to the parent or client concerning appropriate behavior to engage in or provide reinforcement or corrective feedback for desirable or undesirable behavior during these observation sessions. This "bug-in-the-ear" arrangement can help with the supervision of other behavior therapists while they are conducting therapy with their clients.

7.1.1.5. *Toilet Training, Daytime and Nighttime Enuresis Devices*

Azrin and his colleagues (Azrin & Foxx, 1971; Azrin, Sneed, & Foxx, 1973, 1974; Foxx & Azrin, 1973a, b, c) developed a variety of toilet training devices for daytime and nighttime wetting for the retarded child and adult as well as for the normal population of children. When used in combination with the training procedures designed by these applied research scientists, such problems can be minimized or eliminated.

7.1.1.6. *Aversive Control Devices (Farrall Instrument Company, 1983).*

Behavior problems such as smoking, overeating, and sexual deviancy have been dealt with, in part, through the use of aversive conditioning devices such as the shock apparatus. The use of such devices has to be in conjunction with procedures to develop alternative and appropriate behaviors that have been shown to have some success. The therapist must be cautious in the use of this aversive conditioning equipment so as to protect the client from physical harm and ensure that state regulations regarding the use of such instruments are being followed. Use of these procedures constitutes the most, rather than the least restrictive alternatives.

7.1.1.7. *Response Regulation Devices*

There are several devices that have as their purpose the regulation of some behavior to a tolerable level of occurrence. Water Pik's "countdown" device regulates the rate of taking bites of food as well as the time for chewing between bites. In this manner, an individual can lose weight by the manner in which he or she alters eating patterns. In a similar fashion, a standard metronome has been used in the reduction of stuttering by regulating the rate of speech emitted by a stutterer.

7.1.1.8. *Predesigned Charts, Graphs, and Token Systems*

Available through various publishing companies are data recording charts and books, "six-cycle graph paper," and token economy charts for keeping track of points earned, exchanged, and lost. Clinicians may consult Research Press, 2612 North Mattis Avenue in Champaign, Illinois 61820, for a catalog of such materials.

7.1.2. Classical Conditioning Procedures

7.1.2.1. *Cassette Recorders, Slide Projectors, and Slide Presentations for Use in Systematic Desensitization, Covert Sensitization, and Aversive Conditioning*

As part of a treatment regimen, a therapist may wish to present the client with imaginal desensitization coupled with sounds or pictures of the stimuli feared by the client. The use of cassette recorders and slide projectors is very helpful in these treatment modalities. Also, prephotographed slides of various fearful situations are available from commercial companies such as the Farrall Instrument Company.

7.1.2.2. *Relaxation and Sensory Awareness Training Tapes*

It is often helpful for the therapist to make relaxation tapes for the client undergoing desensitization during the initial stages of teaching the client to relax. Clients report better results from such personalized tapes than from commercially available tapes. However, prerecorded tapes are available from such companies as Biomonitoring Applications. One caution is that the client may have a preference for a woman's rather than a man's voice or vice versa so that selection of the right relaxation tape will facilitate training.

7.1.2.3. *Videotaped Vignettes for Use in Assertiveness Training*

Teaching the client to behave assertively may not only require role playing but also some filmed vignettes. In this manner, the client and therapist can role-play using the vignettes, and the therapist can provide reinforcement and corrective feedback as needed.

7.1.2.4. *Packaged Stress Management and Quieting Response (QR) Training for Children and Adults (Budzynski, 1978; Stroebel, Stroebel, & Holland, 1980)*

Available through Biomonitoring Applications are several packaged programs for helping a client understand and reduce stress through a series of taped exercises and recording sheets provided in the treatment package.

7.1.3. Social Learning Procedures

7.1.3.1. *Projection or Videotaping Equipment with Taped Vignettes*

In situations in which the child or adult experiences anxiety when confronted by a fearful stimulus, videotapes of clients about the same age and with similar characteristics as the client could be shown engaging in the handling of that feared stimulus (e.g., guided modeling). The client could then model the more appropriate behavior and obtain reinforcement for this modeled behavior.

7.1.4. Cognitive Restructuring Procedures

7.1.4.1. *Posters That Highlight Important Cognitive Principles*

The Institute of Rational Living, 45 East 65th Street, New York, New York, has available for purchase a variety of posters that emphasize such cognitive concepts and methods as "The Anatomy of Emotions," "Common Irrational Ideas," "The Anatomy of Depression," and "How to Change a Belief." In addition, there are audio and video cassettes demonstrating various cognitive therapeutic strategies for the treatment of diverse clinical problems.

7.1.5. Biofeedback Procedures

7.1.5.1. Electromyographic, Thermal, Electrodermal, and Alpha Training

There are a host of companies that sell biofeedback equipment (Autogenic Systems, 1983; Future Heath, Incorporated, 1985). This equipment is used as part of the treatment of medical as well as psychological disorders. The decision to purchase such equipment should depend on such issues as the sensitivity of the devices to be used in practice, their testability and ease of repair, and their utility for the various clinical and stress-related disorders referred to the private practice. Other and more portable biofeedback equipment that are useful in clinical practice are biotic finger temperature bands (Khemka, 1977) and home-training biofeedback units (Myers, 1980).

7.1.5.2. Audio and Video Cassettes

Like the other areas of behavior therapy, biofeedback clinicians have utilized their expertise in the development of a cassette library for others interested in the various areas of treatment for stress-related disorders via biofeedback. BMA Audio Cassette Publications, 200 Park Avenue South, New York, New York, has an extensive list of cassettes that can be purchased by the clinician for his or her own education or that of the client. The Farrall Instrument Company, the Cyborg Corporation, Autogenic Systems, and the Biofeedback Society of America each have cassettes for purchase on topics involving the assessment and treatment of disorders by biofeedback therapy.

7.1.5.3. Sexual Dysfunction Monitoring and Treatment Equipment (Farrall Instrument Company, 1983)

Plethysmograph equipment for measuring the degree to which a male or female is aroused sexually is a helpful tool to those qualified to do sex therapy. As part of some treatment regimen, such equipment can aid in the measurement, treatment, and evaluation of the problems of sexual dysfunction. Also, videotapes are available for purchase (Focus International, 1984) that attempt to teach intimacy, sexual awareness, and various aspects of human sexuality to reduce sexual dysfunction.

7.2. BOOKS AND JOURNALS

Books and journals based on a behavioral orientation to clinical intervention are very helpful. Such texts aid in the planning of treatment and development of alternative treatment procedures when original procedures are ineffective in correcting the client's maladaptive behavior. Included here is a list of books and journals relevant to various behavior therapy treatment approaches. It is the responsibility of the behavior therapist to review new and current books through mail advertising and at conventions. Professional journals specializing in the field of behavior modification and therapy are also a must for the clinician's library. When writing treatment plans, the therapist may find it very informative to review the various procedures attempted in the literature to correct problems similar to the client's targeted problem behaviors. The therapist can then place the procedures on a continuum of least to most restrictive. The selection of the "treatment of choice" based on the risks and benefits of each procedure, the client's individual or organismic variables, and his or her presenting problems can then be made. The following is a partial list of the books and journals written and edited by behaviorists in the field that are useful in clinical practice. This list of books is not intended to be exhaustive but does attempt to highlight some of the major works that are helpful in clinical practice.

7.2.1. Comprehensive Texts Encompassing All Fields of Behavior Therapy

Within the field of behavior therapy, there are a number of texts that deal with the issue of assessment of behavior disorders, whereas others deal largely with the treatment of various problem areas. There are some texts that deal with the entire field of behavior therapy in a manner similar to that presented in this book. That is, all areas of behavior therapy are represented in these texts with a description of specific behavior disorders and the methods of treatment applied. These texts are listed alphabetically by title, author, publisher, and publication date:

Annual Review of Behavior Therapy: Theory and Practice, edited by G. Terrance Wilson, Cyril M. Franks, Kelley D. Brownell, and Phillip C. Kendall, Guilford Press, 1984

Behavior Therapy, Theory, Techniques and Applications, by David C. Rimm and John C. Masters, Academic Press, 1979

Behavioral Assessment of Adult Disorders, edited by David Barlow, Guilford Press, 1981

Behavioral Assessment of Childhood Disorders, edited by Eric Mash and Leif Terdal, Guilford Press, 1981

Handbook of Behavior Modification and Therapy, edited by Harold Leitenberg, Prentice-Hall, 1976

Helping People Change, edited by Frederick H. Kanfer and Arnold P. Goldstein, Pergamon Press, 1980

International Handbook of Behavior Modification and Therapy, edited by Alan S. Bellack, Michel Hersen, and Alan E. Kazdin, Plenum Press, 1982

Outpatient Behavior Therapy, edited by Michel Hersen, Grune & Stratton, 1983

Progress in Behavior Modification, edited by Michel Hersen, Richard M. Eisler, and Peter M. Miller, Academic Press, 1984

Single Case Experimental Designs: Strategies for Studying Behavior Change, by Michel Hersen and David Barlow, Pergamon Press, 1976

There are, however, specific texts that have been written out of one or a combination of areas of behavior therapy. Of course, these texts are not entirely mutually exclusive in their discussions. Rather, they tend to borrow from the principles that are the foundation for the other areas of behavior therapy. Where applicable, though, these texts are an outgrowth of the specific area of behavior therapy and are listed in this manner.

7.2.2. Traditional Behavior Modification

A Handbook of Research Methods in Applied Behavior Analysis, by Jon Bailey, The Florida State University Press, 1977

Behavior Modification in Mental Retardation, by William I. Gardner, Aldine-Atherton, 1971

Behavior Modification in the Natural Environment, by Roland G. Tharp and Ralph J. Wetzel, Academic Press, 1969

Behavior Modification Procedures for School Personnel, by Beth Sulzer and G. Roy Mayer, The Dryden Press, 1972

Behavioral Counseling: Cases and Techniques, by John D. Krumboltz and Carl E. Thoresen, Holt, Rinehart, & Winston, 1969

Children with Learning and Behavior Problems, by William I. Gardner, Allyn & Bacon, 1974

Families, by Gerald R. Patterson, Research Press, 1971

Habit Control in a Day, by Nathan W. Azrin and Greg R. Nunn, Pocket Books, 1978

Helping the Noncompliant Child: A Clinician's Guide to Parent Training, by Rex Forehand and Robert McMahon, Guilford Press, 1981

How to Use Contingency Contracting in the Classroom, by Lloyd Homme, Attila P. Csanyi, Mary Ann Gonzales, and James R. Rechs, Research Press, 1971

Marital Therapy, by Neil S. Jacobson and Gayla Margolin, Brunner/Mazel, 1979

Operant Behavior: Areas of Research and Application, edited by Werner K. Honig, Appleton-Century-Crofts, 1966

Parents Are Teachers, by Wesley Becker, Research Press, 1970

Principles of Behavior Modification, by Albert Bandura, Holt, Rinehart, & Winston, 1969

Skillstreaming the Adolescent, by Arnold P. Goldstein, Robert P. Sprafkin, N. Jane Gershaw, and Paul Klein, Research Press, 1980

Slim Chance in a Fat World, by Richard B. Stuart and Barbara Davis, Research Press, 1972

Teaching 1: Classroom Management, by Wesley C. Becker, Siegfried Englemann, and Don R. Thomas, Science Resource Associates, 1975

Teaching/Discipline, by Charles H. Madsen, Jr. and Clifford K. Madsen, Allyn & Bacon, 1970

The Token Economy, by Teodoro Ayollon and Nathan Azrin, Appleton-Century-Crofts, 1968

Toilet Training in Less Than A Day, by Richard M. Foxx and Nathan H. Azrin, Simon & Schuster, 1974

Toilet Training the Retarded, by Nathan N. Azrin and Richard M. Foxx, Research Press, 1973

7.2.3. Classical Conditioning Texts

Asserting Yourself, by Sharon Anthony Bower and Gordon H. Bower, Addison-Wesley Publishing Company, 1976

Assertiveness: Innovations, Applications, Issues, edited by Robert E. Alberti, Impact Publishers, 1977

Aversion Therapy and Behavior Disorders, by S. Rachman and J. Teasdale, University of Miami Press, 1969

Behavior Therapy, by Aubrey Yates, John Wiley & Sons, 1970

Behavior Therapy and Beyond, by Arnold A. Lazarus, McGraw-Hill, 1971

Behavior Therapy: Appraisal and Status, edited by Cyril M. Franks, McGraw-Hill, 1969

Depression: Behavioral and Directive Intervention Strategies, edited by John F. Clarkin and Howard I. Glazer, Garland Publishing, 1981

Group Therapy: A Behavioral Approach, by Sheldon D. Rose, Prentice-Hall, 1977

I Can If I Want To, by Arnold Lazarus and Alan Fay, Morrow, 1975

Liking Myself, by Pat Palmer, Impact Press, 1977

Multimodal Behavior Therapy, by Arnold Lazarus, Springer Publishing Company, 1976

Progressive Relaxation Training: A Manual for the Helping Professions, by Douglas A. Bernstein and Thomas D. Borkovec, Research Press, 1973

Responsible Assertive Behavior, by Arthur J. Lange and Patricia Jakubowski, Research Press, 1976

The Mouse, The Monster, and Me, by Pat Palmer, Impact Press, 1977

The Practice of Behavior Therapy, by Joseph Wolpe, Pergamon Press, 1973

Your Perfect Right: A Guide to Assertive Behavior, by Robert E. Alberti and Michael L. Emmons, Impact Publishers, 1974

7.2.4. Social Learning and Self-Control Texts

Behavior Self-Management: Strategies, Techniques, and Outcome, by Richard B. Stuart, Brunner/Mazel, 1977

Helping Couples Change: A Social Learning Approach to Marital Therapy, by Richard B. Stuart, Guilford Press, 1980

Its Up to You, by Eileen Gambrill and Cheryl Richey, Les Femmes Publishing, 1976

Self-Control: Power to the Person, by Michael J. Mahoney and Carl E. Thoresen, Brooks/Cole, 1974

7.2.5. Cognitive Restructuring Texts

A New Guide to Rational Living, by Albert Ellis and Robert Harper, Wilshire Books, 1975

Cognitive-Behavioral Interventions: Theory, Research, and Procedures, by Phillip C. Kendall and Steven D. Hollon, Academic Press, 1979

Cognitive-Behavioral Therapy for Impulsive Children, Phillip C. Kendall and Lauren Braswell, Guilford Press, 1984

Cognitive Therapy and the Emotional Disorders, by Aaron T. Beck, International Universities Press, 1976

Cognitive Therapy of Depression, by Aaron T. Beck, A. John Rush, Brian F. Shaw, and Gary Emery, Guilford Press, 1979

Depression: Causes and Treatment, by Aaron T. Beck, University of Pennsylvania Press, 1967

Handbook of Rational-Emotive Therapy, by Albert Ellis and Russell Grieger,
  Springer Press, 1977
How to Raise an Emotionally Healthy Happy Child, by Albert Ellis, Stuart
  Mosley, and Janet Wolfe, Wilshire Books, 1972
Rational Counseling Primer, by Howard S. Young, Institute for Rational-
  Emotive Therapy, 1974
Various mini- and self-help texts from the Institute of Rational-Emotive
  Therapy, 45 East 65th Street, New York, New York

7.2.6. Biofeedback and Psychophysiology Texts

Biofeedback, by George D. Fuller, Biofeedback Press, 1977
Biofeedback and the Modification of Behavior, by Aubrey J. Yates, Plenum
  Press, 1980
Biofeedback—Principles and Practice for Clinicians, by John V. Basmajian,
  Williams & Wilkins, 1979
Pain and Behavioral Medicine: A Cognitive-Behavioral Perspective, by Dennis C.
  Turk, Donald Meichenbaum, and Myles Genest, Guilford Press,
  1983
Stress Without Distress, by Hans Selye, Harper & Row, 1974

In addition to this list of some of the major texts that are very
helpful for clinicians and their clients, behavioral journals are also important in the formulation of treatment strategies for the client's problems.
It is also vital for the clinician to stay abreast of new developments in
the behavioral literature particularly in the clinician's area(s) of interest.
The following is a list of some of the journals that are available to the
clinician:

Journal of the Experimental Analysis of Behavior	*Child Behavior Therapy*
Journal of Applied Behavior Analysis	*The Behavior Therapist*
Behavior Modification	*Cognitive Therapy and Research*
Behavioral Assessment	*Rational Living*
The Behavior Analyst Newsletter	*Journal of Rational-Emotive Therapy*
Behavior Research and Therapy	*Biofeedback and Self-Regulation*
Journal of Behavior Therapy and Experimental	*Journal of Behavioral Medicine*
Psychiatry	*Behavioral Medicine Update*
Behavior Therapy	*American Journal of Clinical Biofeedback*

7.3. CONTINUING EDUCATION

In January, 1983, the American Psychological Association (APA)
compiled a chart entitled "Summary of Laws Regulating the Practice of
Psychology." At that time, approximately half of the states required

continuing education credits for the renewal of psychologists' licenses and certificates. There has been an increase in the requirement for continuing education to such an extent that APA and AABT now publish a calendar of training seminars for which continuing education credits can be earned. State associations and other public and private agencies are now offering CEU credits for upgrading one's skills and maintaining one's licensure. The emphasis on skill maintenance and development by the practicing clinician certainly increases the quality of therapy. Table 1 is the APA's January, 1983, summary by state of the requirements for licensure certification and continuing education for psychologists. As of 1983, 23 states require continuing education for license or certificate renewal. An up-to-date listing of approved sponsors is available from the APA by writing or calling 1200 Seventeenth Street, NW, Washington, DC, 20036, (202) 833-7592.

Clark, Wadden, Brownell, Gordon, and Tarte (1983) have reviewed sources for continuing education for the behavior therapist. These researchers surveyed the membership of AABT regarding their training, qualifications, and professional and continuing educational activities. Clark *et al.* found that 75% of the members who responded held PhD degrees, 17% held master's degrees, and 7% were psychiatrists and physicians. Further, 29% had 3 to 5 years of experience, 31% had 6 to 10 years, and 35% had over 10 years of experience in the field of behavior therapy and psychology. When these respondents were asked about their clinical activities, 88% indicated that they provided counseling, 48% indicated that they provided consultation and community education, and 20% indicated that they provided residential treatment. With regard to the target populations of individuals and clinical problems treated, the respondents indicated that 85% worked with adult behavioral-emotional problems, 71% worked with marital and couple difficulties, 65% with adolescent behavioral-emotional problems, 64% worked with parent–youth difficulties, 56% dealt with child behavioral-emotional problems, and 59% provided services to adults with sexual problems. The least frequently mentioned target problems treated were child and adolescent substance abuse and adult retardation.

When reviewing the number of behavioral journals being read by the respondents, Clark *et al.* observed that in 1968 there were only two behavioral journals in circulation. However, as of 1981, there are 25 that are widely read. The three journals that respondents rated as the most useful in improving clinical practice were *Behavior Therapy, Journal of Behavior Therapy and Experimental Psychiatry,* and *Behavior Research and Therapy. Cognitive Therapy and Research, Journal of Applied Behavior Analysis,* and *Behavior Modification* were also rated as helpful in enhancing clinical

A Summary of State Laws Regulating Psychological Practice through Licensure (L) or Certification (C)—January, 1983

		First approved	Major Amendments	Coverage	Educational Requirements								Examining Board			"Grandparenting" Ends
					Degree	Post degree	Supervision	Total experience	ABPP Recognized	Mandatory examination	Continuing ed. for renewal	Renewal Every	Psych. Members	Public Members	Terms	
Alabama	L	1963		Practice of psychologists	Doctorate	—	—	0	yes	yes	no	1 yr.	5	—	5	10/1/65
Alaska	L	1967		Psychologist	Doctorate	1	1	1	yes	yes	yes	4 yrs.	3	2	2	1/1/68
				Psychological associate	Masters	1	3	3	—	yes	yes	4 yrs.				
Arizona	C	1965	1978	Psychologist	Doctorate	—	—	0	yes	yes	no	1 yr.	5	2	5	1974
Arkansas	L	1955		Psychologist	Doctorate	—	—	1	—	yes	yes	1 yr.	6	1	5	7/1/57
				Psychological examiner	Masters	—	—	0	—	yes	yes	1 yr.				
California	L	1957	1969	Psychologist	Doctorate	1	2	2	yes	yes	no	2 yrs.	5	3	4	8/20/70
				Psychological assistant	Masters	—	—	—	—	no	no	1 yr.				
Colorado	L	1961		Psychologist	Doctorate	2	2	2	yes	yes	no	2 yrs.	7	2	3	7/1/63
Connecticut	L	1945	1969	Psychologist	Doctorate	1	—	1	yes	yes	no	1 yr.	3	2	5	6/24/69
Delaware	L	1962		Practice of psychology	Doctorate	2	2	2	yes	yes	yes	2 yrs.	6	1	3	6/11/64
Dist. of Col.	L	1971		Practice of psychology	Doctorate	2	1	2	yes	yes	no	2 yrs.	5	0	3	4/8/72
Florida	C	1961	1981	Psychological services	Doctorate	1	2	2	yes	yes	yes	2 yrs.	5	2	4	12/31/81
Georgia	L	1951		Pract. of applied psych.	Doctorate	—	—	1	yes	yes	yes	2 yrs.	5	1	5	5/1/53
Hawaii	L	1967		Practice of psychology	Doctorate	—	1	1	—	yes	no	2 yrs.	5	2	2	6/6/68
Idaho	L	1963		Practice of psychology	Doctorate	—	—	2	—	yes	no	1 yr.	3	0	3	7/1/64

(Continued)

TABLE 1 (Continued)

				Educational Requirements						Continuing ed. for renewal	Examining Board				
		First approved	Major Amendments	Coverage	Degree	Post degree	Supervision	Total experience	ABPP Recognized	Mandatory examination	Continuing ed. for renewal	Renewal Every	Psych. Members	Public Members	Terms	"Grandparenting" Ends
Illinois	C	1963		Psychologist	Doctorate	1	2	2	—	yes	no	2 yrs.	5	0	5	8/15/71
Indiana	C	1969	1981	Psychologist in private practice	Doctorate	1	—	2	yes	yes	no	2 yrs.	5	1	3	7/1/72
		1981		Clinical psychologist	Doctorate	1	1	2			no					7/1/83
		1969		Psychologist (basic)	Doctorate	—	—	—	yes	—	—	—		—		
Iowa	L	1974		Practice of psychology	Doctorate	1	1	1	yes	yes	yes	1 yr.	5	2	3	1976
					Masters	—	2	5	—	yes	yes	1 yr.				
Kansas	L	1967		Psychologist	Doctorate	1	2	2	—	no	yes	2 yrs.	2	1	3	7/1/69
Kentucky	L	1948	1971	Practice of psychology	Doctorate	—	—	1	yes	yes	no	3 yrs.	4	1	4	7/1/65
				Certificand	Masters			—	—							
Louisiana	L	1964		Psychologist	Doctorate	1	2	2	—	yes	no	3 yrs.	5	0	3	7/1/66
Maine	L	1953		Psychologist	Doctorate	—	—	2	yes	yes	yes	1 yr.	5	1	5	10/1/68
				Psychologist examiner	Masters	—	1	1	—	yes	no	2 yrs.				
Maryland	L	1957	1981	Psychologist	Doctorate	1	1	2	yes	yes	yes	1 yr.	5	1	3	12/31/59
Massachusetts	L		1971	Psychologist	Doctorate	1	1	2	yes	yes	no	2 yrs.	5	0	5	12/31/73
Michigan	L	1959	1978	Psychologist	Doctorate	—	—	2	—	yes	yes	1 yr.	5	3	4	10/1/80
				Psychologist (limited license)	Doct./ Masters	—	—									
Minnesota	L	1951	1973	Consulting psychologist	Doctorate	2	2	2	yes	yes	no	2 yrs.	7	4	4	7/1/75
				Psychologist	Masters	2	—	2								
Mississippi	L	1966		Psychologist	Masters	2	—	2	yes	yes	no	2 yrs.	5	0	3	7/1/67
Missouri	L	1977		Psychologist	Doctorate	1	1	1	yes	yes	no	1 yr.				

State		Yr1	Yr2	Profession	Degree											Date
Nebraska	L	1967	1978	Practice of psychology (also specialty cert. for clinical)	Doctorate	—	—	0	—	yes	no	1 yr.	5	0	5	1/1/71
Nevada	L	1963		Practice of psychology	Doctorate	1	4	1	—	yes	yes	2 yrs.	4	1	3	7/1/64
New Hampshire	L	1957	1981	Psychologist	Doctorate	1	2	2	yes	yes	no	1 yr.	5	2	3	7/1/82
				Associate psychologist Psychological assistant	Masters	5	5	5	—	yes	no	1 yr.				7/1/82
New Jersey	L	1966		Practice of professional psychological services	Doctorate	1	2	2	yes	yes	no	2 yrs.	7	3	3	1/1/86
New Mexico	C	1963		Psychologist	Doctorate	2	2	2	yes	yes	yes	1 yr.	5	1	3	12/31/64
New York	C	1956		Psychologist	Doctorate	—	2	2	yes	yes	no	2 yrs.	12	1	5	7/1/59
North Carolina	L	1967		Practicing psychologist	Doctorate	2	2	2	ye	yes	no	1 yr.	5	0	3	7/1/69
				Psychological associate	Masters	—	—	0	—	yes	—	1 yr.				
North Dakota	L	1967		Psychologist	Doctorate	—	—	0	yes	yes	no	1 yr.	5	0	3	7/1/68
Ohio	L	1972	1972	Practice psychology	Doctorate	1	2	2	yes	yes	no	2 yrs.	6	1	5	11/22/76
				Pract. of school psych.	Masters	3	1	4	—	yes	no	2 yrs.				
Oklahoma	L	1965		Practice of psychology	Doctorate	2	2	2	yes	yes	no	1 yr.	5	0	3	6/28/66
Oregon	L	1973		Practice of psychology	Doctorate	—	2	2	yes	yes	yes	1 yr.	7	2	3	1/1/74
	L	(Limited)		Psychologist associate	Masters	—	3	—	yes	yes	—					
Pennsylvania	L	1972		Practice psychology	Doctorate	2	1	2	yes	yes	no	2 yrs.	7	2	3	5/23/72
					Masters	4	2	4	—	yes	no	2 yrs.				

(Continued)

TABLE 1 (*Continued*)

		First approved	Major Amendments	Coverage	Educational Requirements Degree	Post degree	Supervision	Total experience	ABPP Recognized	Mandatory examination	Continuing ed. for renewal	Examining Board Renewal Every	Psych. Members	Public Members	Terms	"Grandparenting" Ends
Rhode Island	C	1969		Consulting psychologist	Doctorate	1	2	2	yes	yes	no	1 yr.	4	1	3	12/31/70
South Carolina	L	1968	1982	Practice of psychology	Doctorate	1	2	2	yes	yes	no	2 yrs.	7	1	5	3/21/69
South Dakota	L	1976	1981	Practice of psychology	Doctorate	2	—	2	—	yes	yes	2 yrs.	4	1	3	1/1/82
Tennessee	L	1953		Psychologist	Doctorate	—	—	1	yes	yes	no	perm.	5	0	5	7/1/55
				Psychological examiner	Masters			0								
Texas	L	1969	1975	Psychologist (also specialty cert. for health service provider)	Doctorate	1	1	2	yes	yes	yes	1 yr.	6	2	6	12/31/79
	C	1981		Psychological associate	Masters (450 clock hours)					yes	yes					
Utah	L	1959		Practice as psychologist	Doctorate	1	2	2	no	yes	yes	1 yr.	5	0	5	12/31/62
Vermont	L	1976	1982	Psychologist-doctorate	Doctorate	2	2	3	yes	yes	yes	2 yrs.	3	2	5	6/30/77
				Psychologist-master	Masters	3	3	4	—	yes	yes	2 yrs.				
Virginia	L	1946		Psychologist	Doctorate	2	2	2	yes	yes	yes	2 yrs.	5	0	5	none
				Clinical psychologist	Doctorate	2	2	2	yes	yes	yes	2 yrs.				

(also certification of qualification-limited lic. below doctorate)
Psychological assistant

State		Year	License title	Degree										Date
West Virginia		1970	Practice of psychology	Doctorate	1	1	yes	yes	yes	2 yrs.	5	1	3	11/12/70
Wisconsin	L	1969	Practice of psychology	Masters	5	5	—	yes	yes	2 yrs.	4	1	3	
				Doctorate	1	1	yes	no	no	2 yrs.				7/1/70
		1979	School psychologist	Masters										
Wyoming	L	1965	Practice of psychology	Doctorate	—	0	yes	yes	yes	1 yr.	5	0	3	12/31/65
CANADA														
Alberta	C	1960	Psychologist	Masters	—	0	—	no	no	—	8	0	1	4/11/62
British Columbia	C	1977	Psychologist	Doctorate	1	1	—	no	no	—	5	2	2	7/6/80
Manitoba	C	1966	Psychologist	Doctorate	2	2	—	yes	yes	1 yr.	7	0	2	12/31/72
New Brunswick	L	1980	Psychologist	Doctorate	1	1	—	yes	no	2 yrs.	5	0	2	6/1/71
				Masters	4	4	—	yes	no	2 yrs.				
Nova Scotia	C	1980	Psychologist	Doctorate	1	2	yes	yes	no	1 yr.	5	0	3	12/18/84
				Masters	4	4								
Ontario	C	1960	Psychologist	Doctorate	1	1	—	yes	no	1 yr.	5	0	5	6/11/66
Quebec	C	1962	Psychologue	Doctorate	—	0	—	yes	no	1 yr.		0	—	
Saskatchewan	C	1962	Registered psychologist	Doctorate	—	0	yes	yes	—	1 yr.	5	0	2	12/31/66

Reprinted by permission of the American Psychological Association, "A Summary of Laws Regulating the Practice of Psychology through (L) Licensure or (C) Certification," Washington, D.C.: American Psychological Association, 1981.

skills. Newsletters that were judged informative by these respondents were *The Behavior Therapist* and *Behavioral Medicine Update.*

The respondents' ratings of conferences and training sessions attended revealed additional information. AABT pre-convention institutes, AABT workshops, and ABA symposia were rated as very useful by at least 80% of those who responded to the questionnaire. AABT symposia, AABT special interest groups, APA Division 25 symposia, and AABT poster sessions were rated by about 70% to 80% as useful to clinical practice and professional development. An additionally interesting finding by these researchers is that informal discussions with colleagues is a valuable source of information for the clinician. Because one of my assumptions is that the behavior therapist is frequently isolated from the rest of the professional community because of his or her chosen identity as a behavior therapist, the need for informal discussions with behaviorally oriented colleagues might suggest a communication network with other such therapists across the nation. Affiliation with the pertinent special interest groups in AABT might be a good method for establishing such a network.

Relative to the behavioral journals available to the clinician, these authors found that journal readership is a frequently utilized source of continuing education for the membership of AABT. However, the most useful source appears to be formal continuing education training during AABT conventions and at other times during the year. The authors conclude that further investigation is needed regarding the adequacy of these formal continuing education programs for the clinician. The form, content, and instructor's mode of presenting information are critical issues to effective training programs. For example, Kuehnel, Marholin, Heinrich, and Liberman (1978) found that there is a negative correlation between the satisfaction ratings by participants and the use of traditional didactic methods of instruction, whereas active teaching methods (role playing, videotaping, and group interaction) were rated very positively.

In light of these findings by Kuehnel *et al.*, it is reasonable for behavior therapists to choose carefully the continuing education workshops to be taken. Conversely, in giving such workshops themselves to other professionals and paraprofessionals, therapists must pay special attention to those methods that promote learning and generalization of the information taught. Keuhnel and Flanagan (1984) have addressed the need for guidelines for effective continuing education workshops. According to these authors, continuing education for behavior therapists is essential due to the explosion of behavior technology, the failure of formal licensure to ensure one's professional competencies, the required periodic renewal of credentials to allow one to continue to provide treatment in facilities governed by peer review committees, the liabilities of malpractice, and positive consequences for the clinician who updates his or her skills from a clinical as well as from a financial standpoint.

There are many active/directive teaching methods for the trainer to use that are key ingredients for effective continuing education workshops proposed by these authors. First, the trainer must set precise objectives that may include attitudinal, cognitive, as well as behavioral objectives for the participants. Second, brief instruction should follow in which information is covered briefly, examples are given to illustrate main points in the presentation, and role-playing vignettes are presented to provide live modeling of the precise clinical skills taught. To teach these skills, a good workshop leader will model those skills and give the trainees the opportunity to rehearse and get performance feedback on the imitation of them. Third, modeling should entail pinpointing for the trainees the specific performance to be learned, showing just enough of the vignette to demonstrate the point, and inviting comments and observations from the participants. The authors suggest that discriminative cuing and directive questioning should be a part of this modeling to promote a clearer picture of the skill to be learned. Fourth, as the trainees begin to rehearse what they have observed, prompting, shaping, and performance feedback need to be given. Finally, generalization and maintenance of the learned skills should be a planned part of the workshop whether training takes place at the on-site facility or at a convention. Use of taped scenes of actual clinical problems pertinent to the training given or *in vivo* experiences might be examples of such generalization and maintenance procedures. Finally, Kuehnel and Flanagan suggest that evaluation of this training occur via one or a combination of ways: a needs assessment for future training in related areas, trainee satisfaction, an actual evaluation of trainee knowledge and skills acquisition, recorded daily utilization of the newly acquired skills, or of the clinical outcomes of the training.

7.4. THE USE OF COMPUTERS IN A BEHAVIORAL PRIVATE PRACTICE

Since the early days of the mainframe computer on which many a graduate student toiled long hours typing their project computer cards and debugging their Fortran programs for class and dissertation credit, professionals have been searching for better ways of handling data. With the advent of the silicon chip, microcomputers have begun to make their way into the business and professional worlds. This symbol of the information age can allow the professional to handle data faster, in greater quantities, more accurately, and with greater flexibility. There are, of course, disadvantages along with these and other advantages that bear consideration. Mental health professionals (DeWeaver, 1983) as well as prominent behavior researchers and practitioners (Klepac, 1984a, b; Romanczyk, 1984; Russo, 1984) have examined the advantages, disadvantages, and applications of the microcomputer in behavior modification and clinical behavior therapy settings as well as its application to business matters of private practice.

DeWeaver indicates that computer application in the mental health field involves information systems management, administrative functions, educational functions, and clinical assessment. Thus, the three main functions of the microcomputer are office management, data manipulation, and clinical assistance. Advantages that DeWeaver sees are that the microcomputer is easy to use, allows for expanded data analysis capabilities, is portable, has great flexibility of programming, and has a relatively low cost to the clinician. The disadvantages that DeWeaver cites are the limitation of memory capabilities when large amounts of data are being gathered and processed (though for the independent practitioner there is little danger of information overload here) and the still limited amount of *reliable* software. Although there are numerous business programs applicable to the mental health profession, there are few software programs on the assessment and treatment of behavioral/emotional disorders. A third disadvantage is that the microcomputer market is such a burgeoning field that computer companies now in fierce competition for the microcomputer dollar may not be around in 5 years. Thus, the professional must be careful to choose the computer with the best track record and one that is most often used by colleagues in that practitioner's local community. This is also true of software that may have been rushed onto a seller's market without proper debugging. DeWeaver's recommendation is to "let the buyer beware." DeWeaver does cite, however, several software companies that have some mental health services software, and lists several newsletters in which are discussed several applicable software programs for the mental health practitioner.

In a series of articles for *The Behavior Therapist*, Romanczyk, Klepac, and Russo each contributed individual comments on the impact of the microcomputer in behavior therapy. Romanczyk has indicated that since the traditional emphasis in behavior therapy has been on precise specification and measurement of the targeted behavior, the microcomputer and behavior therapy fit quite nicely together. Romanczyk lists and discusses many applications in which he has used his computers. Specifically, information management in the tracking of individual educational plan goals and progress of developmentally handicapped children, program planning for a vast number of children being served at his treatment facility, child progress analysis via graphs and a full prose description of such progress, data collection by the staff through several terminals in the residential facility, and direct instruction of the child through pleasant activities that are both fun and educative constitute the variety of his uses for the microcomputer.

Klepac concurs with Romanczyk's observations that the microcomputer is a valuable tool for the behavior therapist. Klepac sees that its utility is as a word processor to handle clerical and administrative tasks, to plan and summarize assessments, and to enable the clinician to tailor the treatment regimens for the client through a clear specification of the procedures to be used. Also, there are some disk programs available that assist the clinician in assessing the level of fears in a child through the use of a joystick and a "gaming" screen. In summary, Klepac indicates that there is some consensus that the potential contributions made by the computer will overshadow its newness, its volatility as a market, and the extensive amount of time needed to learn the basics of the computer.

Another professional in the field of behavior therapy who has extensive knowledge and experience with computers is Dennis Russo. Russo has described the uses of the microcomputer in his private practice and supports the notion that the computer offers the clinician a substantial savings of time, is a guide toward programming improved services to patients, and is useful in the process of evaluation. Russo also sees a need for the microcomputer to serve as a means of data collection, as a data-based management system, and even in conjunction with biofeedback. Not only can the computer store data, but it can analyze and graph it as is needed.

The variety of purposes served by the computer are (a) as a word processor; (b) as a data-based management system; (c) as an information management system; (d) as an assessment tool; (e) as a spread sheet organizer; and (f) as a treatment method (e.g., biofeedback).

When buying a computer, Romanczyk states that there are two ways to make such a purchase: buy one impulsively without understanding its mechanism, or by consulting with colleagues who own the device to determine what capabilities the machine will have and what software will be needed. What follows is a brief discussion of the various purposes of computer programs and some recommended software programs applicable to one's clinical practice. These programs are also reviewed in various computer magazines and books that are commercially available in most retail and wholesale bookstores.

7.4.1. Word Processing

This is a most vital software area for use with the computer. Behavioral evaluations, program development, and specific treatment recommendations can be prepared via word processing packages. In fact, in the case of the "treatment of choice" for a specific problem, such as the use of time-out for childhood disruptive behavior, the word processor can replicate documents from client to client that can be tailored to the individual needs of the client. Thus, the professional office staff do not have to waste valuable secretarial time each time a common treatment approach is recommended. Some popular word processing programs that are easy to use are PFS: Write, Appleworks, and Wordstar 2000.

7.4.2. Data Base Filing

Often, the clinician may wish to analyze his caseload source of referrals, length of treatment, ages of clients, and other such characteristics. With data base software programs, the clinician can access this information quickly and easily. The data base packages also permit the compilation of mailing lists for clients as well as for colleagues. Some popular data base software programs are PFS: File, Appleworks, DB Master, dBase II and III, and Lotus 1-2-3.

7.4.3. Graphs and Charts

The clinician is aware of the need for graphing data collected by the client, the client's representative, or by the clinician himself on his or her client's behavior. Instead of spending priceless professional or clerical time drawing out graphs and charts, the clinician has available several excellent software programs to chart and graph client data. Some popular software programs are PFS: Graph, Visiplot, and Softgraph.

7.4.4. Spread Sheet Analysis

More as a means of analyzing the business end of one's practice, the various spread sheet software programs help the clinician make projections and monitor existing budgets. Some excellent programs in this area are Visicalc, Appleworks, and Supercalc.

7.4.5. Testing Programs

For those clinicians who utilize various behavior rating scales, the MMPI, and various psychometric testing devices, there is a growing supply of programs available to conduct such testing in a computerized format. The major psychological text corporations are beginning to advertise such programs for purchase.

Finally, there are a variety of telecommunication uses of the computer. Community bulletin board services in one's general locale allow for local type–talk conferencing. With a phone modem, one can also call national bulletin board services in the United States at substantially lower rates. These national telecommunications networks allow the caller, with the right phone modem, to connect with others across the country, shop in a store in which one's credit card can be used for membership and purchasing power, peruse the latest stock market rise and fall, arrange for discount flight reservations and, get the latest news in technology, science, and business. CompuServe and the Source are two such telecommunications companies. Charges are made by the minute (from $.10 on up), and such systems minimize loss of valued professional time. Finally, of recent availability is the Knowledge Index, a variety of data bases from which to draw a massive number of articles on a selected topic. Knowledge Index is a small subsidiary of Dialog Services and can reference *PSYINFO, Index Medicus, Mental Health Abstracts, Medline*, pharmaceutical abstracts, and data bases in business, science, and education. Downloading of information from this service to one's disk provides not only a list of up-to-date references but also abstracts of these articles as well. This data base is obviously of vital usefulness to the clinician for referencing the growing body of behavior literature on problems of clinical interest.

8

The Behavior Therapist as Consultant

In Chapter 2, the assumptions governing setting up a behavioral private practice were listed and discussed. One of those assumptions is that the behavior therapist should, for the most part, take on the role of "general practitioner." By doing so, the clinician can work with a diversity of clinical problems, provide a variety of services that affect a greater number of people, establish a wider referral base, and avoid "boredom" and "burnout" (i.e., ratio strain) from seeing individual clients hour after hour each day. Thus, not only does the behavior therapist see individuals and groups of clients, he or she can also serve as a consultant to public and private agencies, hospitals, and schools. The behavior therapist can therefore expand his or her practice and promote this role of general practitioner. A side financial benefit is that, as a consultant, individuals associated with the contracted agencies have an opportunity to work directly with the clinician. Frequently, private referrals result from this exposure over and above one's role as a consultant. Also, such consultant contracts provide a regular source of income that is a hedge against the sometimes seasonal changes or "roller coaster effect" (Browning, 1982) of referrals.

There are disadvantages, of course, to obtaining consultant contracts. First, there is a great deal of professional time given as "in-kind" contributions for program planning, writing reports, and troubleshooting problems over and above the contract hours paid by the agency. Second, the role of the behavioral consultant has changed and now encompasses greater responsibility, as is discussed later in this chapter, so that there are added professional and ethical considerations in the provision of consultant services. Third, agencies, businesses, hospitals, and schools are often on very tight budgets. Thus, fees for services may not match the hourly fee one charges in the office. Rather, one must bid at a lower hourly fee or on a package fee-per-day basis that is usually less than one's daily receivables. In addition, because on-site consultancy is generally more effective than off-site training, there is usually 30 minutes to 1 hour's worth of unpaid travel time expended to get to the consultancy site(s). Although mileage may be provided by the requesting agency, fees are lost to some extent. Despite these disadvantages, consulting can be a very beneficial adjunct to private practice. Its professional benefits, which include private individual referrals resulting from face-to-face involvement with staff who view the consultant as effective, as well as potential for future consulting services, usually outweigh the risks.

8.1. ISSUES AND CURRENT DIRECTIONS IN BEHAVIORAL CONSULTATION

In the late 1960s and early 1970s, the field of behavior therapy enjoyed a great deal of popularity. Schools, retardation facilities, state hospitals, and clinics sought out the services of the behaviorist to consult on a variety of educational, clinical, and social problems. Academic and behavioral problems with children in schools (Ramp & Hopkins, 1971; Sulzer & Mayer, 1972), maladaptive and life-threatening behavior in the retarded (Azrin, Kaplan, & Foxx, 1973; Bostow & Bailey, 1969; Vukelich & Hake, 1971), problems with the psychotic client (Ayllon & Azrin, 1968), and unemployment (Azrin, Flores, & Kaplan, 1975) are some examples of such problems. Unfortunately, the development of effective techniques for resolving the socially and clinically significant problems of individuals and the "mere" dissimination of information regarding the *how-to*'s of these techniques were not sufficient for change agents in these environments to apply the technology efficiently.

In recent years, behaviorists have begun to examine the problems involved in successfully providing consultant services (Bailey & Reiss, 1984; Bernstein, 1982, 1984; Bernstein & Ziarnik, 1984; Brown & Presbie, 1978; Krampfl, 1984; Kratchowill & Van Someren, 1984; Kuehnel & Flanagan, 1984; Linehan, 1980; McDonald, 1983; Ziarnik & Bernstein, 1984). Issues involving the training of behavioral consultants, the structure of continuing education workshops for maximum benefits to other helping professionals, staff and facility problems at consulting sites, and alternative models for consultation have been explored.

Bernstein (1984) has pointed out that research on effective methods for training consultants has lagged behind research on new methods of behavior change. However, in recent years, greater attention has been paid to the need for research and methods of consultant training. Bernstein (1982) has developed a complex model of behavior consultation called the "interactive model of behavioral service delivery," which has great utility for the diversity of problems and populations for which behavioral techniques have been applied.

This interactive model of behavioral service delivery is depicted in Table 2. In this model, the client is the individual whose behavior is to be modified, the behavioral engineer is the designer of the intervention program for this behavior modification, and the behavior manager is the implementer of the designed program. The behavioral consultant is the troubleshooter, and the provider of resources and innovative ideas who will assist the other change agents toward the goals of the intervention program.

This model is dubbed by Bernstein to be both interactive and ecological. That is, not only do the client's behaviors and those of the manager, engineer, and consultant interact and influence one another,

TABLE 2
Ecosystems Analysis[a]

	EcoBehavioral systems	Hypothesis
Macrosystem	Overriding cultural belief and values	A culture which positively consequates work is a culture which survives
Exosystems	Larger social structures (formal & informal)	"Competitive employment" is one way of operationally defining work
Microsystem	Immediate setting in which behavior occurs	A set of specific identifiable skills are required for competitive employment
Individual	Learning history, biological characteristics	People with disabilities who acquire those specific identifiable skills can obtain competitive employment

[a]From "Training Behavior Change Agents in Outcome Selection," by G. S. Bernstein and J. P. Ziarnik, 1984, *The Behavior Therapist, 7*, p. 104. Copyright 1984 by the Association for Advancement of Behavior Therapy. Reprinted by permission.

but there are ecobehavioral systems operating in the context of the behavioral program. First, the individual client comes into this situation with a certain set of behavioral skills, excesses, and deficits, as well as a learning and biological history. Further, the *microsystem* is the immediate setting in which all these individuals are involved, whereas the *exosystem* is the larger formal and informal social structure in which these individuals behave and events occur. Finally, the *macrosystem* is comprised of the beliefs and values the participating individuals hold in each of these systems. Of course, there are many other variations of this model if one individual serves more than one function. These variations are the basis for analyzing all environments in which there are individuals attempting to modify behavior whether the target is for a client's behavior, a group of employees, or the general population. Berstein also discusses the various issues and parameters of the change agent (manager, engineer, and consultant) such as skills, competency and functions, and the contextual parameters that make up the ecobehavioral system. Finally, Bernstein indicates that there must be an emphasis on effective methods of teaching behavior change skills and ensuring that there is lasting maintenance and generalization of the skills conveyed by the behavior change manager, engineer, and consultant.

Kratochwill and Van Someren (1984), Linehan (1980), and Bernstein and Ziarnik (1984) have also explored the issues and directions in training behavioral consultants. Behavioral consultation is viewed as high priority in graduate training. Evidence indicates that merely having effective behavioral procedures alone will not facilitate behavior change. These procedures must be accompanied by a behavioral analytic approach that takes into consideration the change agents' skills, maintenance and generalization of the effective procedures, and considerations in overall program planning of the ecobehavioral systems operating at all levels (Bernstein, 1982). Thus, by teaching behavioral consultants not only the effective methods of treatment but, more importantly, a more thorough and comprehensive approach to the analysis as well as treatment of the problem and overall environment, greater success and influence by the consultant can result.

Kratochwill and Van Someren conceptualize the behavioral consultation model as a problem-solving one. There are four stages that are implemented within the traditional approach of conducting a thorough behavioral assessment, implementing the treatment procedures, and gathering information in formal interviews as a means of troubleshooting treatment intervention. The first stage involves the identification of the problem of the consultee (e.g., agency) and the agency's client. In this stage, the targeted behavior is identified through the problem identification interview (PII) and direct observations in naturalistic settings. Specific performance goals are delineated, and methods of social validation are planned for determining the overall appropriateness and effectiveness of the treatment procedures.

In the problem analysis stage (PAS), the client's problems are validated (i.e., how will continuing these behaviors be harmful to client, agency, community, etc.?). In addition, the consultant specifies and provides, in writing, a treatment program. This information is formulated and provided during the problem analysis interview (PAI).

The intervention stage is the third stage of this problem-solving model. The specific plan developed and discussed in the PAI is put into effect. The important aspects of this stage involve the consultant's monitoring the integrity of the treatment implemented by staff and the review and continuation of data collection on the targeted client behaviors.

The final stage is that of problem evaluation. In the context of the problem evaluation interview (PEI), the consultant must ask such questions as "Was treatment implemented properly during the intervention?", "Was this treatment effective?", and "If not, why not?" In addition, in the PEI, the consultant reviews data collection, overall program effectiveness, and methods of troubleshooting as well as planning and ensuring maintenance and generalization if the procedures have been effective. Consultation services could then be terminated at this point with follow-up planned at a later date, or other clients with problematic behaviors can be reviewed by the consultant.

Kratochwill and Van Someren emphasize that by specifying training procedures, consultation objectives can be developed. Specific curricula and training manuals for teaching behavioral consultants are needed, whereas a sophisticated knowledge of psychology and an emphasis on a broad-spectrum behavior therapy approach are prerequisites for a competently trained behavioral consultant. Didactic instruction that includes modeling, methods of direct observation of behavior, use of audio/videotapes, and role-played situations are necessary. Finally, not only is the cognitive knowledge of the consultative process necessary, but teaching behavioral consultants effective interview skills that (a) emphasize observable behavior; (b) refer to observation and the recording of behavior; and (c) analyze antecedent, consequent, sequential, and ecobehavioral components of the problem is vital.

Bernstein and Ziarnik (1984) have elaborated upon this issue of training considerations for behavior consultations. Specifically, these authors feel that behavior change agents need to be trained in how to select treatment outcomes. Their premise is that behavioral change agents must ask, "To what end is the planned behavior change?" In the past, there have been unsuccessful, arbitrary, or inappropriate methods of selecting targets of change. These include targets selected by consumers such as teachers, rehabilitation specialists, or parents. Also, the change agent typically selects targets most frequently chosen by the agency that the consultant services. The contracted agency is, then, reinforced for selecting a particular outcome and, therefore, frequently chooses those targets without consideration of other possible outcomes. Further, if the change agent selects targets on the basis of his or her own conditioning history and not on the needs of the clients, then the treatment outcome selected is based solely on individual personal values. Such selection of outcomes is unscientific. According to Bernstein and Ziarnik, the "values" and outcomes of behavioral intervention need to be the subjects of scientific study. Behavior change agents should be able to analyze possible consequences, both positive and negative, of selecting various outcomes. The process of outcome selection should be scientifically analyzed and placed in the context of the problem of the client. Although social validation is an important facet of outcome selection, these authors also strongly emphasize a complete contextual analysis that considers all behavioral systems operating on the client. This ecobehavioral systems analysis, as exemplified in Table 2, is a complement to the social validation component in outcome selection. By studying the behavior leading to outcome selection as well as studying methods of changing behavior itself, these authors feel that a more complete system of behavior consultation, analysis, intervention, and evaluation can be developed.

Linehan (1980) has proposed a three-dimensional model useful in conceptualizing the objectives for consultation training. Specific training should focus on teaching in each area so as to train highly effective consultants. The *cognitive* dimension involves the development of the consultant's knowledge of the theoretical and empirical literature in behavior modification. A knowledge base of the ethical and legal aspects of consultation and therapy as well as the ability of the consultant to organize and integrate information gained from written material is also a part of this cognitive area. The consultant must understand the assessment process, gather and analyze data, determine which conditions could influence the attainment of goals for the client, and recognize and recall factual knowledge obtained during interview consults pertaining to overall program development and evaluation. In the *overt behavior* dimension, the consultant should prepare behavioral material useful in the consultative process. In addition, the consultant should have in his or her behavior repertoire, procedural skills, interpersonal clinical skills, facilitative verbal behavioral skills, and self-development and self-management skills. In the *physiologic/affective* dimension, the third area, those affective skills that facilitate and support the entire consultative process are necessary. Linehan indicates that the relationship between the therapist and the client plays a vital role in the actual effectiveness of imposed treatment. Relationship enhancement and rapport building, discussed in Chapter 3, are vital in consultant settings as well.

Ziarnik and Bernstein (1984) and Bailey and Reiss (1984) have explored the issues of the traditional role of the consultant in staff training and in overall facility management. These authors condemn this traditional role and emphasize that how a consultant consults has implications for whether staff charged with carrying out the proven methods of behavior change will, in fact, do so.

Staff training in community-based human services agencies are usually provided by outside consultants paid by the agency. Although there may be good intentions, it is unrealistic, according to these authors, for agency improvement by the administration to be a major factor in obtaining a consultant. Rather, the subtle contingencies involving negative reinforcement may operate to maintain administrative behaviors. These contingencies (loss of federal and state funds, frequent staff dissatisfaction and turnover) prompt the administrator to make an avoidance response of hiring a consultant. By doing so, these consequences are avoided or minimized for a period of time not unlike Sidman's avoidance conditioning (1960). Therefore, hiring a consultant merely makes staff and other agency personnel "happy" without concern for whether real change has occurred in anyone's behavior. Other negative contingencies operating may be that, by hiring an off-site, out-of-geographic-area consultant, staff are impressed, or, at least, have someone else to blame for problems other than the administration. Furthermore, the consultant is a part of this functional analysis of consultant behavior. The consultant must examine his or her reinforcers, which are usually money and social attention, relative to the fact that consultant recommendations usually result in delayed changes or no changes in staff, client, or administration. The ethics of these consequences or lack of consequences are the consultant's responsibility.

Ziarnik and Bernstein (1984) question whether in-service training works. Presently, there are different measures used to demonstrate the effectiveness of staff training: (a) *subjective*—reports of the trainee; (b) *cognitive*—measure of the knowledge gained; (c) *behavioral*—skills acquired by the trainee; (d) *client behavior*—the effects of staff training on client skills; (e) *organizational*—the effects of training staff on overall agency structure; and (f) the *staff skills relative to client outcomes*—the maintenance and generalization of staff skills in the setting so that client behavior is improved. In order for training to be effective, the consultant should consider the outcome of all of these measures.

These methods of consultation services can be placed on a continuum of effectiveness. Table 3 describes the continuum discussed by Ziarnik and Bernstein. Toward the top of this continuum are services that are the least intrusive and least behaviorally costly, but least likely to result in active staff and client behavior change. Staff training strategies toward the bottom of the continuum are considered to be most intrusive and most costly with respect to behavioral output of all change agents, but also most likely to result in staff and client behavior change. Dissemination of information is merely the provision of written materials and lectures for staff to read and attend. Such written and verbal lecturing is highly ineffective, however. Training workshops away from the agency are usually not effective, either, especially if such workshops are attended by hundreds of people together. The case consultation approach is done on a client-by-client basis and is somewhat effective for developing staff skills, but only for the one client. When such consultation results in a written and formalized intervention program for the client that requires staff to follow specific steps, such consultation is a good vehicle for skill acquisition by staff. On-site staff training facilitates the development of behavioral skills *in vivo*, especially when the consultant demonstrates (models) the techniques, requires staff to rehearse the techniques, and provides staff with positive and corrective

TABLE 3
Staff Training Strategies: A Continuum

Effectiveness of services	Consultative strategies
Least instrusive Least behaviorally costly Least likely to result in active staff and client behavior change	1. Dissemination of written and verbally presented information 2. Training workshops away from the agency 3. Case consultation 4. Feedback to staff via written programs and program addenda
Most intrusive Most behaviorally costly Most likely to result in staff and client behavior change	5. On-site staff training 6. Organizational behavioral analysis 7. Total program evaluation

feedback. Such an approach increases the likelihood of maintenance and generalization of staff skills. An organizational behavior analysis by the consultant is one of the most intrusive methods. An agency can take what is learned from the on-site consultant and integrate the newly acquired procedures and skills into the ongoing function of the facility. Finally, a total program evaluation would seek to analyze the behavioral strengths and weaknesses of the facility, program, staff, administrative structure, and client population.

In light of this continuum of services, consultants must consider the ethics involved in providing these various consultative services. Human services organizations usually utilize the least costly, least intrusive, and often least effective methods because of budgetary considerations. Ziarnik and Bernstein contend that the behavioral consultant must develop a "bottom line" of what he or she ethically feels can be provided to a contracted agency. The consultant should consider the usual factors of poor program planning, unreasonable agency demands, the punishing rather than reinforcing environment typically characteristic of agencies to their clients, lack of clear program goals, expectations, and the ineffective use of incentives. Also, the nature of the organizational problems that contribute to the clients' difficulties is a major concern. Consultants should not promise more than they can deliver, avoid giving only a smattering of information, use workshop evaluation methods, and clearly indicate to the agency staff and administration what they are buying and what skills they are likely to come away with. Finally, consultants must conduct an honest appraisal of their own reinforcers and what they will get monetarily versus what long-term benefits will result for the agency from the services provided by the consultant.

Bailey and Reiss (1984) have addressed the problem of consultancy and its benefits to agencies. Although powerful behavioral procedures exist to relieve human suffering, these behavioral procedures, as used in institutions and community facilities, are not being applied on a daily basis by the direct care staff in the manner in which these technologies were intended. Although these therapeutic procedures reduce maladaptive behavior and ultimately provide a healthier and more stimulating environment for the client, most clients still sit idle while staff are congregating together and ignoring their responsibilities and the needs of the client. Further, staff waste time and falsify data just to meet federal regulations. According to these authors, the "Model T," or training model, then operates. Specifically, when staff are not behaving as they "should," send in the in-service consultants, which "should" get them to behave appropriately. Unfortunately, staff do not interact effectively with the clients and are not applying the sometimes formally written programs for their clients. There are several reasons for this lack of compliance by staff.

First, staff typically are hired on the basis of low pay. Thus, people who are hired on this basis have poor educational and work histories, and poor social/interpersonal skills. Few highly motivated and well-organized people would work for such normal wages. Thus, there is high turnover, many sick days taken, and an overall bad work history.

Second, pay and other contrived reinforcers are not related to the work requirement. There is no relation between staff performance and their reinforcers. Unfortunately, this is also true of other work settings. Staff receive no compensation or bonuses for accomplishments shown by clients as a result of their being trained.

Third, there is a lack of structure in many facilities. Programs are run after staff have to complete their custodial duties, and programs are often run by different staff in entirely different ways. When programs are written, they are usually in highly technical language that poorly educated staff do not understand. Staff are not usually given feedback about the qualitative features of their training. Staff may not utilize their voice inflection properly; they may cajole clients into behaving; and/or they may inadvertently deprive clients of all social reinforcement (no smiling, touching, patting, or hugging).

Last, there are no natural consequences to maintain staff performance even when they improve their clients' behaviors. A large percentage of clients in institutions are nonverbal and have extreme behavioral deficiencies and excesses. When change occurs, staff have no consequences for their own behavior that will maintain their consistency in the implementation of the effective procedures for the client. Then, the long history of a client's deficiencies and excesses, by contrast, is more powerful than the brief behavioral change imposed by the staff.

As a result of the failure of the training model to bridge the gap between effective procedures and their implementation, Bailey and Reiss have developed a *behavioral systems management* approach that is a comprehensive system of behavior change for community and institutional facilities. This approach is comprised of several components.

8.1.1. Appropriate and Functional Goals

Social validation is an important variable in this system. By teaching skills from which the client will actually benefit, staff are more likely to comply with training specifications. Efforts are made to review all clients' goals to determine if they are functional and will help them be more independent. In addition, staff time is at a premium so that the number of training goals per client per quarter or per year is kept at a reasonable and practical level. Also, direct teaching sessions with one trainer and one client are better than group training to achieve the functional goals.

8.1.2. Staff Management

Traditional approaches to staff management involve the departmental model in which there is an overall administrator who supervises department heads (e.g., workshop director, preacademics director, or self-care director) who, in turn, supervise direct care staff. Bailey and Reiss have discarded this approach in favor of programming via the *unit* concept. That is, when programming is implemented, monitored, and supervised at the *unit* level, specific areas of the facility are designated as units. With this *unit* concept, there is a greater probability that training will be carried out successfully. In the *unit* approach, programming in an area is scheduled at a precise time and publicly posted on a conspicuous wall of the unit. Programming then proceeds by scheduled times for training rather than at the whim of the trainer. Data are then posted in the unit, and frequent monitoring occurs with greater regularity by all direct and supervisory staff.

8.1.3. Data-Based Decision Making

Early behavior modifiers stressed objectivity through collection and posting an abundance of data day by day on the problem in question. Bailey and Reiss contend that more is not better. Rather, they suggest that data be collected daily, but plotted weekly. They also recommend that criterion lines, which are representative of the habilitation plan goals stated in the initial performance goals for the client, be placed on each client's graph. Then, by viewing the representative weekly data point in relation to the weekly trend and final criterion line, there is a greater chance for staff to understand the data and to see clearly the results of programming.

8.1.4. Quality Control

Accountability at all levels is a basic premise in this *behavior systems management* approach. Weekly client progress is reviewed on publicly posted graphs, which makes direct care staff accountable. The supervisor completes a checklist with the administrator that verifies that graphs have been checked and program deficiencies have been corrected. When staff indicate that a client has reached the performance goal set for him or her, that client is asked to demonstrate the newly acquired skill to an independent observer (i.e., program validation). The trainer is required to carry out a specified number of training sessions and a specified number of validations per month. Finally, the administrator fills out a checklist regularly that rates the quality of programming and, therefore, requires that the administrator stay in close and regular contact with programming implementation, monitoring, progress, and problems. This quality control extends to all facets of training, including skills acquisition programs and maladaptive behavior reduction programs.

Bailey and Reiss have implemented this consultation and facility training model in 14 facilities in the southeastern United States and have found that such behavioral systems management is highly effective. Staff respond well to the structure, monitoring, and feedback. This innovative approach appears highly promising in bridging the gap between technology and staff implementation. Through such a system, consistent rather than spurious influence on the clients' behavior is more likely.

8.2. BEHAVIOR CONSULTATION SETTINGS

There are a variety of applied settings in which a behavioral consultation approach has been used. Research and application has appeared in the behavioral literature in such settings as continuing education workshops (Keuhnel & Flanagan, 1984), geriatric facilities (MacDonald, 1983), and business, industry, and government (Brown & Presbie, 1978). Continuing education in the field of behavior modification and therapy has been increasingly recognized as essential. The expanding behavioral technology, the need for proof of continuing competence professionally, peer review requirements for professionals, risks of malpractice, and other obvious clinical and financial gains for expanding and improving a clinician's therapeutic repertoire demand continuing education.

Keuhnel and Flanagan (1984) have indicated that continuing education workshops in behavior therapy and modification must focus on training skill building. These authors have given a set of guidelines for conducting effective workshops. Participants in such workshops should be given reading assignments. As preparation, workshop goals need to be specified clearly, and assignments need to be given at a regular rate. Well-run workshop programs stress an active and directive teaching model—a model that requires setting process objectives, usually brief didactic instructions, modeling, behavioral rehearsal with performance feedback, generalization and maintenance of skills, and *in vivo* training with real clients.

Kuehnel and Flanagan suggest that the consultant providing in-service training needs to specify the workshop objectives from an attitudinal, behavioral, and cognitive perspective. These authors ask attitudinally, "How will trainees' attitudes change?"; behaviorally, "What kind of new skills or competencies will be learned?"; and cognitively, "What knowledge will the trainess acquire?" In these dimensions, objectives need to be limited and realistic.

To prepare for the workshop, these authors recommend prompting key people as to what services and arrangements must be provided for the consultant. On-site workshops should require that the contracted administrator be present, the format and required readings for the workshop be specified ahead of time, and that the consultant arrive early to inspect the room in which the workshop is to be given. Furthermore, the consultant should check the audio/visual equipment to be used, arrange the seating, and organize the handouts. At all times, the behavior consultant should be flexible if some of these arrangements go wrong. Effectiveness in training programs is somewhat a function of minimizing factors that may interfere with staff learning.

Conducting the workshop is based on the active teaching model. Didactic information is covered briefly, and examples are used to illustrate main points. Role playing and modeling should be arranged and specified clearly. The specific performance to be noted in the modeled vignette is to be pinpointed, and just enough role playing is done to illustrate the skill. The participants are then required to discuss the vignette. Checklists should be used for the participants to rate whether the behaviors observed met the criteria for quality training. Rehearsal by the participants should then follow. Rehearsal scenes should be brief, and multiple practice and feedback should be done. The guiding rule for the workshop participants is that *"perfect* practice makes perfect." Of course, positive feedback should be given, and all negative feedback should be avoided, giving instead, alternative suggestions.

Kuehnel and Flanagan also discuss such special problems in training as participant hesitance to role-play and to rehearse questions or barbs for the consultant, and the consultant's sensitivity to the nonverbal cues of the participants so as to adjust the flow and style of the presentation. Finally, evaluation of training involves what future needs for training exist (i.e., a needs assessment), an evaluation of the knowledge or skills acquired, the degree of training satisfaction, the level to which the skills learned will be utilized, and the clinical outcomes for the clients.

MacDonald (1983) has explored the problems and benefits of the behavioral consultant in geriatric settings. This author contends that there will be an increasing demand for psychological consultative services with geriatric clients. However, consulting in such settings is very difficult, but challenging for several reasons. First, the staff and administrative expectations of the consultant are often unrealistic. Second, nursing homes are generally medical facilities so that staff may feel some ambivalence about the appropriateness of psychological services. Third, staff falsely believe that the elderly are too old to change and have the right to be left alone. Fourth, like other residential facilities, staff are highly transient, and programs would be run inconsistently or not at all. Fifth, most nursing homes are businesses for profit and, therefore, operate on a tight budget with low overhead. Finally, consultation in geriatric settings is challenging because there is only a small body of behavioral research in the literature.

There are several important criteria to be met for successful geriatric consultation. Enthusiastic administrative support, staff motivation, and acceptance by the adult children of the geriatric patient that behavioral services are needed are such prerequisites. A collaborative relationship with the facility medical staff is also necessary due to all the medical problems faced by the elderly, the need for psychotropic and other forms of medication, and tracking the client's behavioral and physical limitations. A consultant should have some expertise with general geriatric psychology, and there should be regular staff meetings for the sole purpose of improving mental health care.

MacDonald suggests that, in staff meetings, the behavioral consultant provide a functional analysis of each client's difficulties. In these meetings, behavior programs are developed and evaluated while staff training on the principles of behavior modification is regularly scheduled. As in other facilities, the focus must be on environmental antecedents, the behavior itself, and its consequences. With the elderly, however, the consultant should be aware of the increasing importance of environmental "props" and instructional prompts. Specifically, the elderly may function better with some behavioral prosthetics (e.g., large-type reading books, improved lighting). Thus, by arranging the environment to be more conducive to the development of appropriate social behavior, there is greater benefit to the elderly client population.

Brown and Presbie (1978) were two of the first individuals to apply principles of behavior modification to business, industry, and government. In their resource guide, these authors provide the consultant with a general format for analyzing employee and supervisor behavior with respect to how they react, their reinforcers, and their punishers. Further, an A(ntecedent)-B(ehavior)-C(onsequence) analysis is provided with a prototype discussion of the ecobehavioral systems operating with business, industry, and government. Through traditional behavioral methods of modeling, prompting, shaping, and reinforcing behavior in the workplace, worker efficiency and overall productivity can increase. The behavioral consultant in big business, industry, and government can provide functional analyses of employee management relations and conduct workshops in leadership training, assertiveness training, and stress management.

John Krampfl is a clinical psychologist turned corporate consultant whose primary responsibility is to do organizational behavioral management (OBM) for large corporations across the country. Krampfl (1984) recently conducted a workshop in organizational behavior and management in which he outlined the considerations and procedures for establishing an organizational behavioral practice.

According to Krampfl, business views psychology as expendable. Therefore, one has to learn marketing and the specific business tactics of organizational management. For psychologists, such marketing involves concept selling rather than product selling, and this form of marketing is a most difficult one to accomplish. Concept selling can be such a nebulous area that business tends to shy away from anything other than issues of dollars and cents. Krampfl advocates finding the "right" person to talk to about OBM services. Talking to the chief executive officer (CEO) or any of the upper crust line managers can begin to make the right contacts that could lead to contracted services to the business.

Selling psychological services to organizations requires the psychologist to be thick-skinned and prepared in the business sense. One has to be prepared to state specifically what will be done, how the company can benefit, and specify these benefits in terms of profit, lowered overhead, and increased worker productivity. If the benefits presented to the company are the least bit theoretical or vague, the business environment will not contract for such services. Rather, the CEOs of business are interested in what such services will do for his employees, how the company stands to benefit financially, how much is it going to cost, what is involved, and how much it will take to get started.

Within his OBM practice, Krampfl and his associates provide several services. First, organizational audits and analyses are done. Within these analyses, questions such as "Who is running the busines?", "What is its structure?", and "What are the problems?" are addressed. Second, the development and training portion of Krampfl's practice involves making up workshop materials, training manuals, and other curricula needed for continued staff training. In the third area, individual employee appraisals of the functions are needed by the corporation with respect to a particular employee's strengths and weaknesses. Krampfl attempts to discuss how the employee's strengths and weaknesses influence the company, how the company may benefit from hiring the employee, and whether the employee fits the need of the company. The fourth service is described as outplacement of displaced executives. In this area, Krampfl works with middle-level and senior-level executives who make $80K and up, who, because of company shake-ups, have been fired. Krampfl attempts to help them deal with what is happening as a result of their severence, look for ways of "retreading" or retraining the executives, identify and treat signs of employee depression and family depression, and help the executives look realistically at their strengths and weaknesses toward alternative placement. As an aside, alcoholism and drug addiction are major areas of concern for top-level management for their employees as well as for themselves.

When conducting the search for alternative placement, the organizational behavior management consultant must be aware of the "goodness-of-fit" approach. That is, the consultant must be aware of the two cultures, that from which the executive looking for the job has come and that of the company who is seeking the services of the severed executive. Matching these two cultures involves, for one, the way in which decisions are made in the company from which the executive was severed and the decision-making process in the company to which the executive is applying. Essentially, one has got to know the "culture" of each company for a successful search service to corporations. As behaviorists, it is useful to analyze the behavior that is occurring—and under what conditions—in these separate environments.

In the organizational work that is done, Krampfl gets started by reading in all the trade magazines about the hot issues and the sources of tension for each industry with whom the consultant plans to work. Such foreplanning prohibits the company from thinking that the consultant/psychologist knows little about the organization or business. Once this preparation is done, Krampfl can then begin the organizational services that his company provides. *Training and development* comprise about 30% of Krampfl's responsibilities. These services involve workshops and seminars that usually are only seen as being perks of employment rather than as an effective tool of employee training. *Materials development* involves the development of written and audiovisual material for the education of the employees in the company. Because one criticism of psychologists is that they know little about the business, knowing all about the environment in which people are having difficulties, department by department, not only gathers helpful information but allows for on-site education through the survey and compilation of information about the company in a book or manual. *Success planning* involves looking at what the company is going to need in several years (which is an actuarial statement) whereas training and development prepare people to move into these programs. The task of the corporate psychologist is to design training programs that will accomplish these tasks. *Productivity evaluations* are important to companies because they are always interested in getting more results for less dollars. The corporate structure sometimes believes that in order for the company to do more financially, the laborers must work harder. However, this is a fallacy. Another consideration should be: What is the effective utilization of first-line supervisors with labor—rather than merely that labor has to produce more.

There are a variety of pointers that Krampfl cites as a means of assisting beginners of corporate consultancy.

1. One must develop a business language repertoire. That is, businesses want to write and to communicate in their own language. When talking with business people, the psychologist should avoid all clinical and behavioral terms. Krampfl advises to speak the business lingo.

2. One must develop quick study skills. Specifically, one has to find out quickly what is critical to the company as well as what is to be sold to the company that will be of benefit.

3. The consultant must think in client's terms, not in psychological terms.

4. Make services brief but effective. Essentially, narrow the time of providing the services, and more referrals will follow. Additional services will also come from satisfied clients.

5. Cold calling when beginning consultancy is brutal and leads to little except frustration. In order to get business, cold calls may be used though they are the least effective. Regardless of the methods chosen, one must set a goal to talk to x number of people about the OBM business each day.

6. One has to be ready to confront the challenging of upper crust employees inside the company who may feel "threatened." Be able to respond strongly to their questions and challenges.

7. When selling stress, the benefits of services are in terms of expense reduction and cost control to the company.

8. There are three types of business that will be generated: renewal business, expansion of existing client work, and new business.

9. Getting started and established in the corporate psychology business is difficult. One should start with at least 12 to 15% of one's monthly salary.

10. The fees charged should be based on out-of-pocket expenses in addition to consultant services.

11. Travel may be a necessary evil to a booming organizational management company. Tailor the method of incurring travel expenses after the big corporations' presidents' methods (e.g., travel coach class or in other inexpensive ways). Keeping costs down is good public relations.

12. One's office does not have to be a showplace to begin with. Renting an extra office from an existing consulting firm may be the least costly. However, one has to consider the effects of having a broken-down car, a bad office location, or looking too hungrily for work.

13. It is a poor business strategy to avoid putting oneself out as being able to do everything, to be all things to all people. Do not tell corporate executives that as a consultant you can solve everything. Therefore, Krampfl advises to determine the nature of the practice in which one will engage and the kinds of activities and services to be performed. Define and limit the areas of work: appraisals, organizational audits, management training and development, or outplacement.

14. For referrals and for getting started, make a list of everyone known in big corporate business. Using a personal/social approach to find out who knows whom and whether they are in a position to help directly with acquiring consultancy contracts is advised.

15. Business referrals should be classified according to the following: (a) *names*—of corporate officers in various companies; (b) *contacts*—someone who could introduce you to someone; (c) *leads*—are anyone that has potential business; (d) *qualified leads*—you know they would be willing to talk to you; (e) *potential clients*—people with whom a great deal of time is spent as they are worth hanging on to, staying in touch with, and maintaining contact with; and (f) *clients*—people whom you sign as consultees.

16. When finalizing contracts, Krampfl cautions to be careful not to underestimate the competition as "It ain't over 'til it's over!" Tenacity is important to maintaining clients.

17. Do not expect to close a deal after the first or second contact. The objective is to have a second meeting, that's all!

18. Referrals can be gotten from corporate people who have received quality individual therapeutic services.

19. Pick out a key industry and know it. Read its trade magazines, go to its local meetings and conventions, go to the library and read any and all other information on the corporation.

20. Sometimes, the beginning consultant can give the company something for nothing. You can say that you want to learn about the company at no expense to it. In return, the next time the company wants a psychological appraisal, it is more likely that this seed principle will generate a return of referrals. In this way, you can get into the company and provide services.

21. In establishing one's fees, it has to be kept in mind that the lower the set fee, the greater will be the likelihood that work will be done with lower echelon people.

22. The consultant can bill by the task, such as by the appraisal, by time, which is usually $500 to $1500 per day, or on contract for some mutually agreed upon figure, time, and conditions.

23. When dealing with heads of corporations, do what upper crust management people do in the company to set an example of frugality.

24. Wear the clothes to fit the business: for manufacturing businesses, wear a sport coat; for insurance or brokerage business, wear a "power" suit, or a gray or black pinstripe suit with wing tip shoes.

25. It is important to do networking. Join the Chamber of Commerce, get on civic boards, and belong to fitness and country clubs where possible contacts and contracts can be obtained and finalized.

Krampfl outlines the beginning process of interviewing a corporate person to obtain consultant contracts. There are several very important things to consider when having the first interview with a potential client. To begin with, Krampfl suggests engaging in brief idle conservation, then demonstrate to the contact person assertiveness by taking control of the situation with such quotes as "There are several things I'd like to accomplish in this visit today," or "Tell me about your business from the inside, what are its problems, and what are your objectives?" Next, spend 3 to 4 minutes informing the potential client of your OBM business.

At the end of the first meeting, Krampfl suggests that the consultant say "I know your time is valuable, but you've told me things that are problems in your company that I think our company can help." Lay out the client company's problems and say "I'd like to come back and talk about these problems and their possibilities in the next visit." Then an appointment can be made at that time for the second meeting with the company contact person.

Before the second meeting, it is important to confirm the appointment because it is a nice touch for building rapport and confidence. Second, it is important to recap the discussion during the first session. Be sure that during this second meeting the individual with whom you are talking is in a position to make a decision. If not, find out who is the next level manager to whom you could speak. Finally, several such meetings may need to occur before a contract is signed.

Other settings in which the behavioral consultant can work are:

1. *Employee assistance programs*—The behavior consultant is in a unique position to provide short-term but effective consultation to industries and their employees on a variety of issues such as child rearing, marital satisfaction, and stress management.

2. *Public and private schools*—In these settings, the behavioral consultant can conduct on-site behavioral evaluations of entire classes or of a problem student. In some public schools, funds are available to provide consultative services to teachers, principals, and guidance counselors for the problems of a particular student.

3. *Hospital staff consultation*—As part of an allied professions team, the behavioral consultant can provide assistance to psychiatric and medical hospitals to establish token economies, develop treatment programs for problem adults and children, and develop medication compliance programs.

4. *Private and public day care and nursery programs*—The behavior problems of children in day care centers are many. A behavioral consultant may be useful to the staff of these centers by providing training and written recommendations that can alter the problems referred.

5. *State and private employment agencies*—Research in the field of job finding (Azrin, Flores, & Kaplan, 1975) has shown that there are important steps one must take in finding employment. By consulting with these agencies, staff can learn these methods and teach their clients how best to locate employment.

6. *Foster parent and adoptive parent training*—Parents who maintain foster homes or who are about to adopt children may need to know the most effective methods of child rearing. As a consultant to these agencies, one can teach parents directly or provide assistance to the agency staff to provide a positive home environment for these children.

7. *Miscellaneous residential facilities*—With the proliferation of behavioral techniques has come their implementation in a variety of settings. Residential facilities for the retarded, halfway houses, substance abuse facilities, and dependent boys' and girls' "ranches" often seek to implement token economies or elaborate contracting for improvements in behavior. The behavioral consultant could help structure such complex systems in these facilities.

9

Business Concerns for the Behavior Therapist

The business and services of independently practicing psychologists is a growing phenomenon. Stapp and Fulcher (1983) and VandenBos and Stapp (1983) have surveyed psychologists to determine the distribution of their employment activities. Stapp and Fulcher's (1983) findings show that the percentage of psychologists who indicated that their primary employment was independent practice has increased from 12.2% in 1976 to 14.7% in 1978, and to 15.8% in 1982. In addition, 54% of those surveyed who were doctoral-level psychologists not in private practice indicated that they were in private practice on a part-time basis.

VandenBos and Stapp's (1983) article reviewed the distribution and nature of the services provided. Organized care settings (hospitals, clinics) had the highest proportion of psychologists (33%) followed by independent practice (23%). However, independent practice was the most frequently cited primary care setting. Psychologists spent an average of 30 to 37 hours in clinical contact with clients, and they tended to see a wide variety of clinically significant problems. These authors' findings provide evidence for this practitioner's view that the clinician needs to be a generalist in serving the referred clients. Additional findings of these authors are that most health service providers deliver services across a range of ages. However, one-third of the psychologists polled indicated that they did not provide services to clients 11 years or younger, and another one third of the psychologists indicated that they did not serve clients 65 years or older. In fact, the most frequently served population of clients was between the ages of 18 and 39 years. Based on the statistics gathered by these authors, they project that approximately 34 million clinical visits are delivered each year. With their mean of 14 visits per client, it is estimated that approximately 2.4 million individuals are served annually by independently practicing psychologists. Based on these statistics, psychological treatment constitutes an area of much-needed health care services.

In a 1982 issue of *Psychotherapy Finances*, the research on therapy and overall health cost was reviewed. The findings suggested that psychological intervention does cut overall medical costs from a reduction of 5% for outpatient physician visits to a reduction of 85% for hospital stays. The median reduction of medical costs following psychological intervention was 20%. These data are further evidence for the continued need for such services.

With the ever-increasing demand for psychological services, the private practice of psychology has become a highly desirable business and profession in which to engage. However, psychologists must be concerned with the financial aspects of clinical practice. Without consideration of office location, support services, marketing, fees, collections, and the size of one's accounts receivable as well as the growing monster of overhead expenses, one's private practice may be short-lived.

There is little research, however, in the behavioral literature on these business issues for the behavior therapist. One article by Drash and Bostow (1981) does address some business concerns for the behavior therapist. These authors offer a comparison of traditional psychotherapy and behavior therapy in the public marketplace. Drash and Bostow conclude that the very factors that make behavior therapy attractive for practitioners, such as its pragmatic approach, efficiency, empirically validated procedures, and rapid client progress may have a negative financial impact because the independent practitioner's livelihood is a function of the number of hours of actual therapy conducted each week. The more efficient the therapy, the more clients are needed to fill the therapist's contact hours each week. Solutions proposed by these authors involve recommendations similar to those proposed in this book, such as developing a broad-based referral source, conducting programs stressing a skills package (parenting, assertiveness training, social skills, job finding, stress management), conducting behavioral group therapy, helping legislate increased insurance coverage for behavior therapeutic services, and, as discussed later in this chapter, becoming involved in prepaid health plans such as health maintenance organizations (HMOs), employee assistance programs (EAPs), and preferred provider organizations (PPOs).

9.1. THE DECISION TO ENTER PRIVATE PRACTICE

Before entering private practice, before spending the first dollar in announcements or business cards, the potential behavioral practitioner would be wise to consider the risks and benefits of private practice (Browning, 1982; Pressman, 1979; Small Business Administration, 1977).

The following is a list of questions that address the business issues of beginning a private practice. From this list, the potential practitioner can evaluate his or her readiness for private enterprise.

1. Am I licensed to provide mental health services?
2. Do I have the skills necessary to render the mental health/ behavioral services to the wide variety of clinical problems referred to me?
3. Do I have professional liability insurance to cover my services to my clients?
4. Am I prepared to devote the long hours needed in marketing my services, in my clinical contact hours, and in report writing and behavior program development?
5. Will my physical health permit such intensive work?
6. Can I organize my time and work, as well as supervise others' schedules efficiently?
7. Do I have effective social skills, decision-making skills, and public relations/successful interpersonal skills?
8. Do I have the skills to persist in clinically providing assistance to others, despite client noncompliance or treatment failure?
9. Do I have the skills to administrate all of the business aspects of my practice while maintaining a high professional level of services to my clients?
10. Am I willing to assume substantial overhead costs, the probable fluctuations of income, and seasonal changes in the flow of client referrals?
11. Am I willing to practice psychology in a fairly isolated environment from my colleagues unlike a university, hospital, or clinic environment?

If the majority of these questions are answered "yes," or by their suggestion have prompted the clinician to obtain the skills and information necessary for beginning private practice, one can then begin to consider the various business concerns for entry into private practice. This information applies to the general private practice community but is equally applicable to the behavioral clinician as well (Browning, 1982; Pressman, 1979).

9.2. OFFICE LOCATION AND FURNISHINGS, LAYOUT, AND HOURS

The location and appearance of the office one selects is an important variable in the nature and flow of referrals one receives. When beginning a practice, the clinician is concerned about holding down costs and may begin practice out of the home. Despite the low cost of engaging in practice from one's home, referrals may be few, and the therapeutic environment may not be professional enough or maintain the needed confidentiality to support such a practice. It is usually better to rent office space, even on a part-time basis to begin with, than to practice out of the home.

The flow of referrals in a newly opened practice is often minimal. Therefore, one approach to entering private practice is to maintain a full-time position (in a clinic, hospital, school, or university setting) and gradually increase the time spent after the workday is over seeing clients in the evenings and on weekends. Thus, renting space or an office from another psychologist, physician, attorney, or businessman on a part-time basis may have maximum advantages. Rental costs are minimal, furnishings and utilities are provided, and the practice is housed in a more professional setting. Also, selecting an office near physicians' offices or hospitals and on a major or well-traveled road with a sign seen by passersby can increase the flow of referrals to the practice. If the part-time practice begins to prosper, the small office space being used will no longer be suitable. The same considerations referred to previously should be taken when seeking a more full-time setting.

After securing more permanent office space, the purchase of furnishings and the arrangement of the office is the next step. Costs must always be kept in mind so as to avoid a larger than tolerable overhead expense. As a practice grows, so does the overhead; so, keeping costs low in the beginning will keep them relatively low as the practice grows. In the larger cities, there are discount office supply companies that sell new and used furniture (desks, chairs, bookcases, filing cabinets, magazine racks, etc.) at a substantial discount. Do not be hesitant to negotiate the asking price of these furnishings as the markup on furniture is usually 50 to 100% of the cost of the merchandise to the wholesaler. Also, when selecting the furnishings, look for what is adequate rather than "showy" or expensive looking. Clients will tolerate used furniture as long as the clinician provides a good service. In short, to paraphrase, "the proof is in the pudding, not in the padding."

The arrangement of the office is important for business as well as for professional reasons. Professionally, the placement of the therapy room(s) as far away from the reception or waiting room as possible affords the greatest amount of confidentiality for the client. Regardless of how soundproof the office is, there is no replacement for distance between office and reception room as a means of maintaining the privacy ethically due your client.

From a business standpoint, the secretary's desk should be near the front entrance of the office. This placement provides the client with a welcoming point, alerts the secretary to the fact that the next client has arrived, and allows the secretary to discuss insurance with the client; it is also the best place for the client to stop after the appointment to schedule the next appointment and to pay the fee for the session. Current practice is that fees are paid when services are rendered.

The office hours selected to see clients will, of course, vary if the clinician is in part- or full-time practice. In part-time practice, hours may be in evenings from 5 or 6 o'clock to 9 o'clock and on Saturdays from 8 A.M. to noon. As the clinician moves more toward a full-time practice, he or she may wish to drop the weekend and part of the evening hours during the week. For the beginning full-time clinician, maintaining hours highly convenient for clients in the evening or weekends can avert scheduling problems around work or school for the client and provide another reason for the client to seek therapy from the beginning clinician who has more flexible hours.

9.3. SUPPORT SERVICES

There are a variety of support services one may need to enlist as aids in establishing and maintaining the practice. Secretarial services are obviously a needed assistance in conducting one's practice. However, the beginning clinician may utilize a secretarial service on a fee-for-service basis while maintaining an answering service to take calls from new clients, current clients, or associated professionals. As the practice grows, the clinician may wish to hire a part-time, then later a full-time, secretary to handle collection of fees, insurance, claims, filing, making appointments, and typing. Maintaining an answering service in addition to having a full-time secretary is important in the event of after-hours emergencies or when the secretary has left the office and the clinician is with a client in session.

Assistance from accountants, bookkeepers, attorneys, and collection agencies may also be needed. Consultation with an attorney may help the beginning practitioner to form a proprietorship, a professional association, or other corporation as well as to serve as a means of assistance in the event a client is very delinquent in the payment of fees. The accountant and bookkeeper can help by advising the clinician as to the best methods of setting up a monitoring system of income and expenses and in keeping watch on cash flow on a week-to-week or month-to-month basis. Finally, the collection agency may be one way of collecting fees if the clinician or his or her agent has given up on calling the client with no success in collecting accumulated back fees.

9.4. OTHER INITIAL AND ONGOING EXPENSES

There are a variety of incidental but regular expenses incurred by the clinician at the onset and in the maintenance of the practice. Professional announcements, business cards, stationery and clinical forms need to be printed, a bookkeeping system such as a ledger card/pegboard system is needed, a filing system and a regular and ongoing supply of office materials (pens, pencils, clips, typewriter ribbons, stamps, files, and folders) have to be maintained. Business equipment for the clinician should include a typewriter, dictation or transcribing equipment, a copy machine, and at least one phone line. It is wise to get prices or bids from several suppliers on a regular basis in order to keep a constant watch on excessive overhead expenditures. Table 4 lists the projected start up "one time" costs of the private practitioner (Kissel, 1983). This form allows the beginning clinician to estimate the amount of monies needed to finance a new practice. Table 5 is a listing of estimated fixed and variable monthly expenses that a clinician incurs (draw, taxes, office expenses, rent, insurances, etc.) and also allows for expense projections. These constitute most of the ongoing costs incurred by the clinician on a month-to-month basis.

9.5. FEES: SETTING, COLLECTIONS, AND PROJECTIONS

In the 1983 VandenBos and Stapp survey, psychologists who are health service providers reported their fees charged and methods of collection. Information gained from this survey indicated that the range

TABLE 4
Private Practice Start-Up "One-Time" Costs

Item	Estimated Cost
Rental security deposit	$____
Start-up professional supplies	____
Office furniture (including phone, answering device, typewriters, computers, chairs, etc.)	____
Office supplies and expenditures	____
Signs for door and building	____
Expenses for business cards, announcements, open house professional gathering	____
Telephone installation	____
Legal and accounting start-up costs	____
Cash for at least 6 months projected "salary" (because there is often a delay in providing services and receiving initial payments of billings)	____
Total	$____

From *Private Practice for the Mental Health Clinician* (p. 57) by S. Kissel, 1983, Rockville, MD: Aspen Systems. Copyright 1983 by Aspen Systems. Adapted by permission.

of hourly fees charged varied from $50 to $60 per hour but usually was not lower than $30 per hour. Thus, the median fee charged for the therapy hour (45 to 60 minutes) is $55 per hour. Third-party payment represented 37 to 46% of fees collected with an equal percentage of fees collected from clients followed by hospitals, courts, and human service agencies for the remainder. Approximately 75% of psychologists surveyed also reported that they based their fees on the ability of the client to pay.

In a more recent survey by *Psychotherapy Finances* (1984), individual and group fees for psychotherapy were polled. The median fee currently stands at $60 per individual therapy hour. The median fee for group therapy was $30 per hour. The length of individual sessions averages 50 minutes, whereas group therapy lasts 90 minutes. In addition to the information supplied by the VandenBos and Stapp study and *Psychotherapy Finances,* the beginning clinician might benefit by surveying the other psychologists' charges in the community in which he or she is to practice so as to be "in line" with the current fees in that geographic area. Each clinician needs to determine whether to charge at the high or low end of that local range of fees. The decision to set fees at the low end of that scale may be based on the fact that the clinician is just beginning practice and that clients sometimes survey the local professionals' fees to determine what they can pay and to whom they will go.

TABLE 5
Estimated Fixed and Variable Monthly Expenses of Private Practice

Item	Estimated Expenses
Monthly "draw" of practitioner	$_____
Social Security taxes for employees	_____
Clerical and other professional wages	_____
State and federal taxes	_____
Unemployment insurance	_____
Office rent or mortgage payment	_____
Office cleaning and maintenance	_____
Office supplies (pens, paper, stationery, typewritter ribbons, photocopying, etc.)	_____
Professional supplies (tests, test protocols, reinforcers)	_____
Professional memberships, books and journals	_____
Continuing education and convention expenses	_____
Postage	_____
Telephone	_____
Utilities	_____
Travel expenses	_____
Professional liability insurance	_____
Medical insurance	_____
Income protection insurance	_____
Comprehensive fire, theft, office liability insurance	_____
Life insurance	_____
Professional services (legal and accounting)	_____
Pension payments (IRA and Keogh)	_____
Depreciation on furniture and office equipment	_____
Miscellaneous (gifts, business lunches, charity, allowance for uncollectable bills, etc.)	_____
Total	$_____

From *Private Practice for the Mental Health Clinician*, (p. 57) by S. Kissel, 1983, Rockville, MD: Aspen Systems. Copyright 1983 by Aspen Systems. Adapted by permission.

The collection of fees is the mainstay of the practice. Without a good cash flow the clinician can only feel comfort in having large receivables. Unfortunately, having this large receivable amount does not pay the bills. Prompt payment and good collections are, therefore, mandatory for the maintenance of the practice.

Fortunately for the clinician, the trend in private health services today is that usual and customary fees are paid at the time services are rendered or soon thereafter. *Psychotherapy Finances* reports that approximately 98% of psychologists polled said their fees were collected within 120 days. Also of note is the fact that 26% of those polled indicate that fees are collected immediately after the session. Posting a sign to this effect in the waiting room is a good method of alerting clients to this policy, but it is no substitute for an assertive request by the secretary for fees to be paid as the client stops at the front desk to make the next appointment.

Insurance reimbursement is playing a greater role in the payment of psychologists' fees. *Psychotherapy Finances* (1984) reports that more than half of psychologists polled indicate that insurance reimbursement accounts for at least 40% or more of their receivables. Most of this reimbursement comes from private insurance companies and Blue Shield with some from CHAMPUS.

Depending on the amount of time the clinician spends in face-to-face contact with the client, a clinician's gross and net income can be very attractive. Drash and Bostow (1981) presented a paper at the Florida Association of Behavior Analysis in which they described the survival potential of the behavior therapist in independent practice. As part of their discussion, they analyzed the number of cases required to produce various gross income amounts, different gross income levels based on the fees charged per session, and net income after overhead expenses were subtracted. Table 6 indicates the number of cases needed for specific gross income levels. The clinician can estimate gross annual income based on how many clients he or she has, how many total hours are

TABLE 6
Number of Cases Required to Produce Specified Gross Annual Income Level[a]

Number of sessions/case	Number of cases ($60/session)							
50	4	6	10	20	30	40	60	80
25	8	12	20	40	60	80	120	160
20	10	15	25	50	75	100	150	200
15	12	20	33	67	100	133	200	267
10	20	30	50	100	150	200	300	400
5	40	60	100	200	300	400	600	800
Gross income	$12,000	$18,000	$30,000	$60,000	$90,000	$120,000[b]	$180,000	$240,000

Note. Adapted by permission from P. Drash and D Bostow, *How to Survive in the Marketplace as a Behavior Therapist or Are We Too Good for Our Own Good?* Paper presented at the 1981 convention of the Florida Association for Behavior Analysis.
[a]Some gross annual income figures are approximations based on the number of cases seen, the number of sessions per case, and the hourly fee charged.
[b]Maximum possible for one individual based on 40 hours/week, face to face contacts.

spent with the client, and on the hourly fee. Using an average hourly fee of $60 per hour (*Psychotherapy Finances,* 1984) the number of cases possible for one therapist (allowing a total of 40 hours/week contact with his clients) varies from a low of 40 cases of five sessions each, which results in a gross annual income of $12,000, to a high of 400 cases at 5 sessions each, resulting in a gross annual income (before expenses) of $120,000. Varying income levels between these two figures depend on having more cases and more sessions per case. Higher income levels above $120,000 per year are based on whether additional clinical personnel also conduct therapy in the office.

Table 7 represents the projections of gross annual income based on the number of face-to-face client hours at various hourly fees charged, which range from $30 per hour to $70 per hour. If, for example, a clinician works 50 weeks per year at 40 hours of face-to-face client contact, this would result in a gross annual income of $140,000 at $70 per hour, or $60,000 if the clinician charges $30 per hour. If the practice is part-time and client contact hours are 10 per week, the clinician would earn $35,000 at $70 per hour and $15,000 at $30 per hour.

Table 8 describes the net income after overhead expenses have been deducted. Drash and Bostow have computed their figures based on an overhead at a 40% level, whereas a 50% level may be more realistic (Jaffe, Shainbrown, & Grenadier, personal communication, 1984). This modification is reflected in Table 8. After expenses, a clinician can earn, annually, as much as $70,000 at an hourly charge of $70 per hour for 40 hours of contact time. Conversely, the therapist can earn as little as $12,000 for 10 hours of contact time at $30 per hour. Of course, taxes on this income would reduce these net amounts. Consultation with an accountant is necessary to familiarize the therapist with the myriad of

TABLE 7
Gross Annual Income: Based on Number of Face-to-Face Client Hours

Client hours/year	Gross annual income					
	Fee/hour					
	$70	$60	$50	$40	$35	$30
2,000	140,000	120,000	100,000	80,000	70,000	60,000
1,150	105,000	90,000	75,000	60,000	52,500	45,000
1,000	70,000	60,000	50,000	40,000	35,000	30,000
500	35,000	30,000	25,000	20,000	17,500	15,000

Note. Adapted by permission from P. Drash and D. Bostow, *How to Survive in the Marketplace as a Behavior Therapist or Are We Too Good for Our Own Good?* Paper presented at the 1981 convention of the Florida Association for Behavior Analysis.

TABLE 8
Net Income (Gross Income Less 50% Overhead)[a]

Client[b] hours/week	Net annual income				
	Fee/hour				
	$70	$60	$50	$40	$30
40	70,000	60,000	50,000	40,000	30,000
30	52,500	45,000	37,500	30,000	22,500
20	35,000	30,000	25,000	20,000	15,000
10	17,500	15,000	12,500	10,000	7,500

Note. Adapted by permission from P. Drash and D. Bostow, *How to Survive in the Marketplace as a Behavior Therapist or Are We Too Good for Our Own Good?* Paper presented at the 1981 convention of the Florida Association for Behavior Analysis.
[a]Income figures based on 50 weeks per year.
[b]Additional time needed for report writing, agency contacts, etc.

taxes (e.g., self-employment tax, social security tax, federal, state and local income tax, and personal property tax) he or she has to pay. In summary, income levels vary according to whether the clinician practices on a part-time or full-time basis, and on how productive the full-time clinician may be. These figures suggest that the full-time clinician can, at least, maintain a comfortable living financially.

9.6. MARKETING PROFESSIONAL SERVICES

Turkington (1984) has addressed the issue of the marketing responsibilities of the psychologist as a clinician and as a consultant. He indicates that psychologists must learn to market themselves effectively if they are to survive and prosper in the changing health care environment. Further, the psychologist must have a marketing plan to be successful, and marketing research is a vital part of a successful practice. Marketing is very important to attract more clients to the practice. In addition, marketing will be an even more critical area in the growing competitive health area environment of alternative mental health delivery systems.

Turkington points out that the level of sophistication of people buying mental health services is increasing in various sectors of the community. Potential clients, insurance companies, employers, and unions are becoming knowledgeable about the effectiveness of mental health services and potential for reducing overall health care costs. Questions that should be asked in doing marketing research are:

1. What is the product (defining all types of services to be provided)?

2. What is the target population or population to be served?
3. What are new populations that could be served?
4. Have referral sources been educated about the clinician and his or her services?
5. For those who have not referred to the clinician, what are the reasons?
6. How can the therapy "product" be improved?

Frederiksen, Brehony, and Riley (1983) have reviewed marketing research and conducted their own extensive market research. In their workshop presentation at the Association for the Advancement for Behavior Therapy in 1983, these authors provide practicing clinicians with necessary information to begin and maintain their practices from a marketing standpoint. According to them, marketing is a managerial process that must continue if one's practice is to flourish. Marketing seeks to bring about a voluntary exchange of the value of services between the service provider and the consumer. Strategies to accomplish this goal include target segmentations, conducting a needs assessment in the various target populations of the community, having an effective marketing mix of "the product," price, place, and promotion, and a system of evaluation by the various market segments.

Target segmentation is a universal marketing strategy that assumes that people have different needs for the services offered in different parts of the population. For example, parents of children in child care centers have different needs for psychological services than do physicians in the community. Specifically, parents of young children may want to obtain advice on effective child management techniques, whereas physicians are seeking assistance for their patients who are in distress as a means of "cure" or control of these patients' stress-related disorders. Similarly, businesses, agencies, attorneys, courts, hospitals, schools, and residential facilities have different needs for psychological and/or behavioral services. Therefore, segmenting the population into areas by the projected needs of the consumer, or agents for the consumer, is the first step toward effective marketing of one's mental health care "product."

Conducting a needs assessment or actually doing the marketing research involves several substrategies. First, collection of demographic data through general information gathering on such issues as economic status, age, sex, race, and geographic characteristics will provide the clinician with a description of the segments of the population targeted. Second, a description of these individuals' life-styles involving such issues as their changing health patterns and habits (excessive eating, drinking, etc.), how much traveling they do, the ages of their children, their occupations and work habits, which people are likely Type A candidates, and what are the overall stressors for each population segment is the next step in conducting this marketing research. Third, describing the behavioral characteristics of each segment is necessary. How the consumers live, that is, how they work and play (i.e., what are their response requirements and reinforcers) and what are their day-to-day behavioral repertoires are other important variables. Fourth, although the market researcher has adequately described his or her target population, finding out what others have done in the way of providing services to the consumers in the various population segments is crucial. What has been tried before in service delivery, what is the competition doing presently, and who is providing these services now are important questions to answer. Finally, the clinician may choose to do a needs assessment to relevant organizations (hospitals, insurance companies, and other businesses). This may be accomplished by surveying current usage of health care services being offered by these organizations, compiling and sharing the results of employees' expenses on health care, and describing the financial impact on these businesses; the clinician may profit from these research/promotional activities via referrals or consulting contracts.

The marketing mix is composed of one's "product," price, place, and promotion. These four *p*'s are all the elements of what any free-enterprise business or profession does. *Product* refers to the tangible goods and services one provides. Individual and group psychotherapy, agency consultation, and seminars/workshops are the intangible services, whereas tapes, books, and other health care products are the tangible goods one can provide to the consumer. According to Fredericksen, *et al.* (1983), the best single thing a practitioner can do is to have a good product, a good practice. *Price* refers not only to the fees one sets for these services but also to the monetary expenditure of energy, inconvenience, and fixed and variable services needed to operate the practice efficiently. The *place* refers to where services are to be delivered. Individuals have a preference for the type of the surroundings inside the office or the location of the office itself. Businesses may not want to send their clients for treatment to the clinician's office but prefer that the clinician work in the consultation rooms housed in the businesses themselves. Issues of confidentiality, privacy, and client comfort need to be taken into consideration here. *Promotion*, of course, refers to the methods of getting referrals, maintaining the flow of referrals, and seeking out new sources of referrals. This area is discussed at length in Chapter 2 of this book, and the reader is referred there for a review of promotional activities for private practice. However, it bears reiteration to indicate that promotional activities can never stop. A clinician needs to plan on approximately 20 to 25% of available time being devoted to such promotional activities as conducting needs surveys, receiving unpaid publicity via appearances on radio or television talk shows, as well as personal contacts through oral presentations, getting listings in the yellow pages and professional or business registries, and following up on referral sources.

Evaluation of one's provision of services to market segments one has targeted is always an important feedback device. Such evaluation involves determining the consumer's response to the "product," or who bought or participated in it. Another variable in evaluation involves whether the participants learn or benefit from the product or service offered. A third variable is utilization. Whether the participants/clients/consumers use their new knowledge and skills to maintain better lives is an important utilization consideration. Finally, evaluation must also involve an estimate of the cost-effectiveness and benefits that ensue from the delivery and utilization of these services.

Fredericksen *et al.* also indicate some common mistakes the clinician makes that can undermine the whole marketing process. Issues such as ineffective or nonexistant promotional activities can produce vacant therapy hours. It is easy to build a practice, but what happens when the referral sources dry up if one has not continued to promote the "product"—one's practice? Second, not proofreading work that is produced in the office and letting it leave the office to the referral source can indicate inefficiency in one's practice or lack of needed attention to detail. Third, having lazy, poor-quality personnel will further erode the practice. Incompetent or barely competent personnel (office or professional) will quickly turn away potential clients or dry up referral sources. Finally, mispricing (over- or underpricing) the "product" can prevent clients from making appointments because the services are too costly or may appear too inexpensive to be attractive to the referral source or consumer.

There are, of course, other issues in marketing one's practice, and the reader is directed to a book by Fredericksen, Solomon, and Brehony entitled *Marketing Health Behavior: Principles, Techniques, and Applications* (New York: Plenum Press, 1985).

9.7. BUSINESS RESOURCES FOR THE PRIVATE PRACTITIONER

Maintaining a private practice from a business standpoint requires continual attention to all aspects of running a business effectively. In addition to consulting one's accountant, there are publications that can aid the practicing psychologist, regardless of orientation, in controlling his or her health care "business." *Psychotherapy Finances* (1985), *The Independent Practitioner* (1985), and *Psychotherapy in Private Practice* (1984) are three such publications. The variety of business and professional problems faced by the private practitioner such as where and with whom to practice, fees, billing and collections, insurance reimbursement, equipment, hiring of employees, bookkeeping and accounting procedures, medical, life and professional liability insurance, building a group practice, taxes, tax shelters, investments, and retirement plans are discussed. Alternatives and solutions to these problems are suggested. These publications are monthly to quarterly and provide the practitioner with business advice not necessarily available through one's accountant.

9.8. PERTINENT BUSINESS QUESTIONS

The following questions summarize the steps needed to be taken by the clinician to help establish an effectively run practice.

1. Where will the practice be set up (in a physician's office, in rented space, or in an office you purchase)?
2. Have start-up and ongoing fixed and variable expenses been projected?
3. How will such a practice be financed?
4. What will be the office hours?
5. What business equipment, furnishings, forms, and materials will be needed?
6. Has adequate professional liability and other office liability insurance coverage been obtained?
7. What services will be provided (testing, consultations, behavioral evaluations, individual and group therapy, etc.)?
8. What fees will be charged for each of these services?
9. How will billing and collections be done for individuals versus agencies where one serves as a consultant?
10. What will be the requirements and duties of the secretary?
11. Will the accounting, bookkeeping, and tax payments be done by an accountant or by yourself?
12. By what methods will the continually growing overhead expenses incurred in the practice be regulated as the practice grows?

9.9. ALTERNATIVE MENTAL HEALTH CARE DELIVERY SYSTEMS: THREAT OR OPPORTUNITY FOR THE MENTAL HEALTH PRACTITIONER?

In the inflation and recession years that occurred from the 1970s to the early 1980s, costs of goods and services rose at an alarming rate. Inflation was frequently at a double digit rate as all areas of goods and services were affected. When the recession began, businesses began looking at ways of reducing their "excess baggage" overhead costs. Because of the rising costs of health care to businesses and to the general public, this huge expense began to be looked at by the business community for ways to cut the high and spiraling costs of health care. What has resulted is an assortment of alternative health care delivery systems that address the health and mental health care needs of the employee, business, and community while at the same time attempting to be more cost-effective. The three major alternative delivery systems for health care are HMOs, PPOs, and EAPs. Each of these systems offers low costs services as well as other advantages to the consumer. It appears inevitable that the status of fee-for-service health care may change drastically in the next decade. Whether these new health care systems will threaten the traditional private practitioner or offer a new market for referrals is still in question. According to Borowy, Buffone, and Kaplan (1985) who have reviewed the literature on these health care delivery systems, clinicians need to be aware of these various innovative models of health care. They must begin to develop and devote at least a portion of practice and promotional time to becoming involved as a service provider in these new systems. Adaptability has to be a key ingredient in the maintenance of one's private practice.

9.10. HMOs

An HMO is a health care plan that delivers comprehensive and coordinated medical services to voluntarily enrolled members on a prepaid basis. These programs are open to individual consumers or as an alternative health care system of enrollment for business employees. There are three basic types of HMOs:

1. *Group/staff (or closed panel staff) HMO* that delivers services at one or more locations through a group of physicians that contract with the HMO to provide care or through its physicians employed by the HMO.

2. *Open-panel IPA (individual practice association)* that makes contractual arrangements with doctors in the community who treat HMO patients out of their offices, usually on a co-payment from the consumer, and reduced fee-for-services basis, with no deductibles.

3. *Closed-panel group model (network)* in which separately incorporated providers' groups accept from the HMO a per member/ per month capitation fee as the principal form of payment for services. If no patients come in for service that month, the payment is still made to the provider just as if the full complement of agreed-upon members came in for services. Conversely, if more clients came in that month, the same fee would be paid that month.

Historically, HMOs began as early as 1929, and there are now at least 300 HMOs serving 13.6 million people. HMOs have grown from 30 plans in 1973 to over 300 presently, and there are HMO locations in 42 states, Guam, and the District of Columbia. This rapid growth is projected at a penetration rate into other communities at between 15 to 25% by 1990.

Cost factors for HMO participants are substantially better than for non-HMO clients. HMO premiums are usually paid monthly by either subscriber or more typically by the employer. The average cost per plan per month is approximately $50, but this may vary from company to company and region to region. Based on current projections, HMO premiums are expected to be lower than traditional health insurance premiums in all regions of the country by 1987. Also, HMO plans are seen as 20% more cost-effective because similar services are provided to the client, but there are no deductibles required. There are also minimal co-payments made by clients.

For the health services provider, the cost benefits are mixed. Generally, the provider can expect that services will be provided at less than a regular rate. Payment is usually paid on a capitation basis (an agreed-upon total amount for the monthly or yearly treatment for an agreed-upon number of clients). Fees are usually paid on a monthly basis to the provider, and the main benefit is that with the capitation monthly payment, income is regular and proves useful in practice expansion.

There are advantages and disadvantages for both patient and provider. For the patient, the advantages are that there are no claim forms necessary; the HMO provides a comprehensive benefit package on a fixed monthly fee basis, paid in advance. Also, the client has ready access to services without having to be reimbursed; there are lower out-of-pocket costs with little or no co-payment, no deductibles; and fees cover nearly all health and mental health care services. Further, the HMO provides preventive care with an emphasis on outpatient treatment as well as a list of qualified providers. Such a panel of available professionals removes the burden from the client of finding a good practitioner.

The disadvantages to the HMO client are that, for those who prefer choosing the provider, their choices are limited to panel members, whereas more choices are offered by traditional health insurance companies. Also, the specialty and mental health services provider must be approved by a "gatekeeper" (usually the HMO-approved family physician), who decides who among the specialty providers will be chosen to treat the client. The client must follow the course of treatment prescribed by the managing physicians. There is always danger of a reduced quality of services due to decreased fees being paid to the provider. Finally, if the client is dissatisfied with the HMO-provided services and seeks help from a nonapproved mental health or health services provider, those full costs will be out of pocket to the client. Of course, the client could then utilize traditional insurance reimbursement under these circumstances.

The advantages of HMO participation for the psychologist/psychiatrist provider are that there is an assured patient flow and volume. Such a regular flow suggests that more group practices will be available. There are also benefits of a steady and regular income useful for basic office overhead revenues. With an emphasis on short-term therapy (ideal for the behavior therapist), the HMO gives the provider the opportunity to practice more prevention-oriented psychology. Finally, through a provider's participation in an HMO, there is increased exposure to referral sources, new avenues for service delivery, and the potential for an expanding referral base.

There are several provider disadvantages. First, patient services have to be provided at a reduced rate, and rates can vary greatly from region to region. Also, there is a definite increase in the range of patients seen that forces the practitioner to expand his or her practice. Though this author advocates a "general practitioner" approach to practice, the HMO almost prohibits the practitioner from choosing whether or not to treat certain types of problems. The practitioner must see everyone and cannot refer out or refuse someone treatment. This forces the practitioner to form a group practice with others who have expertise in these excluded areas of treatment. Thus, the practitioner has to become an administrator over these services. Finally, psychologist providers will now be put into a greater business position to compete with psychiatrists and other mental health professionals (social workers, psychiatric nurses, mental health counselors, and marriage and family therapists) for the therapy dollar.

9.11. PPOs

A preferred provider organization (PPO) is an affiliation or combination of otherwise independent health care providers offering services to third-party payers (insurance companies, employers, and unions) at a discount. It is a second-generation alternative delivery system to HMOs and appears to be growing rapidly and gaining popularity over HMOs. Unlike an HMO, a PPO is more an arrangement than an entity. It is a loosely tied organization of providers who have a contractual arrangement to provide health care services at a discount to a defined pool of patients/clients/employees. These individuals usually also have free choice of providers who are PPO and non-PPO affiliated, and without penalty.

A PPO is composed of various characteristics common to all PPOs but variably expressed. First, there is a provider panel that is comprised of hospitals and physicians in various combinations. Second, there is a negotiated fee schedule for health and mental health services that is based on a discount of the usual and customary fees. Third, a PPO has some form of utilization or claims review and a control mechanism to evaluate the cost-effectiveness of the panel provider. By this review process, the continued inclusion of the professional on the panel is justified. Fourth, the consumer is not "locked in" to a specific provider. Rather, the consumer has freedom of choice to select a panel provider for services or even to go outside of the panel. Last, there are administrative and marketing aims similar to those of HMOs and employee assistance programs (EAPs). Specifically, a PPO is built on sound management principles such as discounting the fee for services for volume, quality control, fast turnaround to maintain cash flow, a performance appraisal of each panel provider, and some contractual arrangements to perform services at a prenegotiated price.

Unlike an HMO, a PPO has no set model or prototype, as this alternative delivery system is being employed in different variations among professionals, hospitals, clinics, and insurance carriers from state to state. There are, however, three general forms of structure this health care delivery system can take. A PPO can be a free-standing medical and mental health services group or organization, such as a hospital or clinic, that contracts directly with the payer (insurance company, union, corporation, or government). A PPO can also be structured in such a way that the organization contracts with the payer and acts as a middleman or broker handling bills, paperwork, and appointments for a loose association of health care providers. Finally, the PPO can act as a broker and sign up health care providers for a fee. The PPO can then contract with a payer for a higher fee, and guarantee the enrolled providers a steady flow of referrals.

The model of service delivery in a PPO is very straightforward. Usually there is no deductible to be met by the consumer, there is a low payment for a doctor's visit (some as low as $10 per visit), and prescription costs are minimal. There are no forms to fill out; subscribers simply show a membership card at the time of their visit to the doctor's office. In the California PPO that operates under the name of the California Psychological Health Plan (CPHP), the first five visits are 100% paid, and the next five visits are paid 85% by the plan with 15% paid by the consumer. The next five visits are paid 75% by CPHP and 25% by the subscriber. Then the balance of sessions is shared equally on a 50% basis.

There are a variety of advantages and disadvantages of a PPO to both client and therapist. The client benefits from the PPO in that services are being provided by efficient physicians, hospitals, and health services providers. The idea behind the PPO is to cut out the top 20 to 40% of inefficient providers. Consequently, there are significant reductions of medical and health-related costs such as deductibles, cost per visit, hospitals, and reduced or no co-payment. Further, the client has reduced time in the hospital. There are lower premiums to the subscriber, and rate increases from one year to the next are lower than traditional insurance rate hikes each year. As mentioned previously, the subscriber has a great deal more freedom of choice for selecting the service provider than in HMOs, there is an ongoing peer and utilization review to ensure greater protection of the subscriber, and there is greater dialogue between lobbying business coalition groups and provider groups to negotiate more cost-effective health care.

There are a few disadvantages to enrolling in a PPO. Controversy still exists as to whether quality health care is being compromised to a level of only "adequate" health care. A PPO may be based on a closed panel because there is no one organizational structure currently operating and recognized as the most efficient. Lastly, the PPO is a business, and like all businesses, it could go out of business due to mismanagement, poor estimates of costs versus profit-earned ratios in the contracting for services, and other such problems.

There are few advantages to date for the provider and many disadvantages in enrolling as a panel member in a PPO. It is of benefit that despite reduced fees, there is little or no cash flow problem, which means greater liquidity and fewer accounts receivable. Also, payments to the provider are made by the PPO in a very timely manner. Last, it is of benefit that as one's client load increases, so does the volume of fees. This is especially true in a group practice.

Unfortunately, the PPO could place unwanted restrictions on one's practice. A provider may be locked into participating in one PPO. In "gatekeeper" PPOs, the primary care physicians control utilization and, therefore, only refer to a limited number of professionals or hospitals. This may be especially true of physicians referring to psychiatrists more than to psychologists (though with lower psychologists' fees, they are more likely to survive the cost-saving measures of HMOs, PPOs, and EAPs). Another disadvantage of the PPO for the provider is that the PPO can place limits on one's dealing with patients. For example, if a PPO client was persistently noncompliant in treatment, the PPO may not allow the client to be referred out to another professional. Further, the fees for non-PPO clients could be affected if insurance profiles of an area or service provider are generally lower. With a PPO, paperwork could increase, meaning more administrative costs to the provider. Other considerations are that the PPO could go out of business. The legal issues of restraint of trade claims being lodged against PPOs are still undecided; the PPO, like hospitals, can be held liable in malpractice suits, and the IRS has yet to decide on the tax status of the PPO. Finally, the individual practitioner who is successful may not really need more patients/clients. Why work harder for less money to see more clients? In doing so, the PPO provider could gradually and accidentally plot his or her own demise. That is, by taking part in a PPO at a reduced fee, the provider may be ignoring the continual rise of overhead costs. With a contracted reduced fee, an individual practitioner who services a large-volume PPO practice may ultimately be unable to meet overhead costs as his or her profit margin might be eroded by the rise of overhead. It may be that there will be fewer sole practitioners in the field of psychology in the next 10 to 15 years. Those providers who turn out to be winners in PPOs will be the ones who have had much experience and efficiency in prepaid health care services. Other individual practitioners may be unable to compete effectively and efficiently in the changing mental health care deliver system.

9.12. EAPs

An employee assistance program (EAP) is a legal entity that contracts with various businesses to provide cost-free assistance to troubled employees and their families. Services may involve screening and referral for alcohol and substance abuse by employees, brief (under 10 sessions) individual therapy, and various training programs for all employees of a company. Employees who exhibit deteriorating work performance are financial, medical, and safety risks to the business. The U.S. Department of Health, Education, and Welfare estimates that approximately 10% of any work force are "troubled" employees on the job. A troubled employee is defined as any employee having serious behavioral/emotional/medical problems that directly affect job performance. To deal with such employees, companies can fire them, transfer them, retire them early, or tolerate lost efficiency, none of which is really a desirable alternative, as they sap resources from companies at a significant cost. EAPs provide a positive, productive alternative that offers both human and fiscal benefits.

Presently, 55% of all companies with more than 5,000 employees offer EAP services, whereas 70% of Fortune 500 companies maintain EAP services. With EAPs there is a 50 to 80% recovery rate for employees, meaning a substantial savings to the business in health care benefits and increased revenue due to increased manpower and worker efficiency.

The impact of EAPs on psychology is growing. There are several million employees currently under EAPs, and there are many nonpsychologist providers handling EAPs. Thus, there is increased competition, which will diminish referrals, lower fees, and possibly "starve out" inefficient practitioners. However, the energetic psychologist is likely to benefit from such programs.

There are various ways for psychologists to get involved with EAPs (*Psychotherapy Finances*, 1982). Psychologists can (a) set up and run in-house programs on a part-time basis; (b) serve as a resource professional doing testing or counseling at a company location or at one's office; or (c) obtain regular referrals for therapy from the company's in-house program coordinator with the fees covered by the family's regular health insurance, the separate EAP budget, or both. Therapy done within an EAP is usually short-term and tailored to the behaviorally oriented psychotherapeutic approaches. Family counseling, training supervisors, assertiveness training, substance abuse, stress management, and child–parent relations are services typically provided to EAP participants.

GLS Associates, Inc. (1983) in Philadelphia, Pennsylvania, has prepared documents that explain HMOs, PPOs, and EAPs. These individuals have also targeted five markets in which psychologists can provide mental health services. These markets are nonpsychiatric physicians, HMOs, EAPs, employers, and unions. They cite strategies for obtaining referrals, contracts, and consultation that include establishing a professional relationship with primary care physicians in HMOs who can help get the professional on the closed panel of mental health service providers, target various companies or unions who do not yet have an EAP for the purpose of developing a contract with them, submit a proposal for services that addresses business issues of cost-effectiveness for the employer, engage in competitive bidding, and follow-up with calls and correspondence showing interest during the consideration time and bidding process by the union or employer.

In summary, the private practice of psychology is rapidly changing in light of these new and rapidly developing alternative health and mental health delivery systems. Still health care is now consuming 10.5% of the gross national product and is rising to 12% in 1985. The effects of the growing demand for these and other alternative health care delivery systems have made an impact on mental health services. Around the United States, HMOs, PPOs, and EAPs are including psychologists and other mental health professionals on a limited to a very large basis. The impact that these alternative mental health delivery systems will have on the private practitioners is projected to be so great in the next decade that private practice may be nonexistent in its current from by the 1990s. By 1990 there will be some form of contract care accounting for about 40% of fee-for-service income, according to some experts. There will be more group practices, and there will be a 20 to 30% drop in income for physicians. The demand for only "adequate" services combined with reduced fees may make it impossible for independent sole practitioners to conduct their practices. The end result may very well be that the number of independent and sole practitioners currently in practice may drop, and group practices comprised of psychologists, psychiatrists, social workers, and mental health counselors may be common.

Case Illustrations from a Behavioral Practice

In this chapter, six cases are presented as examples of the "general practitioner" approach to an independent practice of behavior therapy. These cases have been selected from the variety of individuals treated by this author and attempt to represent a wide range of clinical problems, populations, and the broad-spectrum approach to behavior therapy. Of course, the names of these individuals and other revealing information have been altered for the purpose of confidentiality.

Some of the descriptions of these clients include graphic presentation of the data regarding the presenting problems. Though these A-B design studies may not be methodologically sound, they are useful to both client and therapist as feedback. However, the fact that clients and their representatives took careful data, implemented the recommended procedures, and worked with the therapist toward the targeted goals is perhaps more important than the data and results presented here.

10.1. BILLY: A CHILD EXHIBITING DISRUPTIVE BEHAVIORS

Billy is a 7-year-old second grade child who was referred by his parents upon the recommendation of physicians from a local military family services center. The family was often transferred to and from various parts of the world due to their commitment to the armed forces, and reported that Billy had had counseling previously in other residences. Billy behaved in a disruptive manner not only at home but also at school and had done so since the first grade. This young boy had been diagnosed by other mental health and medical professionals as experiencing a severe oppositional disorder. Specific complaints that the parents expressed were that their son was highly noncompliant with rules and would violate the rules at home and at school. In addition, Billy would avoid responsibilities assigned to him at home and would fight frequently with his younger brother. Methods used by these parents previously involved restriction to his room or to the yard, removing privileges and objects that he enjoyed, and spanking. All of these punitive measures were applied inconsistently.

In a 1-hour interview with Billy's parents, they described the full extent of their son's disruptive behavior. They reported that Billy would avoid following instructions given by his mother and would, instead, yell at her. This defiance was more typically present when she was alone with her son than when her husband was either at home or having full responsibility for Billy and his brother. Further, Billy would behave inappropriately outside the home. For example, during the summer, Billy would be reprimanded by day camp officials for his noncompliance; he played on railroad tracks near his home and had been brought home by the police twice for throwing rocks at cars.

Developmentally, Billy had a normal birth and delivery, but his mother took the drug Bendectin, because of nausea, for 6 months during her pregnancy. Development was, however, normal, with the exception of difficulties in potty training in which Billy was extremely defiant. Socially, Billy had little difficulty with his friends and, for the most part, played appropriately with them. However, Billy behaved very aggressively toward his brother and would often yell at and hit him. Academically, Billy had no difficulty. His teacher reported that he maintained above-average grades and scored well on standardized achievement tests. An additional problem that was identified was that Billy's mother was experiencing difficulty coping with the stress of her son's disruptive behaviors especially at times when her husband was away on sea duty. At that time the burden for parenting rested solely on her.

A 1-hour observation was conducted in Billy's home for the purpose of analyzing the relationship between Billy's behavior and its consequences. During the course of this observation, it was evident that Billy's mother gave frequent beta or inappropriate commands (Forehand & McMahon, 1981), attended only to her son's disruptive behavior, did not talk to him at appropriate times, and provided no instances of verbal praise, physical contact or closeness, smiles, positive facial expressions or gestures, or more tangible incentives. In fact, when Billy was noncompliant, his mother would begin yelling back at him, at which point she would move toward him to force him to comply. Billy would then run from her and laugh while his mother was "chasing" him.

Billy was also seen for a 1-hour interview in which additional information was obtained. Billy reported that he did not always follow the instructions that his parents gave to him. Further, he indicated that his parents spanked him for not doing what he was asked to do. Of significance was this boy's statement that his mother yelled at him "all the time" for things he did not do as well. There was no evidence of hyperactivity during the interview, and teacher reports indicated that this youngster did not switch tasks frequently and remained on task for long periods of time. There was no evidence of learning problems either. Finally, a reinforcement survey and a fear survey were conducted. A variety of reinforcers including edibles, arts and crafts, desired excursions, forms of entertainment and sports and games, and social activities and incentives were indicated. There were no indications of extreme fears noted by Billy though his parents did report the occurrence of night terrors when Billy was much younger. However, these nighttime fears were not ongoing at the time Billy was being seen for his disruptive behavior.

Billy's parents were seen for the follow-up session in which a written evaluation of the presenting problems was given. It was indicated that Billy's behavior was a function of the lack of appropriate cuing techniques, the combination of an absence of reinforcers for Billy's appropriate behavior and reinforcing attention for Billy's disruptive behavior, and the lack of consistent use of effective negative consequences for his behavior. Following this analysis, the therapist spent a great deal of time explaining the concepts of reinforcement, punishment, and other behavioral methods for correcting problem behaviors in children. Billy's parents were given a book, *Parents Are Teachers* (Becker, 1971), to read and about which they would be tested (O'Dell, Tarler-Benlolo, & Flynn, 1979). They were also required to use objective data collection measures of the number of instructions not followed by their son for charting and monitoring purposes. The therapist then outlined a treatment procedure that involved compliance training, special privileges for completed tasks, and time-out (Forehand & McMahon, 1983). In addition, Billy's mother was taught relaxation training as a means of desensitizing her to her son's disruptions. Biofeedback was used to enhance and make the relaxation response more objective.

Figure 6 is a graph of the number of instructions not followed by Billy during the course of his and his mother's treatment. During baseline, Billy was observed to behave in a noncompliant manner approximately four times per day. In addition, it can be seen that the frequency

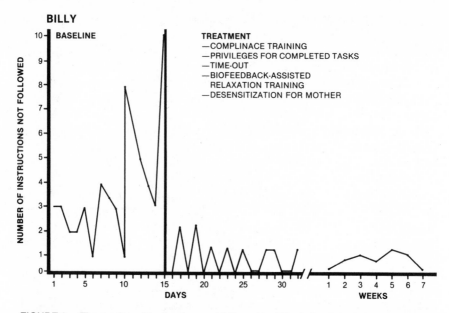

FIGURE 6.   The number of instructions not followed by Billy during Baseline and Treatment conditions. Treatment consisted of compliance training with privileges for tasks assigned and instructions followed. Biofeedback, relaxation training, and desensitization were used as treatment for Billy's mother.

of Billy's defiance was increasing across this baseline condition. During treatment, Billy showed an immediate drop in his noncompliance to a level of approximately one instance of noncompliance every 2 days. This low level of disruptive behavior persisted for a 2-month period after sessions with his family were gradually diminished. Follow-up data indicate that noncompliance has been maintained at an acceptable level of about once per day. Anecdotal reports from Billy's parents were that his behavior had significantly improved in public situations and in school though no formal attempt had been made to target and modify the disruptive behavior in these situations.

10.2.   PAULA: A CASE OF PERSISTENT HAIR PULLING (TRICHOTILLOMANIA)

Paula was a 2-year-old blond-haired girl referred by her pediatrician for persistent hair pulling. Paula's mother stated that her daughter pulled her hair out to such an extent that she was completely bald on one side of her head. Observation of this child's head confirmed the severity of this problem. In questionnaires completed by her parents, Paula was rated as a talkative young girl who was cooperative with her friends and followed the instructions of her parents. This child's birth was full term and normal with no significant illnesses and accidents to date.

In the 1-hour interview with her parents, they reported that their daughter started to pull her hair out after she contracted a cold and, although the cold had since passed, the hair pulling continued. Her hair was shoulder length before she began this trichotillomania, but she was bald on one side of her head at the time of her referral. Photographs supplied by Paula's mother confirmed the absence of problems when Paula was 18 months of age.

A functional analysis of Paula's difficulties was conducted with her mother. The hair-pulling response occurred typically when Paula was tired, inactive, when she was about to fall asleep, about to wake up in the morning or after her afternoon nap, or when she was riding in the car. Paula did not pull her hair out when her parents played with her or read her stories but did pull when more attention was shown Paula's sister, when Paula was ill, or when Paula's parents would go out of town. The specific topography of the hair-pulling response never just involved hair pulling, but a critical component involved thumb sucking as well. That is, Paula would pull her hair out of her head with her left hand, usually holding one or several small strands, place the pulled hair intertwined in the fingers of the right hand whose thumb she was sucking, and rub the hair gently in an up-and-down motion across the side of, or on top of, her nose. This response topography never varied, according to Paula's mother, and always involved her thumb sucking. Paula's parents did not, however, wish to eliminate the thumb sucking response but preferred to allow this response to be reduced in its frequency over the passage of time. Paula's physician also concurred with this position regarding her thumb sucking. Obviously, there were concerns that by eliminating the thumb-sucking response some developmental stage would be interrupted. In order to follow the wishes of these parents, a treatment program would have to be designed that would both accomplish a reduction or elimination of the trichotillomania as well as allowing for the maintenance of the thumb-sucking response. In addition, there were some financial difficulties that prevented regular sessions so that it was necessary to develop a treatment program that the parents could understand and implement on their own with only brief, periodic phone consultations with this therapist. After the parents were assigned to collect data on the frequency with which they observed the hair-pulling response as well as the number of hairs found in Paula's bed (to account for times when the observation of the hair pulling was not possible), a reinforcement survey was completed. A written plan of treatment was then submitted for review and explanation to Paula's parents. The proposed procedures were based on the least restrictive alternative rule and on the available literature of techniques used to treat this problem (Azrin, Nunn, & Frantz, 1980; Gray, 1979; Rosenbaum & Ayllon, 1981). This evaluation specified the problems in operational terms, the criteria for success, various alternative procedures for treatment, their risks and benefits, and overall projected length of intervention. After a thorough discussion of behavior modification procedures, fully informed consent was obtained, and therapy was begun.

Figure 7 is a graph of the data collected by Paula's parents during the baseline and treatment conditions of her therapy. During baseline, Paula was observed to pull her hair an average of approximately five times per day. This behavior appeared to be increasing during baseline though only a week's worth of data were collected before treatment procedures were implemented.

A combination of procedures was used for this young girl. Paula received reinforcement on a DRO schedule for gradually longer periods

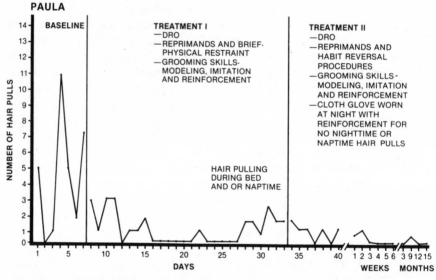

FIGURE 7.   The number of hair pulls by Paula during Baseline, Treatment I, and Treatment II. These treatment conditions utilized such procedures as DRO, reprimands, brief physical restraint, grooming skills education, habit reversal techniques, modeling and instruction, and the use of a cloth glove.

in which hair pulling was absent. In addition, reinforcement for cooperative behavior was given. It was determined that Paula's mother had reinforced many dependent behaviors emitted by her daughter so that when the mother would leave the house, Paula would be fearful, anxious, and then pull her hair. Tantrums would occur, and time-out was used for this behavior. Paula also received instructions in grooming skills, and a doll was purchased for her to practice these good-grooming behaviors on her doll and then on herself. The mother would participate in these activities with her daughter and thus reinforced her appropriate behavior. Of course, praise was an integral part of these self-care sessions. At times when Paula would pull her hair, response interruption, social disapproval, and brief physical restraint would follow. As seen in Figure 7, hair pulling gradually declined and was eliminated during the day from Day 7 through Day 27 but increased during bedtime and naptime hours and remained stable at two hair pulls per day from Day 28 through Day 33. At that point the decision was made to proceed to the next level of restrictiveness, Treatment II. Because hair pulling persisted in Paula's bed, it was determined that tactile reinforcement caused by Paula's brushing her hair against her face was still available and the opportunity was greater when Paula was in bed than at other times. Paula's bed began to take on properties of a discriminative stimulus for hair pulling because it was a condition in which her mother was absent, and there was a low probability of punishment and a high probability of this tactile reinforcement. Consequently, in Treatment II, not only were those procedures used in Treatment I continued, but two additional procedures—habit reversal techniques (Azrin, Nunn, & Frantz, 1980) and the use of a cloth glove during bedtime and naptime—were added. Specifically, at the infrequent times during the day that Paula did pull her hair, habit-reversal procedures were used. Positive practice and competing response activity were used that were especially contingent on instances of the hair-pull response. These habit-reversal procedures were assumed to be more restrictive and, therefore, would be more of a deterrent as well as having an educative effect on the nighttime and naptime instances of trichotillomania.

During night- and naptime, Paula was also required to wear a cloth glove with the hole cut out of the thumb portion to allow the thumb-sucking response. This cloth glove reduced the tactile reinforcement obtained by rubbing the hair pulled across her face and made such rubbing impossible due to the bulkiness of the glove. Reinforcement was provided to Paula for no instances of hair found in her bed or no observation of hair pulling by her mother upon coming into Paula's room after naptime. Hair pulling quickly declined at Day 34 to a near-zero level and during follow-up, across a 6-week period of time. With the continued reinforcement, grooming skills training, reprimands, habit-reversal techniques, and use of the cloth glove, hair pulling was eliminated in one office visit and five phone consultations of one-half to 1 hour each during a 3-month period of time. Gradually, the cloth glove was eliminated from use. Paula's physician was regularly apprised of the progress and problems, and graphs were sent to him, all with the permission of Paula's parents. Follow-up at 12, 18, and 24 months revealed that there were two instances of spontaneous recovery, but immediate reimplementation of the treatment procedures reduced the behavior to zero. This young girl, over the course of therapy and follow-up, now has a full head of long blond hair with no signs of balding spots on her head. Incidentally, her mother reports that Paula reduced her own thumb sucking and now no longer engages in that behavior.

10.3. ROBERT: A PHYSICALLY AGGRESSIVE MENTALLY RETARDED ADULT

As part of this "general practitioner" approach, this author is also a consultant to a nearby intermediate care facility for the mentally retarded (ICF/MR). In this facility are lodged 60 severely and profoundly retarded adults who have been selected from a variety of state institutions to be eligible to enter a less restrictive environment aiming toward the goal of group home placement. Many of these clients come to this and similar facilities with many skills deficits, excesses, and inappropriate behaviors for which training via skills acquisition or behavior reduction programs are needed. Robert is a 24-year-old client who demonstrated extremely severe aggressive behavior toward staff and other clients. Specifically, when given instructions he did not want to follow or when he or a fellow client whom Robert befriended was given a verbal reprimand for some disruptive behavior, he engaged in frequent and, many times, highly dangerous physically aggressive behavior. Typically, Robert would simultaneously bite his own hand while engaging in a swift kicking motion that would often make contact with a staff member or fellow client. At other times this client would pick up heavy metal chairs and throw them in the direction of others or physically attack others with his hands, fists, and teeth. The staff and other clients in the cottage in which Robert lived were very afraid of him and, instead of attempting to intervene with him, the staff would avoid him, thus reinforcing this aggressive behavior. Because there was no formal programming on this client and because his behavior posed extreme danger for others around him, immediate attention was given to this problem. In addition to the behavioral observations conducted on this client, reinforcement surveys were conducted with the staff members most familiar with Robert, and baseline data were collected. Then a formal treatment program was written after consulting the behavioral and retardation literature for the least restrictive treatments of choice. Staff were given in-service training on the appropriate use of the methods prescribed by the maladaptive behavior reduction program. Baseline measures indicated that this client engaged in approximately 12 episodes of aggressive behavior per day that either involved actual physical contact or motions directed toward others as described previously.

Figure 8 is a graph of the frequency of Robert's aggression. The last 7 to 10 days of each condition are plotted. Actual time of programming from the beginning to the end for this client was approximately 9 months.

As prescribed by the written behavior program, the staff, who had major responsibility for this client, would not only have to intervene with him when he engaged in disruptive and dangerous behavior, but they also had the responsibility to teach Robert compliance. Therefore, during Treatment I the staff were first required to provide frequent praise

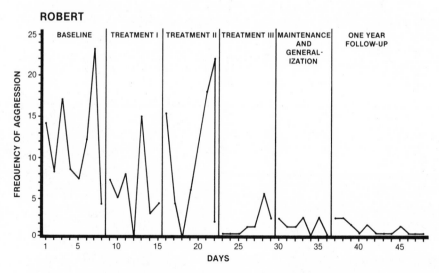

FIGURE 8.   The frequency of aggressive responses by Robert during Baseline, Treatment I, II, and III, Maintenance and Generalization, and at a 1 year Follow-up. Due to the duration of the reduction program, only the last 7 to 8 days of each condition are plotted.

to this client because it was determined that there was low frequency of praise due to his high-frequency aggressive behavior and staff avoidance of him. In addition to this rather simple, but often forgotten procedure, the staff were required to arrange a series of 10 instructions that would be given to Robert approximately three to five times per day (compliance training). By giving Robert the frequent opportunity to comply with requests made by others around him, it was hoped that this would decrease his frequency of aggression. Initially, the experienced members of the psychology department implemented this program, whereas later, general and direct care staff were brought into the training program to ensure maintenance and generalization. Not only did staff provide him with praise, but they also provided Robert with incentives, stickers exchangeable for time on a three-wheeler adult bicycle, and riding in the facility van on local errands.

As shown in Figure 8, Robert's frequency of aggression was reduced by approximately half during Treatment I. Once these reinforcement conditions were being implemented, negative contingencies were then begun. Specifically, in Treatment II, whenever Robert engaged in the initial responses of aggression (which the staff could reliably identify), he was given a verbal reprimand following each episode of aggression. What resulted was wide variability in his frequency of aggression to a level almost returning to that of baseline. It was decided that Treatment III would require Robert to go into a 10-minute time-out period in his room for his disruptive behavior in addition to the positive consequences already available. The results of Treatment III as shown in Figure 8 were that there was an immediate and significant drop in the frequency of aggression. Maintenance and generalization procedures were imposed before the formal program was terminated. Ultimately, Robert's aggressive responses were reduced to a zero or near-zero level, and follow-up measures indicate that these results are still maintained after a 2-year period of time. Occasionally, Robert will become aggressive, but his responses are infrequent, manageable, and staff are no longer avoiding him.

10.4. MARIE: A CASE OF HETEROSEXUAL ANXIETY AND SEXUAL DYSFUNCTION

Marie is a 25-year-old elementary school teacher who was self-referred. Her presenting complaints were that she was nonorgasmic and, in fact, had never been orgasmic via intercourse. She did report that orgasm was, however, achieved through masturbation. Of most concern to her was that in the sexual relationship with her boyfriend, as with previous boyfriends, she experienced intense anxiety. Intercourse for her was laden with anxiety and recurring upsetting thoughts that always prevented her from sexual satisfaction. In the initial interviews with Marie, it was learned that she had experienced a long history of sexual abuse as a child from an uncle with whom she lived after her parents were killed in an auto accident when she was very young. This abuse was ongoing from the time she was 9 years old until shortly after her 16th birthday. In the midst of the episodes of this incestual relationship, Marie reported that she would often attempt to think of more mundane things so as to avoid the overwhelming feelings of guilt, anxiety, fear, and anger. From this ongoing abuse, Marie indicated that the thoughts of what she was forced to do as a young girl recur anytime she begins to develop an intimate relationship with a man in such a way that touching, kissing, and sexual intercourse are characterized by the same thoughts and feelings she had when she was younger.

In paper/pencil questionnaires completed by Marie, she rated herself as an otherwise assertive woman who engaged in excellent self-control and had normal self-sufficiency as indicated by the Bernreuter Self-Sufficiency Scale. The Fear Survey Schedule (Wolpe & Lang, 1969) did include anxiety in sexually related areas but also ratings of anxiety in social situations such as those in which she was rejected by others and/or hurting others' feelings. On Cautela's (1977) Sexual Behavior Survey, Marie rated herself as having varying degrees of anxiety to almost all of the items. Other paper/pencil questionnaires provided background information that was helpful in the development of a treatment regimen for this client.

After a thorough analysis of the presenting and other possible problem areas, a written evaluation was presented to Marie for her fully informed consent. This evaluation discussed the problems she was experiencing, gave a functional analysis of each problem, presented a list and a description of the recommended procedures indicated in the professional literature as the treatments of choice, specified the goals of treatment, and the projected overall duration of therapy with an indication of time intervals at which a review of problems and progress in therapy were to be discussed before therapy would continue. The specific methods of treatment selected involved relaxation training and systematic desensitization, imagery development and cognitive restructuring techniques, thought stopping and sexual education, and highly structured sex therapy that involved graded and nonthreatening sexual assignments to Marie and her boyfriend as therapy proceeded.

Figure 9 is a chart of the number of instances of orgasm achieved

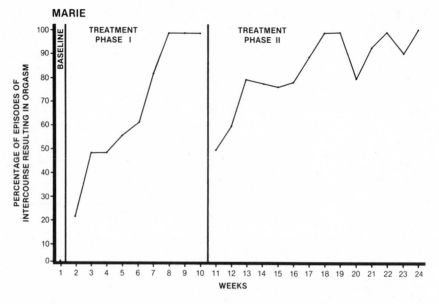

FIGURE 9. The percentage of episodes of intercourse that resulted in orgasm by Marie during Baseline, Treatment Phase I, and Treatment Phase II.

by Marie through intercourse with her boyfriend. During baseline, no instances of orgasm were recorded. In Treatment Phase I, Marie was asked to increase her frequency of masturbation, engage in positive imagery relating to her sexual fantasies, and to engage in self-stimulation during intercourse because she was orgasmic during her own masturbation. In Treatment Phase II, Marie was then asked to cease her masturbation during intercourse and allow her boyfriend to take gradually more responsibility for her satisfaction through physical guidance, verbal feedback, and demonstration. Consults with Marie's boyfriend were arranged to discuss these recommendations. As treatment proceeded, the percentage of episodes of sexual intercourse in which orgasm occurred compared to the total number of instances of sexual intercourse increased steadily from 50% after the initial sex therapy assignments had been implemented, to a 90 to 100% level at the end of Treatment I. Treatment Phase II generated an initial drop to a 50% level, perhaps due to greater reliance by Marie on her boyfriend, but soon returned to a 90 to 100% level of orgasm. The other components of therapy were also completed successfully, and follow-up contact with this client indicates that therapy benefits are still being maintained. Marie has few instances of intrusive thoughts during heterosexual activities; she reports that her anxiety has diminished to a near-zero level, and she continues to be orgasmic.

10.5. JENNIFER: A CASE OF DEPRESSION WITH MEDICAL COMPLICATIONS

Jennifer is a 36-year-old housewife whose presenting complaints were of depression, "foggy" thoughts, difficulty sleeping, and frequent periods of spontaneous crying. She was referred by her husband. In the Life History Questionnaire, Jennifer reported experiencing depression for extended periods that was recognized when her daughter was born but did also occur with the significant amount of ridicule and little praise she received from her parents when she was a young child. Jennifer estimated that her depression ranged in its severity from mildly upsetting to totally incapacitating when problems with her children, her husband, and herself occurred. Other complaints that Jennifer indicated involved dizziness, anxiety, headaches, bowel disturbances, tension, concentration difficulties, fatigue, and insomnia. The Beck Depression Inventory, Cautela's Cues for Tension and Anxiety Survey Schedule, The Self-Rating Behavioral Scale, the Revised Willoughby Questionnaire for Self-Administration, and the Benreuter Self-Sufficiency Scale all indicated depression, anxiety, somatic complaints, and insomnia. Further, Jennifer had been evaluated by a psychiatrist who administered the Minnesota Multiphasic Personality Inventory. This test indicated that Jennifer was moderately depressed, socially sensitive, overly concerned about her somatic complaints, had a "low-energy level," and had difficulty completing her responsibilities or engaging in desirable activities.

In the clinical interview with Jennifer, she reported that she was very sensitive to criticism due to the frequency of criticism levied on her by both her parents whom she saw as cold, non-nurturing people. This sensitivity to criticism was evident in almost every setting that Jennifer entered, such as at a party with her husband, on her job, around strangers, and with her children. This sensitivity to criticism was especially evident around the time of Jennifer's period. When queried, Jennifer reported that she had a history of symptoms similar to those that characterize premenstrual syndrome (PMS). Further, eating certain foods was also correlated with these symptoms. At this point, it was decided to refer Jennifer to her internist for a complete physical evaluation. In consultation with Jennifer's physician, it was learned that Jennifer experienced symptoms of hypoglycemia in addition to PMS, and medication with a strict dietary regimen was prescribed in conjunction with therapy.

In the evaluation session, the therapist and Jennifer discussed the antecedents, consequences, and the nature of her depression, sensitivity to criticism, and irrational statements about the events and individuals in her life. It was decided that the depression and irrational thinking would be dealt with through rational emotive therapy (RET), whereas her sensitivity to criticism would be reduced via systematic desensitization and assertiveness training. Over a period of 12 sessions, Jennifer's difficulties decreased in their frequency and duration. RET occurred the first four sessions, whereas systematic desensitization and assertiveness training occurred during the next six sessions. The final two sessions were used for review and generalization to other minor problems Jennifer presented. These sessions were extended over a 2-month period as improvement was shown. Readministration of the Beck Depression Inventory and other paper/pencil questionnaires and her own self-report revealed significant improvement.

10.6. MATT: A CASE OF HYPERTENSION AND INTERPERSONAL DIFFICULTIES

Matt is a 34-year-old engineer who was referred by his internist due to essential hypertension, which was uncontrolled even by massive doses of medication. Matt was divorced for several years and had custody of his children. In consultatioon with Matt prior to treatment, it was reported that this young man experienced blood pressures as high as 200/110, but the average level of his blood pressure was approximately 170/100.

In the variety of paper/pencil questionnaires completed by Matt, he gave additional information about himself. At the time of this referral, Matt indicated that his difficulties were moderately severe. He had difficulty coping with his job, and he was very dissatisfied with his position. He reported further stresses of being a single parent as well as having interpersonal difficulties that prevented him from socializing with fellow employees and acquaintances. Matt also indicated that he had difficulty making decisions, had feelings of inferiority, was tense and anxious, had concentration difficulties, saw himself as overly ambitious or having a "Type A personality," and was very shy with people. Most of his learning history was characterized by little socializing, a father whose behavior he characterized as nonsocial, and receiving little praise but much criticism from both his parents. Historically, Matt has always viewed himself as tense, anxious, and serious. He was the subject of ridicule as a youngster and also experienced social difficulties. Further, there was a history of heart disease in both parents. Matt's major goal in therapy was to be able to lower his blood pressure and to learn techniques that would maintain this lowered blood pressure level. Matt also saw himself as highly anxious and had a goal to reduce this anxiety.

After Matt completed his series of questionnaires and an interview, it was determined that episodes of high blood pressure occurred when he was stressed. Times in his life such as when he was divorced, took custody of his two small children and became a single parent, changed jobs that were not satisfactory to him, and moved his residence were cited by Matt as episodes in which his blood pressure soared to dangerous levels. After a written evaluation detailing a functional analysis of Matt's problems and proposed treatment was provided, the risks and benefits of treatment were discussed. Therapy involved three phases: first, biofeedback and relaxation training to lower his blood pressure; second, rational emotive psychotherapy (RET) to eliminate the negative cognitions concommitant to his stress reactions; and, lastly social skills training that involved role playing and didactic training to improve Matt's skills in his interactions with others. Matt's physician was regularly informed by phone of his progress, and graphs of blood pressure and EMG readings were sent to him.

During the first phase of treatment, a psychophysiological profile was done to assess if Matt was a muscular or vascular responder to his stress. Figure 10 is a graphic presentation of the psychophysiological profile that includes both Matt's EMG readings as well as his temperature during the various stages of his profile. This profile comprised six phases: (a) Matt was told to relax the best he could though no formal relaxation training methods had been taught to him; (b) he was given imagery that related to warming his hands while hand temperature and EMG readings were being taken; (c) he was required to count backward by 7's from 999; (d) he was again asked to relax to the best of his ability; (e) a significant emotional stressor such as a frightening and highly descriptive scene was presented that involved him or his children; (f) he was again asked to relax; and (g) he was taught specific relaxation training procedures involving the five major muscle groups. It can be seen from Figure 10 that Matt's hand temperatures changed little across these various phases (87 to 89 degrees), whereas muscle tension gradually increased from approximately 2 microvolts initially, to a high of approximately 7 to 8 microvolts of tension. As relaxation was again imposed at Stage 6 and Matt was taught progressive relaxation in Stage 7, his tension dropped to below the baseline level to approximately 1.8 microvolts of

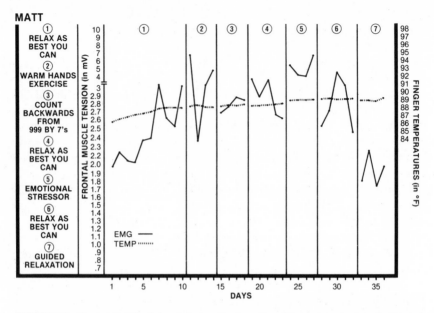

FIGURE 10. The level of frontal muscle tension (in mv) and finger temperature (in °F) during the psychophysiological profile of Matt. This profile involved seven conditions: (a) "relax-as-best-you-can" instructions; (b) a hand warming exercise; (c) Matt counting backwards from 999 by 7's; (d) "relax as best you can"; (e) an emotional stressor; (f) "relax-as-best-you-can" instructions; and (g) guided deep muscle relaxation training. EMG levels are indicated by the solid line; finger temperatures are indicated by the broken line.

tension. On this basis, Matt was deemed a muscular responder to stress, and therapy was begun.

After a baseline measure had been taken prior to the first session of treatment, biofeedback and relaxation training involved making a relaxation tape during the therapy hour that Matt could listen to and practice with each day outside the office as well as downward shaping of his muscle tension. Data were plotted each session for him to review. After the beginning of treatment, it was decided that Matt's blood pressure would be taken before each session began and after each session had been completed. Feedback and discussion occurred after these sessions to answer any questions he had and to explore other strategies for enhancing his relaxation response. During the downward shaping phase, Matt was taught to lower his tension levels through the use of gradually lowering the threshold level of the offset of the feedback stimulus. Consequently, as Matt would relax to below threshold levels more frequently and for longer durations, the threshold level would be lowered toward the goal of less than 1 microvolt of tension across his frontalis muscle. Once Matt had reduced his level of tension to less than 1 microvolt for most of the session, speed training (muscle tension release to a very low level in a brief period of time) and generalization (relaxing in different settings at the desired level) techniques were begun. Figure 11 is a graph of the course of treatment and the results of Matt's therapy. During baseline, Matt's muscle tension was at 2 microvolts in the resting state. When downward shaping was begun, he showed an immediate and steadily lessening level of muscle tension both before and after each session. Matt's post-EMG readings were consistently lower than his pre-EMG readings for each session prior to speed and generalization training. When this next phase was implemented, Matt continued to maintain a very low and consistent level of muscle tension (1 microvolt or less).

Table 9 details the pre- and postsession blood pressure readings taken on Matt. In baseline, his blood pressure readings were 170/110. After the first treatment session in which Matt was taught complete

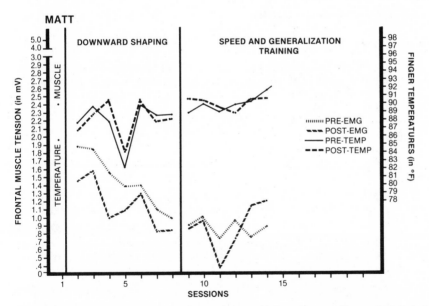

FIGURE 11. The level of frontal muscle tension and finger temperatures of Matt during biofeedback training. After Baseline, Downward Shaping was indicated through Session 8 while Speed and Generalization Training was begun. Pre- and postsession EMG and temperature levels were taken each session for the duration of therapy.

TABLE 9
Pre- and Postsession Blood Pressure Measures during Biofeedback
Training for Matt

Condition	Session number	Pre	Post
Baseline	1	170/110	
Downward shaping	2	—	—
	3	140/90	118/70
	4	120/85	125/85
	5	140/89	120/82
	6	126/88	110/78
	7	130/88	130/85
	8	125/90	130/85
	9	127/80	118/70
Temperature training	10	130/92	110/80
	11	132/88	120/80
	12	120/82	118/78
	13	122/70	118/75
	14	110/80	109/65

deep muscle relaxation, his presession reading dropped to 140/90 and
then to 118/70 postsession. This pattern was consistent throughout both
phases of treatment. In fact, in 10 of the 12 data points plotted on
Figure 11, Matt showed a corresponding drop in his blood pressure in
either systolic, diastolic, or both, as shown on Table 9. At this point, he
was assigned to relax for brief periods during the day, placing colorful
stickers on often-looked-at objects (e.g., mirror, wristwatch, telephone)
to cue the relaxation response. Other such generalization methods facilitated continued improvement. The results of this treatment were that
Matt learned to relax, and his resulting blood pressure was within the
normal range for both systolic and diastolic measures before and after
each treatment session occurred. Matt was then assigned to take his
own blood pressure twice per day at home. When his blood pressure
levels were maintained at this normal level, his physician was contacted
and, based on these results, as well as the physician's own measures of
Matt's blood pressure, the drugs he was taking were gradually lowered
until medication was at minimum dosages.

Cognitive restructuring using RET as well as social skills training
were implemented toward the speed and generalization training phases
of treatment for Matt. Total therapy time was 16 sessions, and follow-
up was done after 1 year. Matt reported maintenance of these effects

and that persistently practicing the relaxation training methods learned in therapy facilitated this maintenance.

10.7. SUMMARY

Billy, Paula, Robert, Marie, Jennifer, and Matt were clients who received a variety of services from the different areas of behavior therapy in an effort to minimize the difficulties experienced by them and by the significant individuals in their lives. These cases demonstrate the capability for utilizing a behavioral analysis approach in private practice in order to treat such problems as were presented here. Data collection and evaluation were made possible by the client's self-monitoring, the client's representative keeping data, as well as the therapist's collecting the data. All clients or their guardians were provided with a written analysis and evaluation of the presenting problems and the proposed treatments with their risks and benefits. Using such an evaluation, fully informed consent was obtained so as to maintain the ethical standards needed for treatment. By maintaining a sound data-oriented treatment program, the therapist is more accountable for the success or failure of the program (i.e., the treatment procedures), and the client is better informed as to what methods are being used and with what rationale. Thus, the client can participate more in treatment and, eventually, learn the skills necessary to become his or her own therapist.

11

Current Trends and Future Directions in the Practice of Behavior Therapy

In recent years, the field of behavior therapy has seen a burgeoning of research and techniques in each of the five major areas of influence on the field. With the growing body of literature indicating that behavior therapy is a viable clinical discipline and even the treatment of choice for many difficulties, individuals from the variety of the helping professions are increasingly implementing behavioral techniques in efforts to ameliorate the clinically and socially significant problems that are presented to them. Professional organizations and governmental agencies such as the American Psychiatric Association, the Alcohol, Drug Abuse, and Mental Health Administration, and the National Institute of Mental Health now also recognize that behavior therapy has much to offer therapists and clients in the effort to relieve human suffering (Birk *et al.*, 1973; Brown, Wienckowski & Stolz, 1975).

As with any growing science, there are a number of issues still to be addressed about the goal of greater efficiency and refinement of the field. Clinical issues, such as the least restrictive alternative model, the appropriateness and effectivess of treatment, certification, and peer review make up one such area of current concern. Applied research issues, such as the analysis of setting events and ecobehavioral systems, scientific and social validation, and the need for a convergence of research and therapy are also trends under investigation. Finally, on a much larger scale, there is a move within the behavioral field to affect social policy in the political and social arenas that may have a lasting influence on the field in the years to come. These and other related trends are the topics of discussion in this final chapter.

11.1. CLINICAL ISSUES

11.1.1. The Least Restrictive Alternative Model

In the 1970s, abuses of prison inmates and residents of retardation and psychiatric institutions were charged against practitioners of behavior modification (Goldiamond, 1975b). These charges resulted in court cases that set precedents regarding whether and how a client is to receive treatment. Court cases such as *Wyatt v. Stickney* (1971), which mandated due process, set limits on specific types of treatments allowable, fully informed consent, and review of treatment by a physician prior to treatment and needs for human rights committees; *Donaldson v. O'Conner* (1974), which held that institutionalized clients have a constitutional right to treatment; and *Lake v. Cameron* (1968), *Covington v. Harris* (1969), and *Welch v. Likens* (1974), which required that officials responsible for the care and treatment of institutional clients place them in facilities and provide them treatment in such a manner so as to be least restrictive of their physical liberties and human rights (Brown, Wienckowski, & Stolz, 1975), are examples of the justifiable efforts made to protect the rights of clients. Thus, the concept of the least restrictive alternative model was born and was made a permanent part of behavioral intervention. The least restrictive alternative model applies both to the treatment selected as well as the environment in which the client is to be treated. In short, the least restrictive approach applied to a clinical behavioral practice would require that, initially, treatment procedures be selected that are easily applied and pose little or no distress to the client. If that treatment is only minimally effective, then a slightly more restrictive technique would be selected based on the same premise, and so on, until the goal of treatment was reached.

This least restrictive alternative model should be used in the planning of treatment for clients within one's independent practice. There are several ways in which this can be accomplished. First, according to Foxx (1982) and this author, the behavior therapist must review all the available literature on the presenting problem and select the various procedures for treating the difficulty. Next, these various approaches should be prioritized, and the first treatment approach should be implemented according to this least restrictive alternative model. Third, accurate data must be collected on a regular (preferably daily) basis to evaluate the effectiveness of the treatment applied. Though Foxx recommends using the next level of least restrictiveness if the originally selected treatment fails to produce the desired outcome, Kaplan (1984) suggests that at least one addendum to the initial method of treatment be attempted before moving on to the higher level of restrictiveness. Finally, as the need for aversive procedures arises with a client, fully informed consent must be obtained. In this manner, the client is ensured of reasonable attempts to protect him or her from undue restriction of emotional and physical liberties.

11.1.2. Appropriateness and Effectiveness of Treatment

DeLeon, VandenBos, and Cummings (1983) indicate that most psychotherapy is, certainly, more effective than no treatment at all and that various types of psychotherapy are appropriate for different types of clinical problems. Though these authors suggest that treatment should be brief and focused on the presenting problem, little is known about what kind of therapy is most appropriate for what kind of problem. It is the therapist's responsibility to make this determination according to the least restrictive approach. However, a major concern in the behavior therapist's compliance to the least restrictive alternative rule involves determining the appropriate and effective method of treatment for specific problems. The therapist must make this determination based on his or her appraisal of the degree of restrictiveness or intrusiveness versus the projected effectiveness of the selected procedures.

According to Reese (1982), there has to be a balance between the intrusiveness and the effectiveness of treatment. Specifically, Reese cites several dimensions of intrusiveness and several dimensions of treatment effectiveness. Within the realm of intrusiveness, Reese indicates that there has to be public acceptability of the proposed treatment. That is, the clinician must determine, objectively or by judgment, that the informed lay community would indicate that the treatment proposed was fair and reasonable. Second, the therapist must also consider how much restriction of liberty is needed to implement the treatment procedure. Whether the proposed treatment involves confinement, as in seclusion time-out procedures, or use of noxious stimuli, such as the use of shock or chemical agents for severely dangerous and highly deviant behavior, it is the therapist's responsibility to ensure a reasonably minimal level of restriction of liberty. Last, the therapist must also consider the amount of discomfort and stress the application of the treatment procedure produces. In this manner, intrusiveness is defined by the public acceptability and by the therapist's consideration of the restrictive nature of the procedure on the client.

Reese's dimensions of effectiveness must also be considered in the planning of treatment. These dimensions of effectiveness interact and covary with the dimensions of intrusiveness. The first dimension involves the probability that the procedure will be effective with the client being treated. A review of the client's history, consultation with the significant others in the client's environment, and initial assessment and observation of the client in naturalistic settings, as well as a review of the current literature on the proposed treatment help to provide a basis for making this probability statement about the client and the selected procedures. Time in treatment is the second dimension of effectiveness to consider as the client may be involved in extended periods of treatment in which aversive methods are being used. The third dimension of effectiveness involves the positive and negative side effects of the procedure. Of course, considering whether a treatment is going to be effective depends on the risks and benefits of that procedure for the client. A treatment procedure's positive and negative side effects can interact with intrusiveness if it causes other inappropriate behaviors requiring additional treatment. Thus, time in treatment would be increased leading possibly to a reduction in overall treatment effectiveness. The durability and generality of the behavior change is the fourth dimension to be considered. The treatment procedures that work rapidly but have only short-term effects may become more intrusive if the client has to return for treatment time after time. Last, the cost associated with treatment that includes therapist and significant others' time in therapy, the amount of time the client has to wait for therapy, and the time of actual implementation of the prescribed procedures must be reviewed. Excessive "costs" such as these may undermine treatment effectiveness by generating increased intrusiveness.

As indicated by Reese, a therapist's decision on the best treatment to use is often a very difficult and perplexing one. There has to be a balance between the amount of intrusiveness of the procedure and the degree to which the procedure is going to be effective for the client. Problems arise in this decision-making process, however, as those procedures that are not intrusive may not be effective, whereas those that are effective are very often intrusive and require close scrutiny by review committees and other sanctioning bodies. Such intrusive but effective procedures increase the therapist's liability as well. Also, the therapist must consider the degree of intrusiveness and effectiveness on an individual basis and not strictly on a procedural basis. Despite all these difficulties, when the therapist considers all these dimensions of intrusiveness and effectiveness, the client, his or her guardians, and where appropriate, human rights committees, are more assured of quality therapy based on the consideration of the client's liberties.

11.1.3. Certification of Behavior Therapists or Behavior Therapy Procedures: Issues of Regulation of the Field

Among a number of applied researchers and clinicians, there has been an ongoing debate as to the advisability of certifying individuals and/or the use of behavioral procedures in the practice of behavior therapy (Agras, 1973; Hutchinson & Fawcett, 1981; Lubetkin, 1983; Sajwaj, 1977; State of Florida, 1982; Stolz, 1977; Thomas & Murphy, 1981). Agras (1973) argued that certification would foster a greater separation between the experimenter and the behavioral clinician. Further, Agras suggested, as an alternative to certification of behavioral practitioners, that behaviorists get appointed to the current state licensing and certification boards of their professions so as to strengthen guidelines within their respective disciplines, rather than forming a separate regulating body to certify individuals, procedures, or to grant licenses. Lubetkin (1983), as a member of an AABT task force on certification, indicated that AABT has considered the possibility of some certification procedures for its members. However, in a recent survey of members in APA and AABT on whether to certify or not certify individuals as behavior therapists in the role as behavioral community psychologists (Hutchinson & Fawcett, 1981), results indicate that most of the membership of these organizations polled voted not to certify on the grounds that such certification would be premature, could be exclusionary, is impractical, and is inconsistent with the public interest. Rather, those polled indicate a preference to establish guidelines in general behavioral analysis rather than to certify or license individuals in the narrowly defined field of behavior therapy.

Stemming from this issue of greater regulation of the behavior therapy profession is the subject of establishing guidelines or competencies. Individuals and treatment facilities could be required to adhere to a set of guidelines for the proper implementation of treatment programs for precise data collection and for the use of appropriate procedures for the referred problems. There has, however, been much debate as to the viability of having such guidelines. Stolz (1977) indicates that imposing such guidelines on professionals and treatment facilities would have undesired side effects. Stolz contends that such guidelines for behavior modification are unnecessary and impractical. She cites several reasons for this position. First, any prescriptive and proscriptive guidelines would interfere with clinical creativity and innovation in the formulation of treatment plans and program development. Second, if behavior modification is regulated, then procedures outside the realm of behaviorism would be used to a greater extent, instead of those regulated procedures, in order to avoid and reduce the aversive paperwork and the required peer review. Third, such guidelines may be used to protect the practices that meet the letter but not the spirit of the regulating rules. Fourth, Stolz indicates that there are critical aspects of behavioral intervention that vary across settings and populations and that it would be difficult to write guidelines applicable in all cases. Last, it would be extremely difficult to write guidelines that would adequately handle the complexity of the interaction between the psychologist's and the client's priorities regarding treatment.

Stolz suggests that an alternative to a written set of guidelines and competencies would be found in the various checklists published by AABT, APA, and the *National Register of Health Services Providers in Psychology* (Survey of Psychological Services, 1979). Use of the *Ethical Standards of Psychologists* (APA, 1979), *Standards for Providers of Psychological Services* (APA, 1974) and its *Specialty Guidelines for the Delivery of Services* (APA, 1980), and AABT's *Ethical Issues for Human Services* (1977) is sufficient, according to Stolz.

Although it is Stolz's opinion that guidelines for the use of behavior therapy procedures are impractical and possess several undesirable side effects, it is the position of Sajwaj (1977), the State of Florida (1982), and Thomas and Murphy (1981) that such guidelines are needed. However, these authors do suggest that caution should be taken in too tightly restricting the professional activities of behavior therapists. These authors have discussed the importance of more objectivity in the designation of which individuals are qualified to practice behavior therapy, which procedures to use for what maladaptive behaviors, what methods will be used to monitor and evaluate these procedures, and what steps will be taken to protect client rights. These and other considerations are currently being made in the development and implementation of such guidelines.

In response to this concern for a greater regulation of behavioral procedures, several states have begun to consider certifying individuals and procedures in the general field of behavioral analysis. Two such states are Minnesota and Florida. Thomas and Murphy (1981) provided a list of competencies that individuals would have to master in order to be certified to act under the Minnesota behavior management guidelines. Through funding by the National Institute of Mental Health, Thomas and Murphy attempted to compile a set of competencies and objective assessment measures for determining those who were at the outset and who continue to be qualified to provide services in the public sector for clinics, retardation facilities, and psychiatric institutions. What is unique about these competencies and guidelines is the objective measures used involve not only a written test, but more important, videotaping in naturalistic settings, case presentations, and simulation exercises with the practitioner applying for certification to use the behavior procedures. This objectivity enhances the credibility of such certification guidelines and further protects the public.

In the state of Florida, the guidelines jointly sponsored by the National Association of Retarded Citizens and the State of Florida (1982) have been implemented for the last 8 years in state facilities for the developmentally disabled. In the last 4 years, individuals have been certified by the Florida Association of Behavior Analysts and the state of Florida to utilize the variety of basic nonrestrictive, mildly restrictive, moderately restrictive, and severely restrictive procedures listed in its manual. A basic nonrestrictive procedure might be differential reinforcement of other behavior (DRO), whereas a mildly restrictive procedure is positive practice. A moderately restrictive procedure is exemplified by a token economy, whereas a severely restrictive procedure is, of course, seclusion time-out. Within this manual are also listed treatment considerations and contraindications for the use of the variety of behavioral procedures, requirements of training, and proficiency scales to utilize these procedures, and the list of federal and state objectives used to evaluate various behavioral programs in publicly funded facilities. These guidelines appear to sufficiently safeguard client rights, while, at the same time, they allow for the behavior therapist to have some flexibility in the selection of procedures for the reduction of certain maladaptive behaviors and the increase of appropriate social and behavioral skills.

The Minnesota and Florida guidelines are certainly positive steps toward proper regulation of the behavior therapy profession. It is my opinion that such guidelines and certification procedures are needed in the private as well as in the public sector. Psychologists, psychiatrists, mental health counselors, and social workers active in private practice as well as in private hospitals and clinics may be unskilled in the use of behavior techniques. These individuals may only be familiar with behavior principles through coursework in a few graduate classes or continuing education workshops. Nonetheless, they attempt to use these procedures, which appear surprisingy and conceptually simple, but are technically difficult to implement. It is not uncommon that some of these individuals misuse these procedures and have few skills in functionally analyzing behavior or "troubleshooting" when a treatment program is ineffective. They, therefore, deprive the client of proper behavioral intervention services. Regulating who uses these procedures would certainly benefit and protect the client and the general public.

11.1.4. Peer Review and Human Rights Committees in the Public and Private Sectors

With the sweeping changes that occurred within the mental health field during the 1970s, greater attention has, therefore, been shown to the provision of quality care to clients. Though Stolz (1980) might contend that guidelines and peer review in behavior therapy are unnecessary and redundant, peer review makes the therapist accountable on a continuing basis, which promotes greater self-discipline. Theaman (1984) suggests that long before any review of a professional for his or her practices occurs, that professional should question himself regarding what his colleagues would think about how he was handling the case in question. More realistically, self-monitoring cannot be the only approach to ensuring quality human services. The need for peer review and the protection of the client's human rights are ongoing and vital processes to the provision of care (Theaman, 1984).

The era of peer review and human rights committees is quite young, and the criteria for what peer review and other such committees should review are gradually evolving and have not yet entirely solidified. Professionals in the field have attempted to address the issue of what standards are needed for these committees (Florida Psychological Association, 1985; Goldiamond, 1974, 1975b; Griffin, 1980; Risley & Sheldon-Wildgen, 1980a, 1980b; Stolz, 1980; Theaman, 1984). Much of what is written has been directed toward the review and regulation of services by public facilities, whereas peer review in the private sector is still in its infancy.

Griffin (1980) has suggested a set of procedures for ensuring a legally safe environment in residential facilities. These procedures are written for administrators to use in safeguarding the rights of the residents living in their facilities. Because one of the primary responsibilities of an administrator is to monitor programs that might place a client "at risk" for physical or psychological harm, these guidelines help to ensure client rights and reduce liability.

Griffin outlines a variety of components of a legally safe environment. The first consideration should be a statement of policy regarding the facility's adherence to the least restrictive alternative model of treatment and living conditions. All program development must be consistent with this policy statement and must include alternatives for treating the client's problems, the risks and benefits of treatment, anticipated outcomes, and any special precautions to be taken in treatment. As part of this program development consideration, documentation must involve a system of data collection that must be ongoing and provide a data base for all program decisions. The peer review component requires that any procedures to be used that pose physical and psychological danger to the client should be reviewed by a committee of knowledgeable professionals and, possibly, by informed lay individuals for the purpose of determining the feasibility of such procedures.

Another component of this legally safe environment consists of the issue of consent. That is, the client or the client's representatives must grant consent to the use of potentially "at-risk" procedures. Fully informed consent involves the capacity of the client or representative to make decisions and the degree to which the client or representative is aware of the exact nature of the proposed progam and its risks and benefits. Consent must be granted without coercion, and it must be obtained after peer review approval. The client or his or her representative has a right to withdraw consent at any time. Human rights committees must also be in place to be an external source of review and represent public consent. The purpose of these committees is to ensure that programs ongoing at a facility are generally palatable and defendable to the public at large.

Griffin also indicates that staff training and consultant involvement must be provided. All staff must be trained in order to provide the level of professional competency necessary to implement the treatment procedures prescribed. The use of consultants is needed for the administrator to obtain second opinions regarding controversial programs. However, to avoid further situations in which abuse might occur, Griffin also suggests that the administrator define *abuse* in the facility's policy statement. This definition of abuse would include what procedures must be followed for what violations of clients' rights.

In her response to Griffin's suggestions for these guidelines, Stolz (1980) criticizes his position of the need for such guidelines on the premise that clinicians and those in the position to make treatment recommendations would make such choices regarding the treatments of choice for a client's difficulty based on what is least effortful and not always on what is in the best interest of the client. Similarly, Stolz indicates that the client's representatives are usually going to act in ways that are more reinforcing to themselves rather than in ways that are good for their wards. Whether this position is a universal one is certainly in doubt, but it is subject to empirical determination. However, having human rights committees does go one step further in monitoring what is good for the client over and above the peer review and client's representative's opinion of what is in that client's best interest.

Risley and Sheldon-Wildgen (1980b) have provided a list of suggested procedures for human rights committees (HRC) to follow, particularly in cases involving controversial treatment programs. At the inception of the formation of a HRC, there are several procedures to follow. First, there must be a written statement of purpose with objectives and goals delineated. Second, members of the newly formed HRC should acquaint themselves with the various guidelines and standards of advocacy groups relevant to the clients whose rights the HRC are protecting (e.g., National Association of Retarded Citizens, mental health boards). Third, where necessary, outside experts and advocates in the area should be contacted in pertinent cases for their review as well as for their input in upgrading the HRC guidelines. Fourth, there must be a formal review process for determining the HRC's position on the use of aversive procedures to include what constitutes controversial and noncontroversial procedures, what procedures require HRC review and approval, and those that do not. Fifth, the HRC must establish a formal review process to periodically evaluate and assess the treatment and progress of each client. Sixth, whenever a case is being reviewed, Risley and Sheldon-Wildgen suggest that the committee always take a position advocating the opposite type of treatment to the one being proposed. In this manner, those proposing a certain treatment have to make a convincing case for the treatment, present supporting literature, indicate what has been tried, and detail the safeguards to be written into the proposed methods. Seventh, these authors suggest that the HRC meet and deliberate as an independent body and be as autonomous as possible from the rest of the staff of the facility. Finally, the HRC should provide all relevant staff and facilities with a description of its policy and review procedures.

AABT has begun to be involved in the concept of peer review in the private as well as in the public sectors (Risley & Sheldon-Wildgen, 1980a). The association has begun to serve in the role as an assistant and reviewer to those writing guidelines for facilities, for on-site review of noncontroversial and controversial programs, and to provide testimony in, or provide professional assistance to, investigations for lawsuits concerning the appropriateness of treatment to a client or residents in a facility. In the private sector, AABT can serve in the role as a "clearinghouse" by providing to therapists who do not have access to professional colleagues in their local area consultation with other behavioral clinicians to discuss unique, perplexing clinical problems. In this manner, AABT assists the behavioral clinician in providing quality services to his or her clients.

Peer review in the private sector is a double-edged sword, however. On the one hand, the clinician is not as isolated from his colleagues and can communicate more freely through such vehicles as AABT. In this way, the client is assured of greater protection of his rights and to quality services. However, as Theaman (1984) points out, the impact of peer review on private professional practice makes such private practice less private than ever before. Theaman exemplifies this concern by his description of the various levels of review that are now in place in the CHAMPUS operations. The mental health treatment report that CHAMPUS now requires is quite explicit and asks for a great deal of information about the client, his or her difficulties, what type of treatment is planned, projected treatment duration, and the rationale for each treatment method proposed. Such peer review does provide more competency and thoroughness on the part of the clinician, but there is a point at which peer review becomes a violation of the client's right to privacy and confidentiality. These and other related issues certainly need exploration in the future.

11.2. APPLIED RESEARCH ISSUES

There are a variety of issues within the field of applied research that are beginning to have impact on the field of behavior therapy as well as on independent behavioral practice. These issues are briefly discussed in this chapter to highlight current research concerns in the application of behavior therapy.

11.2.1. Ecobehavioral Systems and the Analysis of Setting Events: A Study of More Complex and Subtle Social Contingencies

An integration of behavioral technology and ecology such as the one projected by Willens (1974) has been the focus of recent research (Tertinger, Greene, & Lutzker, 1984). The behavioral/ecological impact that behavior therapy has on the client, on the client's family, and on the interaction of other features of the environment has also been the subject of recent study. Willens suggests that there is a larger ecological system that behaviorists have to consider in their overall planning for therapeutic change for a client. Second and third order contingencies and consequences resulting from the implementation of certain procedures should be projected by the behavior therapist before intruding on the complex behavioral ecosystem in place, prior to treatment. According to Willens, the behaviorist and ecologist have to work together to formulate a method of conducting a behavioral/ecological analysis of the referred problems.

Tertinger, Greene, and Lutzker (1984) studied home safety as a component of an overall ecobehavioral treatment program for children of abuse and neglect. This study attempts to validate various categories of home safety and tests the results of an educative treatment approach encompassing behavioral and ecological procedures and consequences. Studies such as these and the many shared "values" held by the behaviorist and the ecologist such as objectivity, pragmatism, and principles of behavior suggest that an integration of behavioral technology and ecology is possible. There is still much debate about behavioral ecology. However, future directions in behavior therapy point toward this approach as well as to an improvement in the assessment and treatment in accord with the ongoing ecosystem.

A related research issue involves the influence of setting events on social contingencies or "networks" (Wahler & Graves, 1983). *Setting events* are defined as immediate conditions that tend to influence which of the various stimulus-response relationships will occur within some ongoing social network. Wahler and Graves (1983) define a *social network* as a bidirectional process of the interaction of the behaviors of parents, teachers, children, siblings, and peers. A setting event is assumed to be an additional variable to be considered in the functional analysis of, for example, a parent–child problem, over and above the ongoing contingencies, the conditioning history of the child, and the topography of the child's behavior. The analysis of setting events is similar to Bernstein's (1984) exosystem and macrosystem analysis in whch higher order contingencies can affect the lower order contingencies and therefore influence the behavior of concern. Unfortunately, little is known about the principles of setting events that would allow the researcher or practitioner to better analyze and predict the behavior of a parent and child, for example. Wahler and Graves indicate that setting events analysis should be the focus of inquiry to assist the clinician in better analyzing the clinical problems of the clients he or she sees. Through such an investigation, a more thorough analysis of the variables influencing behavior from first as well as higher order contingencies can result in greater predictability of the outcome of various behavioral interventions.

11.2.2. Research and Therapy: Toward a Better Integration of Disciplines

Researchers in the field (Barlow, 1980; Bornstein & Rychtarik, 1983; Goldfried, 1983) indicate that the future trend in the private practice of behavior therapy is in a greater association of research with therapy. Through such efforts, the scientist-practitioner can better know what are effective behavioral techniques for what clinical problems. Such an approach would provide the clinician as well as his or her colleagues with information that would narrow the use of certain procedures to certain populations and better define the parameters of the procedures for the private practitioner.

Goldfried (1983) emphasizes that, in a clinical behavioral practice, there are often no set guidelines for selecting the appropriate behavioral procedure for referred clinical problems. On the contrary, clinical behavior therapy is more of an art than a science because the clinician is left to select from "intuition," educated guessing, or by laboriously reading through all the literature on the referred problem those procedures that appear to be viable methods of ameliorating the presenting problems. Goldfried strongly recommends that there be a pooling of clinical observations of successes as well as failures of practicing behavior therapists to provide a balance of what more puristic research indicates are the "treatments of choice." Finally, Goldfried reiterates that neither behavioral research nor clinical behavior therapy can alone advance the field. Rather, both of these groups need each other to validate scientifically, clinically, and ecologically the methodology currently available to researchers and clinicians.

Levy (1984) has discussed the integration of research with therapy in an article advocating the formation of a new subfield of psychology called "human services psychology." This branch of psychology, Levy contends, would be a "metamorphosis" of present-day clinical psychology and should be based on a biopsychosocial model of human behavior. Levy proposes a three-dimensional matrix of clinical services which is analogous to the broad-spectrum approach of behavior therapy advocated in this text and in current behavioral literature. The axes of this matrix are made up of (a) *content*, to include the knowledge and skill base of clinical psychology; (b) *levels of intervention*, which involve social/community contingencies, psychobehavioral contingencies, and biopsychological contingencies; and (c) *modes of intervention*, which include direct therapy, program development and evaluation, and consultation and education.

11.2.3. Scientific and Social Validation and Consumer Satisfaction: Research and Clinical Accountability

Accountability in the field of research and therapy has been a growing concern. Accountability can be viewed from different perspectives such as from the researcher's scientific validation of the clinical significance of a treatment approach, the social validation or determination of significance of treatment to a client, and to overall client/consumer satisfaction with therapy.

At the simplest level, practitioners should require themselves to take data within an A-B design, such as is reported in Chapter 10, in order to demonstrate treatment effectiveness. The objective data and the clinical observations of the practitioner may aid the researcher in conducting a component analysis of what works in therapy. Such information exchange would then influence the conduct of individual therapy by specifying the important variables of treatment.

In the behavioral literature, there are many claims of procedural effectiveness. In accord with the issue of accountability, there is now a greater need for scrutiny of claims that various treatment procedures are effective without subjecting them to rigorous behavioral analysis. As Barlow (1980) points out, some procedures are a part of treatment packages but, other than face validity, they have little research supporting their inclusion in the treatment of the client's difficulties. It is the responsibility of the behavioral clinician/researcher to conduct evaluative studies based on single-subject research to validate the use of these various procedures. Without this self-examination, behavior therapy may lose its gradually earned credibility in the professional community as an accepted broad-spectrum approach to eliminating human suffering.

Jacobson, Follette, and Revenstorf (1984) have emphasized, in their treatise on scientific validation, the need for greater accountability in the reporting of variability and clinical significance of psychotherapy outcome research. There are several ways in which applied researchers can more accurately and representatively report their results. Jacobson and Follette support current views of the need for developing, validating, and using single-subject experimental designs; they suggest the development of adequate norms for comparative purposes and various within-subject and normative indexes of progress by a client. Specifically, indexes should be developed that reflect how a client has progressed during therapy relative to control group clients, locate the client somewhere in the distribution of change scores achieved by other clients given the same treatment, show how different the client is from what would be predicted by a linear regression analysis based on pretest scores, and reflect the percentage of the control group that the client had surpassed while in therapy. In summary, Jacobson and Follette contend that in order to make accurate judgments regarding the "goodness" or "badness" of a clinical procedure, the psychotherapy research must more clearly reflect significant clinical improvement or deterioration of the results of therapy. Only in this manner can the field and the clinician claim more accountability.

Social validation is another method for determining accountability in research and therapy. Validation is defined by Kazdin (1977) as the demonstration of the clinical and social significance of some behavioral excess, deficiency, or stimulus control difficulty as well as the treatment selected for this problem. Wolf (1978) indicates that treatment acceptability (i.e., social validation) refers to the judgments about the treatment methods by nonprofessionals, lay persons, clients, and other consumers of therapy. Treatment is deemed appropriate according to whether the consumer views the treatment procedures as fair, reasonable, and based on the least intrusive/most effective rule for the selection of therapeutic procedures. Social validation is obtained by various methods such as videotaping the client's engaging in the maladaptive behavior and obtaining ratings as to the degree of social deficiency of the behavior being rated, or, after treatment had been successfully completed, having the client demonstrate the appropriate behavior in the critical setting in which the behavior was deemed inappropriate and then having the client rated by significant others as well as by independent observers on some dimension of appropriateness. Despite the fact that some researchers question the theoretical integrity of the social validation procedure due to contentions that too much subjectivity is involved in the determination of social validation (Woods, 1983), the current literature indicates an increase in the number of studies incorporating the use of social validation in their procedures (Fawcett & Miller, 1975; Finney, Rapoff, Hall, & Christophersen, 1983; Kazdin, 1980; Minkin et al., 1976; Wolf, 1978).

Consumer satisfaction with therapy is also a component of therapeutic accountability not only with the individual client and his or her family but also for the purposes of insurance reimbursement and peer review committees. Bornstein and Rychtarik (1983), Garfield (1983), Kiesler (1983), McMahon and Forehand (1983), and Parloff (1983) have discussed this issue at length in a miniseries on consumer satisfaction that appeared in *Behavior Therapy*. These authors concluded that behavior therapists must be cognizant of assessing consumer satisfaction in their research and therapy programs. Assessment needs to be multifaceted to include not only direct and moment-to-moment data but also ratings of satisfaction from the consumer, representatives, and the lay public. The therapist is urged by these researchers to keep detailed descriptions of treatment and therapy as well as to note the types of treatments helpful to which types of clients. With this data, the behaviorist in private practice can then consult with the behavioral researcher for the purpose of examining new methods for validating and increasing consumer satisfaction.

11.3. BEHAVIOR THERAPISTS' ROLE IN SHAPING SOCIAL POLICY

In the years that followed the early 1970s during which there were many abuses of human rights lodged against individuals for misusing behavior modification, the public image of behavior therapy was gradually tarnished in the media, both in the newspapers and on television. Turkat (1979) has cited many references in the public media as well as from other behavioral researchers that indicate that there was a stronger negative image of the field held by professionals and the lay public at that time. In response to this crisis of confidence in the profession, representatives of AABT met in 1980 to outline the long-range plan for the future of AABT and the profession. O'Leary (1983), in his message to the membership of AABT, specified the long-range objectives of that overall plan for AABT's future. As part of its objectives, AABT has planned to enhance its public and professional image in several ways. This long-range plan recommends promoting positive and accurate mention of behavior therapy in the print media, making behavior therapy an insurance reimbursable clinical service, increasing the number of federal, state, and third-party payments, increasing the representation of behavior therapists on state licensing boards, advisory committees, and peer review committees, developing a positive image of behavior therapy by 50% of those recognized in the field, having positive mention made about behavior therapy in national columns, having at least one segment per month on a health cable network on behavior therapy, and developing a valid mechanism for evaluating the quality of research, service, and education by behavioral scientists, clinicians, and academicians.

O'Leary (1984), in his presidential address to the 17th Annual Convention of AABT, has encouraged the membership to "take a stand" and strive for a more positive image of behavior therapy on the part of the public, the media, and other professions. According to O'Leary, statistics indicate that there is a greater preference for the use of behavior therapy among psychologists. Professionals such as pediatric psychologists and pediatricians, professional schools of psychology, and a sample of practitioners from the national register and the American Psychiatric Association Task Force report on behavior therapy all indicate that behavior therapy is a viable clinical approach useful in a variety of settings and for a variety of populations. Not only do professionals in the field indicate an acceptance of behavior therapy but the professional research literature has shown a dramatic increase in the number of studies and position papers in the application of behavioral techniques to various problems. According to O'Leary, the number of research grants awarded to behavior therapists/researchers far outweigh the number granted to other psychologists. The reason for this fact, O'Leary states, is that behavior therapists have a greater expertise in designing sound treatment outcome studies. In opposition to Turkat's (1979) position that behavior therapy has a strongly negative public and professional image, O'Leary reviewed newspaper articles between the years 1968 and 1983 and found that although behavior therapy was rated in negative terms in the media up to 1978, articles in major newspapers since that time have described behavior therapy in very positive terms. Hence, it can be said that the lay and professional public now generally view behavior therapy with greater acceptance as a viable treatment approach. From this and other evidence, O'Leary contends that it is now time to push for greater recognition by the public as well as in the political arena. In order to facilitate greater research grants and funds from the federal government, behavior therapists and AABT must take an active role in influencing the political powers that be toward the view that behavior therapy is a very effective and major theoretical orientation having a great deal to offer the public. In this manner, social policy and decision making can be strongly influenced by this view.

AABT formally recognized the need for developing a working relationship between itself and political and social service policymakers at the state and federal levels (Jones, Czyzewski, Otis, & Hannah, 1983). With the formation of a network of experts in the field of behavior therapy as representatives of AABT, the organization is now in a position to significantly affect social policymaking involving the appropriate use and growth of behavior therapy. There is now a Committee on Legislative Affairs to monitor state and federal policies that in some way may have impact on the field in general. Not only is this committee seeking regional liaisons to testify on various policy issues in the making, but the members of this committee are also able to serve as consultants to administrative officials to help design and evaluate treatment programs with the appropriate safeguards. In summary, the Committee on Legislative Affairs is one of the first steps forward to assert the role of behavior therapy in the helping professions.

It is time to take a stand; to assert ourselves as viable clinicians who meet the needs of our clients in an effective, ethical, and accountable fashion. A greater integration and meeting of the minds between research and therapy is needed. A continued upgrading of the peer review system in the private as well as in the public sectors is crucial. The therapist's continued adherence to the needs of the client, maintaining responsibility and accountability for competent assessment, evaluation, and treatment is vital. With such affirmative steps forward, the future of behavior therapy can only get brighter.

References

Achenbach, T. M., & Edelbrock, C. S. (1979). The child behavior profile, II. Boys aged twelve to sixteen and girls aged six to eleven and twelve to sixteen. *Journal of Consulting and Clinical Psychology, 47,* 223–233.

Agras, S. (1973). Toward the certification of behavior therapists? *Journal of Applied Behavior Analysis, 6,* 167–172.

Alberti, R. E. (Ed.). (1977). *Assertiveness: Innovations, applications, issues.* San Luis Obispo, CA: Impact Publishers.

Alberti, R. E., & Emmons, M. L. (1974). *Your perfect right: A guide to assertive behavior.* San Luis Obispo, CA: Impact Publishers.

American Psychiatric Association. (1980). *Diagnostic and Statistical Manual of Mental Disorders* (3rd ed.), Washington, DC: Author.

American Psychological Association. (1974). *Standards for providers of psychological services.* Washington, DC: Author.

American Psychological Association. (1979). *Ethical standards of psychologists.* Washington, DC: Author.

American Psychological Association Committee on Professional Standards. (1980). *Specialty guidelines for the delivery of services.* Washington, DC: Author.

Anrep, G. V. (1920). Pitch discrimination in the dog. *Journal of Physiology, 53,* 367–385.

Association for Advancement of Behavior Therapy. (1977). *Ethical issues for human services.* New York: Author.

Autogenic Systems. (1983). *Biological feedback instrumentation catalog.* Berkeley, CA: Author.

Ayllon, T., & Azrin, N. H. (1968). *The token economy: A motivational system for therapy and rehabilitation.* New York: Appleton-Century-Crofts.

Azrin, N. H., & Foxx, R. M. (1971). A rapid method of toilet training of the institutionalized retarded. *Journal of Applied Behavior Analysis, 4,* 89–99.

Azrin, N. H., & Foxx, R. M. (1973). *Toilet training the retarded.* Champaign, IL: Research Press.

Azrin, N. H., & Foxx, R. M. (1974). *Toilet training in less than a day.* New York: Simon & Schuster.

Azrin, N. H., & Holz, W. C. (1966). Punishment. In W. K. Honig (Ed.), *Operant behavior: Areas of research and application* (pp. 380–447). New York: Appleton-Century-Crofts.

Azrin, N. H., & Lindsley, O. R. (1956). The reinforcement of cooperation between children. *Journal of Abnormal and Social Psychology, 52,* 100–102.

Azrin, N. H., & Nunn, G. R. (1973). Habit reversal: A method of eliminating nervous habits and tics. *Behavior Research and Therapy, 11,* 619–628.

Azrin, N. H., & Nunn, G. R. (1978). *Habit control in a day.* New York: Pocket Books.

Azrin, N. H., & Powers, M. A. (1975). Eliminating classroom disturbances of emotionally disturbed children by positive practice procedures. *Behavior Therapy, 6,* 525–534.

Azrin, N. H., & Wesolowski, M. D. (1974). Theft reversal: An overcorrection procedure for eliminating stealing by retarded persons. *Journal of Applied Behavior Analysis, 7,* 577–581.

Azrin, N. H., Hutchinson, R. R., & Hake, D. F. (1966). Extinction-induced aggression. *Journal of Experimental Analysis of Behavior, 9,* 191–204.

Azrin, N. H., Kaplan, S. J., & Foxx, R. M. (1973). Autism reversal: Eliminating stereotyped self-stimulation of retarded individuals. *American Journal of Mental Deficiency, 78,* 241–248.

Azrin, N., Naster, B., & Jones, R. (1973). Reciprocity counseling: A rapid learning-based procedure for marital counseling. *Behavior Research and Therapy, 11,* 365–382.

Azrin, N. H., Sneed, T. J., & Foxx, R. M. (1973). Dry bed: A rapid method of eliminating bedwetting (enuresis) of the retarded. *Behavior Research and Therapy, 11,* 427–434.

Azrin, N. H., Sneed, T. J., & Foxx, R. M. (1974). Dry-bed training: Rapid elimination of childhood enuresis. *Behavior Research and Therapy, 12,* 147–156.

Azrin, N. H., Flores, T., & Kaplan, S. J. (1975). The job finding club: A group assisted approach for obtaining jobs. *Behavior Research and Therapy, 13,* 17–27.

Bailey, J. (1977). *A handbook of research methods in applied behavior analysis.* Tallahassee, FL: The Florida State University Press.

Bailey, J. S., & Reiss, M. L. (1984). The demise of the "model-T" and the emergence of systems management in human services. *The Behavior Therapist, 7,* 65–68.

Bandura, A. (1962). Social learning through imitation. In M. R. Jones (Ed.), *Nebraska Symposium on Motivation,* pp. 211–269. Lincoln: University of Nebraska Press.

Bandura, A. (1965). Vicarious processes: A case of no-trial learning. In L. Berkowitz (Ed.), *Advances in experimental social psychology* (Vol. 2, pp. 1–55). New York: Academic Press.

Bandura, A. (1968). Modeling approaches to the modification of phobic disorders. In R. Porter (Ed.), *CIBA Foundation Symposium: The role of learning in psychotherapy* (pp. 201–217). London: Churchill.

Bandura, A. (1969). *Principles of behavior modification.* New York: Holt, Rinehart & Winston.

Bandura, A., & Huston, A. C. (1961). Identification as a process of incidental learning. *Journal of Abnormal and Social Psychology, 63,* 311–318.

Bandura, A., & Kupers, C. J. (1964). Transmission of patterns of self-reinforcement through modeling. *Journal of Abnormal and Social Psychology, 69,* 1–9.

Bandura, A., & Walters, R. H. (1959). *Social learning and personality development.* New York: Holt, Rinehart & Winston.

Bandura, A., & Whalen, C. K. (1966). The influence of antecedent reinforcement and divergent modeling cues on patterns of self-reward. *Journal of Personality and Social Psychology, 3,* 373–382.

Bandura, A., Ross, D., & Ross, S. A. (1963). Vicarious reinforcement and imitative learning. *Journal of Abnormal and Social Psychology, 67,* 601–607.

Bandura, A., Grusec, J. E., & Menlove, F. L. (1967). Some social deterimants of self-monitoring reinforcement systems. *Journal of Personality and Social Psychology, 5,* 449–445.

Bandura, A., Blanchard, E. B., & Ritter, B. (1969). The relative efficacy of desensitization and modeling approaches for inducing behavioral, affective, and attitudinal changes. *Stanford University, 13,* 173–199.

Barlow, D. H. (1973). Increasing heterosexual responsiveness in the treatment of sexual deviation. A review of the clinical and experimental evidence. *Behavior Therapy, 4,* 655–671.

Barlow, D. H. (1980). Behavior therapy: The next decade. *Behavior Therapy, 11,* 315–328.

Barlow, D. H. (Ed.). (1981). *Behavioral assessment of adult disorders.* New York: Guilford Press.

Basmajian, J. V. (1974). *Muscles alive: Their function revealed by electromyography* (3rd ed.). Baltimore: Williams & Wilkins.

Basmajian, J. V. (1979). *Biofeedback—principles and practice for clinicians.* Baltimore: Williams & Wilkins.

Beck, A. T. (1964). Thinking and depression: II. Theory and therapy. *Archives of General Psychiatry, 10,* 561–571.

Beck, A. T. (1967). *Depression: Causes and Treatment.* Philadelphia: University of Pennsylvania Press.

Beck, A. T. (1976). *Cognitive therapy and the emotional disorders.* New York: International University Press.

Beck, A. T. (1978a). *Daily log of dysfunctional thoughts.* Philadelphia: Center for Cognitive Therapy.

Beck, A. T. (1978b). *Depression Inventory.* Philadelphia: Center for Cognitive Therapy.

Beck, A. T., Ward, C. H., Mendelson, M., Mock, J. E., & Erbaugh, J. K. (1961). An inventory for measuring depression. *Archives of General Psychiatry, 5,* 462–467.

Beck, A. T., Rush, A. J., Shaw, B. F., Emery, G. (1979). *Cognitive therapy of depression.* New York: Guilford Press.

Becker, W. C. (1970). *Parents Are Teachers.* Champaign, IL: Research Press.

Becker, W. C., Engelmann, S., & Thomas, D. R. (1975). *Teaching 1: Classroom management.* Chicago: Science Research Associates.

Bellack, A. S., Hersen, M., & Kazdin, A. E. (Eds.). (1982). *International handbook of behavior modification in therapy.* New York: Plenum Press.

Benson, H. (1975). *The relaxation response.* New York: Morrow.

Bernstein, D. A., & Borkovec, T. D. (1973). *Progressive relaxation training: A manual for the helping professions.* Champaign, IL: Research Press.

Bernstein, G. S. (1982). Training behavior change agents: A conceptual review. *Behavior Therapy, 13,* 1–23.

Bernstein, G. S. (1984). Training of behavior change agents. In M. Hersen, R. M. Eisler, & P. M. Miller (Eds.), *Progress in behavior modification* (pp. 167–199). New York: Academic Press.

Bernstein, G. S., & Ziarnik, J. P. (1984). Training behavior change agents in outcome selection. *The Behavior Therapist, 7,* 103–104.

Birk, L., Stolz, S. B., Brady, J. P., Brady, J. V., Lazarus, A. A., Lynch, J. J., Rosenthal, A. J., Shelton, W. D., Stevens, J. B., & Thomas, E. J. (1973). *Behavior therapy in psychiatry.* Washington, DC: American Psychiatric Association.

Biomonitoring Applications, Incorporated. *BMA books and cassettes catalog.* (1983). New York: Author.

Bornstein, P. H., & Rychtarik, R. C. (1983). Consumer satisfaction in adult behavior therapy: Procedures, problems, and future perspectives. *Behavior Therapy, 14,* 191–208.

Borowy, T., Buffone, G., & Kaplan, S. J. (1985, March). *EAPs, PPOs, HMOs: A growing opportunity for private practice.* A workshop presented at the Southeastern Psychological Association, Atlanta, Georgia.

Bostow, D. E., & Bailey, J. B. (1969). Modification of severe disruptive and aggressive behavior using brief time-out and reinforcement procedures. *Journal of Applied Behavior Analysis, 2,* 31–37.

Bower, S. A., & Bower, G. H. (1976). *Asserting yourself.* Reading, MA: Addison-Wesley.

Brady, J. V., & Hunt, H. F. (1955). An experimental approach to the analysis of emotional behavior. *Journal of Psychology, 40,* 313–324.

Brady, J. V., Porter, R. W., Conrad, D. G., & Mason, J. W. (1958). Avoidance behavior and the development of gastroduodenal ulcers. *Journal of Experimental Analysis of Behavior, 1,* 69–72.

Brown, B. (1974). *New mind, new body—biofeedback: New directions for the mind.* New York: Harper.

Brown, B. S., Wienckowski, L. A., & Stolz, S. B. (1975). *Behavior modification: Perspectives on a current issue.* Washington, D.C.: National Institute of Mental Health.

Brown, R. L., & Presbie, R. J. (1978). *Behavior modification in business, industry, and government.* New Paltz, NY: Behavior Improvement Associates.

Browning, C. H. (1982). *Private practice handbook: The tools, tactics, and techniques for successful practice development.* Los Alamitos, CA: Duncliff's International.

Budzynski, T. (1978). *Relaxation training program.* New York: Biomonitoring Applications.

Cautela, J. R. (1977). *Behavior analysis forms for clinical intervention* (Vols. 1 & 2). Champaign, IL: Research Press.

Cautela, J. R., & Upper, D. (1975). The Process of Individual Behavior Therapy. In M. Hersen, R. M. Eisler, & P. M. Miller, (Eds.) *Progress in Behavior Modification* (Vol. 1, pp. 275–305). New York: Academic Press.

Clark, H. B., Wadden, T. A., Brownell, K. D., Gordon, S. G., & Tarte, R. D. (1983). Sources of continuing education for behavior therapists: The utility of journals, conferences, and other informational sources. *The Behavior Therapist, 6,* 23–26.

Clarkin, J. F., & Glazer, H. I. (Eds.). (1981). *Depression: Behavioral and directive intervention strategies.* New York: Garland.

Covington v. Harris, 419 F.2d 617 (D.C. Cir. 1969).

Cower, E. L., Huser, J., Beach, D. R., & Rappoport, J. (1970). Parental perceptions of young children and their relation to indexes of adjustment. *Journal of Consulting and Clinical Psychology, 32,* 97–103.

Craighead, W. E., Rogers, T., & Bauer, R. M. (1979). A scene-presentation flowchart for systematic desensitization proper. *The Behavior Therapist, 2,* 22.

DeLeon, P. H., VandenBos, G. R., & Cummings, N. A. (1983). Psychotherapy—Is it safe, effective and appropriate? *American Psychologist, 38,* 907–911.

DeWeaver, K. L. (1983). Evolutions of the microcomputer: Technological implications for the private practitioner. *Psychotherapy and Private Practice, 1,* 59–69.

DiCara, L., & Miller, N. E. (1968). Instrumental learning of vasomotor responses by rats: Learning to respond differentially in the two ears. *Science, 159,* 1485–1486.

Donaldson v. O'Connor, 493 F.2d 507 (5 Cir. 1974).

Drash, P., & Bostow, D. (1981). *How to survive in the market place as a behavior therapist or are we too good for our own good?* Paper presented at the 1st Annual Florida Association of Behavior Analysts (FABA) Convention, Orlando.

Edelson, J. O., & Rose, S. D. (1978). *A behavior role-play test for assessing children's social skills.* Paper presented at the 12th Annual Convention of the Association of Behavior Therapy, Chicago.

Ellis, A. (1962). *Reason and emotion in psychotherapy.* New York: Stuart.

Ellis, A. (1970). Posters of rational terms, rational self-analysis forms, and common irrational ideas. New York: Institute for Rational Living.

Ellis, A. (1971). *Growth through reason.* Palo Alto, CA: Science and Behavior Books.

Ellis, A. (1976). Rational self-help form. New York: Institute for Rational Living.

Ellis, A., & Grieger, R. (1977). *Handbook of rational-emotive therapy.* New York: Springer Press.

Ellis, A., & Harper, R. (1975). *A new guide to rational living.* North Hollywood, CA: Wilshire Books.

Ellis, A., Mosely, S., & Wolfe, J. L. (1972). *How to raise an emotionally healthy, happy, child.* North Hollywood, CA: Wilshire Books.

Estes, W. K., & Skinner, B. F. (1941). Some quantative properties of anxiety. *Journal of Experimental Psychology, 29,* 390–400.

Eysenck, H. J. (1960). *Behavior therapy and the neuroses.* Oxford: Pergamon Press.

Eysenck, H. J. (1964). *Experiments in behavior therapy.* Oxford: Pergamon Press.

Farrall instruments catalog. Grand Island, NB: Farrall Instruments.

Fawcett, S. B., & Miller, L. K. (1975). Training public speaking behavior: An experimental analysis and social validation. *Journal of Applied Behavior Analysis, 8,* 125–135.

Ferster, C. B., & Skinner, B. F. (1957). *Schedules of reinforcement.* New York: Appleton-Century-Crofts.

Finney, J. W., Rapoff, M. A., Hall, C. L., & Christopherson, E. R. (1983). Replication and social validation of habit reversal treatment for tics. *Behavior Therapy, 14,* 116–126.

Fishman, S. T. (1978). *Sensory awareness relaxation* (G. C. Davison, consultant). New York: Biomonitoring Applications.

Fishman, S. T., & Lubetkin, B. S. (1983). Office practice of behavior therapy. In M. Hersen (Ed.), *Outpatient behavior therapy* (pp. 21–41). New York: Grune & Stratton.

Florida Psychological Association. (1985). *The Florida Psychologist.* Tallahassee, FL: Author.

Flowers, J. V., & Borream, C. D. (1980). Simulation and role-playing methods. In A. P. Goldstein & F. H. Kanter (Eds.), *Helping people change* (pp. 159–194). Oxford: Pergamon Press.

Focus International catalog of films, video, filmstrips, and slides. (1984). New York: Focus International.

Ford, J. D. (1978). Therapeutic relationship in behavior therapy: An empirical analysis. *Journal of Consulting and Clinical Psychology, 46,* 1302–1314.

Ford, J. D., & Kendall, P. C. (1979). Behavior therapists' professional behaviors: Converging evidence of a gap between theory and practice. *The Behavior Therapist, 2,* 37–38.

Forehand, R. L., & McMahon, R. J. (1981). *Helping the noncompliant child: A clinician's guide to parent training.* New York: Guilford Press.

Foxx, R. M. (1982). *Decreasing behaviors of severely retarded and autistic persons.* Champaign, IL: Research Press.

Foxx, R. M., & Azrin, N. H. (1973a). *Toilet training the retarded: A rapid program for day and nighttime independent toileting.* Champaign, IL: Research Press.

Foxx, R. M., & Azrin, N. H. (1973b). Dry pants: A rapid method of toilet training children. *Behavior Research and Therapy, 11,* 435–442.

Foxx, R. M., & Azrin, N. H. (1973c). The elimination of autistic self-stimulatory behavior by overcorrection. *Journal of Applied Behavior Analysis, 6,* 1–14.

Foxx, R. M., & Azrin, N. H. (1974). *Toilet training in less than a day.* New York: Simon & Schuster.

Franks, C. M. (Ed.). (1969). *Behavior therapy: Appraisal and status.* New York: McGraw-Hill.

Fredericksen, L. W., Brehony, K. A., & Riley, A. W. (1983). *Marketing professional services.* A workshop presented at the Association for Advancement of Behavior Therapy.

Fredericksen, L. W., Solomon, L. J., & Brehony, K. A. (1984). *Marketing health behavior: Principles, techniques, and applications.* New York: Plenum Press.

Fuller, G. (1977). *Biofeedback: Methods and procedures in clinical practice.* San Francisco: Biofeedback Press.

Future Heath, Incorporated. (1985). *Future Heath equipment catalog.* Bensalem, PA.

Gambrill, E. D., & Richey, C. A. (1975). An assertion inventory for use in assessment and research. *Behavior Therapy, 6,* 550–561.

Gambrill, E. D., & Richey, C. A. (1976). *It's up to you.* Millbrae, CA: Les Femmes Publishing.

Gardner, W. I. (1971). *Behavior modification in mental retardation.* Chicago: Aldine-Atherton.

Gardner, W. I. (1974). *Children with learning and behavior problems: A behavior management approach.* Boston: Allyn & Bacon.

Garfield, S. L. (1983). Some comments on consumer satisfaction in behavior therapy. *Behavior Therapy, 14,* 237–241.

GLS Associates, Incorporated. (1983). Philadelphia, PA.

Goldfried, M. R. (1983). The behavior therapist in clinical practice. *The Behavior Therapist, 6,* 45–46.

Goldfried, M. R., & Merbaum, M. (Eds.). (1973). *Behavior change through self-control.* New York: Holt, Rinehart & Winston.

Goldfried, M. R., & Padawer, W. (1982). *Current status and future directions in psychotherapy.* New York: Springer.

Goldiamond, I. (1974). Toward a constructional approach to social problems: Ethical and constitutional issues raised by applied behavior analysis. *Behaviorism, 2,* 1–38.

Goldiamond, I. (1975a). Toward a constructional approach to social problems: Ethical and constitutional issues raised by applied behavior analysis. In C. M. Franks & G. T. Wilson (Eds.), *Annual review of behavior therapy* (pp. 21–63). New York: Brunner/Mazel.

Goldiamond, I. (1975b). Singling out behavior modification for legal regulation: Some effects on patient care, psychotherapy, and research in general. *Arizona Law Review, 17,* 105–126.

Goldstein, A. P. (1980). Relationship enhancement methods. In A. P. Goldstein & F. H. Kanfer (Eds.), *Helping people change* (pp. 15–49). Oxford: Pergamon Press.

Goldstein, A. P., Sprafkin, R. P., Gershaw, N. J., & Klein, P. (1980). *Skillstreaming the adolescent.* Champaign: IL: Research Press.

Griffith, R. G. (1980). An administrative perspective on guidelines for behavior modification: The creation of a legally safe environment. *The Behavior Therapist, 3,* 5–7.

Hake, D. F., & Vukelich, R. (1973). Analysis of the control exerted by a complex cooperation procedure. *Journal of the Experimental Analysis of Behavior, 19,* 3–16.

Hake, D. F., Vukelich, R., & Kaplan, S. J. (1973). Audit responses: Responses maintained by access to existing self or coactor scores during non-social, parallel work, and cooperation procedures. *Journal of the Experimental Analysis of Behavior, 19,* 409–423.

Hardy, M. W. (1976). What every psychologist should know about P.S.R.C. *The Florida Psychologist,* 21–29.

Hartje, J. (1981). Flowchart and headache tracking forms. Unpublished raw data.

Hauck, P. A. (1967). *The rational management of children.* New York: Libra Publishers.

Heinrich, R. (1978). Clinical behavioral assessment. In S. Fishman (Chair), *Clinical behavior therapy*. An Institute presented at the Association for the Advancement of Behavior Therapy Annual Convention, New York.

Hersen, M. (Ed.). (1983). *Outpatient behavior therapy: A clinical guide*. New York: Grune & Stratton.

Herson, M., & Barlow, D. H. (1976). *Single-case experimental designs: Strategies for studying behavior change*. New York: Pergamon Press.

Hersen, M., Eisler, R. N., & Miller, P. M. (Eds.). (1984). *Progress in behavior modification*. New York: Academic Press.

Holland, D. J. (1970). An interview guide for behavioral counseling with parents. *Behavior Therapy, 1*, 70–79.

Holland, M., Stroebel, C. F., & Stroebel, E. (1980). *Q.R. (Quieting reflex training) for young people*. Tampa, FL: QR Institute-South.

Homme, L., Csayni, A. P., Gonzales, M. A., & Rechs, J. R. (1969). *How to use contingency contracting in the classroom*. Champaign, IL: Research Press.

Honig, W. K. (Ed.). (1966). *Operant behavior: Areas of research and application*. New York: Appleton-Century-Crofts.

Hull, C. L. (1943). *Principles of behavior*. New York: Appleton-Century-Crofts.

Humphreys, L., & Beiman, I. (1975). The application of multiple behavioral techniques to multiple problems of a complex case. *Journal of Behavior Therapy and Experimental Psychiatry, 6*, 311–315.

Hutchinson, W. R., & Fawcett, S. B. (1981). Issues in defining the field of behavior community psychology and certifying (*or not* certifying) its members. *The Behavior Therapist, 4*, 5–8.

Independent Practitioner, The. (1985). Teaneck, NJ: Psychologists in Independent Practice.

Jacobson, E. (1938). *Progressive relaxation*. Chicago: University of Chicago Press.

Jacobson, N. S., & Margolin, J. (1979). *Marital therapy: Strategies based on social learning and behavior exchange principles*. New York: Brunner/Mazel.

Jacobson, N. S., Follette, W. C., Revenstorf, D. (1984). Psychotherapy outcome research: Methods for reporting variability and evaluating clinical significance. *Behavior Therapy, 15*, 336–352.

Jones, N. L., Czyzewski, M. J., Otis, A. K., & Hannah, G. T. (1983). Shaping social policy: Developing a national social policy information network. *The Behavior Therapist, 6*, 149–151.

Kanfer, F. H., & Goldstein, A. P. (1980). *Helping people change*. New York: Pergamon Press.

Kanfer, F. H., & Saslow, G. (1969). Behavioral diagnosis. In C. M. Franks (Ed.), *Behavior therapy: Appraisal and status* (pp. 417–444). New York: McGraw-Hill.

Kaplan, S. J. (1982). *Survey and follow-up of six years of charts from private practice. Establishing and maintaining a private practice in behavior therapy*. AABT convention workshop, Los Angeles.

Kaplan, S. J. (1983). *AABT private practice special interest group informal survey*. Unpublished survey, Jacksonville, FL.

Kaplan, S. J. (1984). The private practice of behavior therapy. In M. Hersen, R. M. Eisler, & P. M. Miller (Eds.), *Progress in behavior modification* (pp. 201–240). New York: Academic Press.

Kaplan, S. J., & Kuhling, S. D. (1984). Unpublished termination report form.

Kazdin, A. E. (1977). Assessing the clinical or applied importance of behavior change through social validation. *Behavior Modification, 1*, 427–452.

Kazdin, A. E. (1978). *History of behavior modification: Experimental foundations of contemporary research*. Baltimore: University Park Press.

Kazdin, A. E. (1980). Acceptability of alternative treatments for deviant child behavior. *Journal of Applied Behavioral Analysis, 13*, 259–273.

Kazdin, A. E. (1984, November). *Approaches to the diagnosis of childhood disorders*. A workshop at the Association for the Advancement of Behavior Therapy Convention, Philadelphia, Pennsylvania.

Kazdin, A. E., & Wilson, G. T. (1978). *Evaluation of behavior therapy*. Cambridge, MA: Ballinger.

Keane, R. M. (1983). AABT's media committee. *The Behavior Therapist, 6,* 69.

Keller, P. A., & Ritt, L. G. (Eds.). (1983). *Innovations in clinical practice: A sourcebook* (Vols. 1 & 2). Sarasota, FL: Professional Resources Exchange.

Kendall, P. C., & Braswell, L. (1984). *Cognitive-behavioral therapy for impulsive children*. New York: Guilford Press.

Kendall, P. C., & Hollon, S. (Eds.). (1979). *Cognitive-behavioral interventions: Theory, research, and procedures*. New York: Academic Press.

Keuhnel, T. C., & Flanagan, S. G. (1984). Training and professionals: Guidelines for effective continuing education workshops. *The Behavior Therapist, 7,* 85–87.

Keuhnel, T. G., Marholin, D., II, Heinrich, R., & Liberman, R. (1978). Evaluating behavior therapists continuing education: The AABT, 1977 Institute. *The Behavior Therapist, 1,* 5–8.

Khemka, K. C. (1977). *Biotic-band II: A finger temperature indicator for thermal biofeedback training*. Indianapolis: Biotemp Products.

Kiesler, C. A. (1983). Social psychological issues in studying consumer satisfaction with behavior therapy. *Behavior Therapy, 14,* 226–236.

Kissell, S. (1983). *Private practice for the mental health clinician*. Rockville, MD: Aspen.

Klepac, R. K. (1984a). Micro-computers in behavior therapy: A sampler of applications. *The Behavior Therapist, 7,* 79–83.

Klepac, R. K. (1984b). Trends in computerdom. *The Behavior Therapist, 7,* 151–152.

Knaus, W. (1974). *Rational emotive education: A manual for elementary school teachers*. New York: Institute of Rational Living.

Krampfl, J. (1984, November). *Organizational behavior*. An Institute presented at the Association for the Advancement of Behavior Therapy Convention, Philadelphia, Pennsylvania.

Krasner, L. (1982). Behavior therapy: Roots, contexts, and growth. In G. P. Wilson & C. M. Franks (Eds.), *Contemporary behavior therapies*. New York: Guilford Press.

Kratochwill, T. R., & Van Someren, K. R. (1984). Training behavioral consultants: Issues and directions. *The Behavior Therapist, 7,* 19–22.

Krumboltz, J. D., & Thoresen, C. E. (1969). *Behavioral counseling: Cases and techniques*. New York: Holt, Rinehart & Winston.

Lake v. Cameron, 373 F.2d 451 (D.C. Cir. 1968.)

Lange, A., & Jakubowski, P. (1976). *Responsible assertive behavior: Cognitive-behavioral procedures for trainers*. Champaign, IL: Research Press.

Lazarus, A. A. (1958). New methods in psychotherapy: A case study. *South African Medical Journal, 33,* 660.

Lazarus, A. A. (1966). Broad-spectrum behavior therapy and the treatment of agoraphobia. *Behaviour Research and Therapy, 4,* 95–97.

Lazarus, A. A. (1967). In support of technical eclecticism. *Psychological Reports, 21,* 416.

Lazarus, A. A. (1971). *Behavior therapy and beyond*. New York: McGraw-Hill.

Lazarus, A. A. (1976). *Multimodal behavior therapy*. New York: Springer.

Lazarus, A. A., & Fay, A. (1975). *I can if I want to*. New York: Morrow.

Leitenberg, H. (Ed.). (1976). *Handbook of behavior modification and behavior therapy*. New York: Appleton-Century-Crofts.

Levy, L. H. (1984). The metamorphosis of clinical psychologist: Toward a new charter as human service psychology. *American Psychologist, 39,* 486–494.

Levy, R. L. (1984). Therapist-recorded and audiotaped-coded client homework assignments. *The Behavior Therapist, 7,* 122, 128.

Lieberman, M. A. (1980). Group methods. In F. H. Kanfer & A. P. Goldstein (Eds.), *Helping people change* (pp. 433–485). Oxford: Pergamon Press.

Linehan, M. M. (1980). Supervision of behavior therapy. In A. K. Hess (Ed.), *Psychotherapy supervision: Theory, research, and practice* (pp. 148–180). New York: Wiley.

LoPiccolo, L., & Heiman, J. (1978). *Handbook of sex therapy.* New York: Plenum Press.

Lubetkin, B. (1983). How to establish and maintain a behavioral practice. *The Behavior Therapist, 6,* 61–64.

MacDonald, M. L. (1975). Multiple impact behavior therapy in a child's dog phobia. *Journal of Behavior Therapy and Experimental Psychiatry, 6,* 317–322.

MacDonald, M. L. (1983). Behavioral consultation in geriatric settings. *The Behavior Therapist, 6,* 172–174.

Madsen, C. H., Jr., & Madsen, C. K. (1970). *Teaching/Discipline.* Boston: Allyn & Bacon.

Madsen, C. H., Jr., & Madsen, C. K. (1972). *Parents/children/discipline: A positive approach.* Boston: Allyn & Bacon.

Mahoney, M. J. (1974). *Cognition and behavior modification.* Cambridge, MA: Ballinger.

Mahoney, M. J., & Thoresen, C. E. (1974). *Self-control: Power to the person.* Monterey, CA: Brooks/Cole.

Marlatt, G. A. (1976). The drinking profile—a questionnaire for the behavioral assessment of alcoholism. In E. J. Mash & L. G. Terdal (Eds.), *Behavior therapy assessment: Diagnosis, design and evaluation* (pp. 121–137). New York: Springer.

Mash, E. J., & Terdal, L. G. (Eds.). (1981). *Behavioral assessment of childhood disorders.* New York: Guilford Press.

Masserman, J. M. (1943). *Behavior and neuroses.* Chicago: University of Chicago Press.

Masters, W. H., & Johnson, V. E. (1966). *Human sexual response.* Boston: Little, Brown.

McMahon, R. J., & Forehand, R. L. (1983). Consumer satisfaction in behavioral treatment of children: Types, issues, and recommendations. *Behavior Therapy, 14,* 209–225.

Meichenbaum, D. H. (1977). *Cognitive behavior modification: An integrative approach.* New York: Plenum Press.

Miller, N. E. (1969). Learning of visceral and glandular responses. *Science, 163,* 434–445.

Miller, N. E., & Banuazizi, A. (1968). Instrumental learning by curarized rats of a specific visceral response: Intestinal or cardiac. *Journal of Comparative and Physiological Psychology, 65,* 1–7.

Miller, N. E., & Carmona, A. (1967). Modification of a visceral response, salivation in thirsty dogs, by instrumental re-training with water reward. *Journal of Comparative and Physiological Psychology, 63,* 1–6.

Miller, N. E., & DiCara, L. (1968). Instrumental learning of the urine formation by rats: Changes in renal blood flow. *American Journal of Physiology, 215,* 677–683.

Minkin, N., Braukman, C. J., Minkin, B. L., Timbers, G., Timbers, B. J., Fixsen, D. L., Phillips, E. L., & Wolf, M. M. (1976). The social validation and training of conversational skills. *Journal of Applied Behavioral Analysis, 9,* 127–139.

Myers, H. K. (1980). *GSR Temp 2 Device.* Montreal, Canada: Thought Technology.

Nelson, R. O., & Barlow, D. H. (1981). Behavioral assessment: Basic strategies and initial procedures. In D. H. Barlow (Ed.), *Behavioral assessment of adult disorders* (pp. 13–43). New York: Guilford Press.

National Register of Health Service Providers in Psychology. (1979). *Survey of Psychological Services.* Washington, DC: Author.

Nelson, R. O., & Hartmann, D. P. (1981). *Behavioral assessment for the clinician*. AABT Convention Workshop, Toronto.

Nordheimer, I. (1974, May 28). Experts feel Miss Hearst may have undergone brainwashing. *The New York Times*, p. 30.

O'Dell, S. L., Tarler-Benlolo, L., & Flynn, J. M. (1979). An instrument to measure knowledge of behavioral principles as applied to children. *Journal of Behavior Therapy and Experimental Psychiatry, 10,* 29–34.

O'Leary, K. D. (1983). President's message: Charting the future of AABT. *The Behavior Therapist, 6,* 199.

O'Leary, K. D. (1984). The image of behavior therapy: It is time to take a stand. *Behavior Therapy, 15,* 219–233.

Palmer, P. (1977a). *Liking myself*. San Luis Obispo, CA: Impact Press.

Palmer, P. (1977b). *The mouse, the monster, and me*. San Luis Obispo, CA: Impact Press.

Parloff, M. B. (1983). Who will be satisfied by "consumer satisfaction" evidence? *Behavior Therapy, 14,* 242–246.

Patterson, G. (1971). *Families*. Champaign, IL: Research Press.

Pavlov, I. P. (1927). *Conditioned reflexes: An investigation of the physiological activity of the cerebral cortex* (G. V. Anrep, trans.). London & New York: Oxford University Press.

Peterson, D. R. (1961). Behavior problems of middle childhood. *Journal of Consulting Psychology, 25,* 205–209.

Phillips, D., & Mordock, J. B. (1970, November). *Behavior therapy with children: Some general guidelines and specific suggestions*. Paper presented at the annual convention of the American Association of Psychiatric Services for Children, Philadelphia.

Pressman, R. M. (1979). *Private practice: A handbook for the independent mental health practitioner*. New York: Gardner.

Psychotherapy and private practice. (1984). Binghamton, New York: The Hawthorne Press.

Psychotherapy finances. (1985). Ridgewood, NJ: Ridgewood Financial Institute.

Rachman, S., & Teasdale, J. (1969). *Aversion therapy and behavior disorders: An analysis*. Coral Gables, FL: University of Miami Press.

Ramp, E. A., & Hopkins, B. L. (1971). *A new direction for education: Behavior analysis 1971*. Lawrence, KS: The University of Kansas Press.

Rathus, S. A. (1973). A 30-item schedule for assessing assertive behavior. *Behavior Therapy, 4,* 398–406.

Reese, M. (1982). Helping human rights committees and clients balance intrusiveness and effectiveness: A challenge for research and therapy. *The Behavior Therapist, 5,* 95–99.

Rimm, D. C., & Masters, J. C. (1979). *Behavior therapy: Techniques and empirical findings*. New York: Academic Press.

Risley, T. R., & Sheldon-Wildgen, J. (1980a). Invited peer review: The AABT experience. *The Behavior Therapist, 3,* 5–8.

Risley, T. R., & Sheldon-Wildgen, J. (1980b). Suggested procedures for human rights committees of potentially controversial treatment programs. *The Behavior Therapist, 3,* 9–10.

Romanczyk, R. G. (1984). Micro-computers and behavior therapy: A powerful alliance. *The Behavior Therapist, 7,* 59–64.

Rose, S. D. (1977). *Group therapy: A behavioral approach*. New York: Prentice-Hall.

Russo, D. C. (1984). Computers as an adjunct to therapy and research in behavioral medicine. *The Behavior Therapist, 7,* 99–102.

Sajwaj, T. (1977). Issues and implications of establishing guidelines for the use of behavioral techniques. *Journal of Applied Behavior Analysis, 10,* 531–540.

Schwartz, G. E. (1972). Voluntary control of human cardiovascular integration and differentiation through feedback and reward. *Science, 175*, 90–93.

Schwitzgebel, R. K. (1975). Use and regulation of psychological devices. *Behavioral Engineering, 2*, 44–46.

Selye, H. (1974). *Stress without distress*. New York: Harper & Row.

Sheldon-Wildgen, J. (1982). Avoiding legal liability: The rights and responsibilities of therapists. *The Behavior Therapist, 5*, 165–169.

Shelton, J. L., & Levy, R. L. (1981a). A survey of the reported use of assigned homework activites in contemporary behavior therapy literature. *The Behavior Therapist, 4*, 13–14.

Shelton, J. L., & Levy, R. L. (Eds.). (1981b). *Behavioral assignments and treatment compliance: A handbook of clinical strategies*. Champaign, IL: Research Press.

Sherrington, C. S. (1906). *Integrative action of the nervous system*. New Haven: Yale University Press.

Sidman, M. (1960). *Tactics of scientific research*. New York: Basic Books.

Skinner, B. F. (1938). *The behavior of organisms*. New York: Appleton.

Skinner, B. F. (1953). *Science and human behavior*. New York: Macmillan.

Small Business Administration. (1977). *Checklist for going into business*. Washington, DC.

Smith, D. (1982). Trends in counseling and psychotherapy. *American Psychologist, 37*, 802–809.

Spangler, P. F. (1979). Certification of behavior therapists: A step in which direction? *The Behavior Therapist, 2*, 25–26.

Spielberger, C. D. (1973). *Manual for the State-Trait Anxiety Inventory for Children*. Palo Alto, CA: Consulting Psychologists Press.

Stapp, J., & Fulcher, R. (1983). The employment of APA members: 1982. *American Psychologist, 38*, 1298–1320.

State of Florida. (1982). *Behavior programming and management*. Tallahassee, FL: Department of Health and Rehabilitative Services.

Stolz, S. B. (1977). Why no guidelines for behavior modification? *Journal of Applied Behavior Analysis, 10*, 541–547.

Stolz, S. B. (1980). A legally safe environment is not necessarily an ethical one. *The Behavior Therapist, 3*, 7–8.

Stolz, S. B., Wienckowski, L. A., & Brown, B. S. (1975). Behavior modification: A perspective on critical issues. *American Psychologist, 30*, 1027–1048.

Stroebel, C. F. (1982). *Quieting reflex training for adults*. New York: Biomonitoring Applications.

Stroebel, C. F., & Sandweiss, J. (1979). *Handbook of physiological feedback* (Vol. 1). San Francisco: Pacific Institute.

Stroebel, E., Stroebel, C. F., & Holland, M. (1980). *Kiddie Q.R.: A choice for children*. Tampa, FL: QR Institute-South.

Stuart, R. B. (Ed.). (1977). *Behavioral self-management: Strategies, techniques, and outcome*. New York: Bruner/Mazel.

Stuart, R. B. (1980). *Helping couples change*. New York: Guilford Press.

Stuart, R. B., & Davis, B. (1972). *Slim chance in a fat world*. Champaign, IL: Research Press.

Stuart, R. B., & Stuart, F. (1973). *Marital Pre-Counseling Inventory*. Champaign, IL: Research Press.

Subcommittee on Constitutional Rights of the Senate Subcommittee on the Judiciary, 93rd Congress, 2nd Session. (1974). *Individual Rights and the federal role in behavior modification*. Washington, DC: U.S. Government Printing Office.

Sulzer, B., & Mayer, G. R. (1972). *Behavior modification procedures for school personnel*. Hinsdale, IL: The Dryden Press.

Swan, G. E., & MacDonald, M. L. (1978). Behavior therapy in practice: A national survey of behavior therapists. *Behavior Therapy, 9,* 799–807.

Tarasoff v. Regents of University of California. (1976). 17KCAL. 3d 425 551 P. 2d 334 131 Cal. Rptr. 14.

Tertinger, D. A., Greene, B. F., & Lutzker, J. R. (1984). Home safety: The development and validation of one component of an ecobehavioral treatment program for abused and neglected children. *Journal of Applied Behavioral Analysis, 17,* 159–174.

Tharpe, R. G., & Wetzel, R. J. (1969). *Behavior modification in the natural environment.* New York: Academic Press.

Theaman, N. (1984). The impact of peer view on professional practice. *American Psychologist, 39,* 406–414.

Thomas, D. R., & Murphy, R. J. (1981). Practitioner competencies needed for implementing behavior management guidelines. *The Behavior Therapist, 4,* 7–10.

Thorndike, E. J. (1932). *The Fundamentals of Learning.* New York: Teacher's College, Columbia University.

Tower, E. L., Huser, J., Beach, D. R., & Rappaport, J. (1970). Parental perceptions of young children and their relation to indexes of adjustment. *Journal of Consulting and Clinical Psychology, 32,* 97–103.

Turk, D. C., Meichenbaum, D., & Genest, M. (1983). *Pain and behavioral medicine: A cognitive-behavioral perspective.* New York: Guilford Press.

Turkat, I. D. (1979). The image of behavior therapy. *The Behavior Therapist, 2,* 17.

Turkat, I. D., & Brantley, P. J. (1981). On the therapeutic relationship in behavior therapy. *The Behavior Therapist, 4,* 16–17.

Turkat, I. D., & Feuerstein, M. (1978). Behavior modification and the public misconception. *American Psychologist, 33,* 194.

Turkington, C. (1984). Marketing called essential to success. *APA Monitor, 15,* 16.

VandenBos, G. R., & Stapp, J. (1983). Service providers in psychology: Results of the 1982 APA Human Resources Survey. *American Psychologist, 38,* 1330–1352.

Vukelich, R., & Hake, D. F. (1971). Reduction of dangerously aggressive behavior in a severely retarded resident through a combination of positive reinforcement procedures. *Journal of Applied Behavior Analysis, 4,* 215–225.

Wachtel, P. L. (1977). *Psychoanalysis and behavior therapy: Toward an integration.* New York: Basic Books.

Wahler, R. G., & Graves, M. G. (1983). Setting events in social networks: Ally or enemy in child behavior therapy: *Behavior Therapy, 14,* 19–36.

Walker, H. M. (1976). *Problem Behavior Identification Checklist.* Los Angeles: Western Psychological Services.

Water Pik Company. (1977). *Countdown: Permanent weight loss system.* Fort Collins, CO: Teledyne.

Watson, J. B., & Rayner, R. (1920). Conditioned emotional reactions. *Journal of Experimental Psychology, 3,* 1.

Welch v. Likens, 373 F. Supp. 487 (M.D. Minn. 1974).

Whalen, S. (1978). *The private practice of behavior therapy.* Symposium of the 12th Annual Association for the Advancement of Behavior Therapy Convention, Chicago.

Wicker, T. (1974, February 8). A bad idea persists. *The New York Times,* p. 31.

Widiger, T. A., & Rorer, L. G. (1984). The responsible psychotherapist. *American Psychologist, 39,* 503–515.

Willens, E. P. (1974). Behavioral technology and behavior ecology. *Journal of Applied Behavior Analysis, 7,* 151–165.

Williamson, D., Labbé, E. E., & Granberry, S. W. (1983). Somatic disorders. In M. Hersen (Ed.), *Outpatient behavior therapy* (pp. 143–172). New York: Grune & Stratton.

Wilson, G. T., & O'Leary, K. D. (1980). *Principles of behavior therapy*. Englewood Cliffs, NJ: Prentice-Hall.

Wilson, G. T., Franks, C. M., Brownell, K. D., & Kendall, P. C. (1984). *Annual review of behavior therapy: Theory and practice* (Vol. 9). New York: Guilford Press.

Wolf, M. M. (1978). Social validity: The case for subjective measurement of how applied behavioral analysis is finding its heart. *Journal of Applied Behavior Analysis, 11,* 203–214.

Wolpe, J. (1958). *Psychotherapy by reciprocal inhibition.* Stanford, CA: Stanford University Press.

Wolpe, J. (1973). *The practice of behavior therapy.* Oxford: Pergamon.

Wolpe, J., & Lang, P. (1969). *Fear Survey Schedule.* San Diego, CA: Educational and Industrial Testing Service.

Woods, T. S. (1983). A note on the theoretical integrity of social validation. *The Behavior Therapist, 6,* 19.

Woolfolk, R. L., & Richardson, F. C. (1984). Behavior therapy and the ideology of modernity. *American Psychologist, 39,* 777–786.

Wyatt v. Stickney, 325 F. Supp. 781 (M.D. Ala. 1971), 334 F. Supp. 1341 (M.D. Ala. 1971), 334 F. Supp. 373, 343 F. Supp. 387 (M.D. Ala. 1972), 368 F. Supp. 1383 (M.D. Ala. 1974), affirmed in part, modified in part, Sub. Mon. Wyatt v. Aderholt, 503 F. 2d 1305 (5 cir., 1974).

Yates, A. J. (1970). *Behavior therapy.* New York: Wiley.

Yates, A. J. (1980). *Biofeedback and the modification of behavior.* New York: Plenum Press.

Young, H. S. (1974). *Rational counseling primer:* New York: Institute for Rational-Emotive Therapy.

Ziarnik, J. P., & Bernstein, G. S. (1984). Effective change in community-based facilities: Putting staff trainee in perspective. *The Behavior Therapist, 7,* 39–41.

Index